Black Week

The British Army and Defeat in the Anglo-Boer War 1899–1900

Quintin Barry

Helion & Company

Helion & Company Limited
Unit 8 Amherst Business Centre
Budbrooke Road
Warwick
CV34 5WE
England
Tel. 01926 499 619
Email: info@helion.co.uk
Website: www.helion.co.uk
Twitter: @helionbooks
Visit our blog at https://helionbooks.wordpress.com/

Published by Helion & Company 2024
Designed and typeset by Mach 3 Solutions (www.mach3solutions.co.uk)
Cover designed by Paul Hewitt, Battlefield Design (www.battlefield-design.co.uk)

ISBN 978-1-804511-86-2

British Library Cataloguing-in-Publication Data.
A catalogue record for this book is available from the British Library.

Contents

List of Illustrations

Plates

Maps

Glossary

berg	mountain
Boer	literally farmer; Dutch speaking burgher of the Transvaal or Orange Free State
bult	hill; rising ground; literally hump
burg	town
burgher	citizen of the Transvaal or Orange Free State
donga	cutting caused by action of water; often dry
dorp	town, village
drift	ford
fontein	spring
modder	mud
kloof	ravine or gorge
kopje, kop	hill, peak
kraal	cluster of native huts
krantz	overhanging cliff face
Krigsraad	Council of War
laager	camp
nek	saddle or pass between hills;
pan	pond
pont	ferry
poort	gap or pass; literally gate
rand	ridge; edge of plateau
riet	reed
schanz	stone entrenchment or breastwork
sluit	watercourse; artificial ditch
span	team of animals
spruit	watercourse feeding larger stream or river
stad	town
veld	open plain
vlei	hollow or valley: marsh; small lake
Volksraad	legislative assembly of the Transvaal and Orange Free State

Acknowledgements

As always, Duncan Rogers and his team at Helion have been extremely supportive in preparing this book for publication. I should like also to thank George Anderson, who drew the maps; and Tim Readman, who read the book in draft and made a number of valuable suggestions. I should also like to acknowledge the enormous resource represented by the vast literature on the South African War on which I have been able to draw.

Preface

The reasons for the series of British defeats in December 1899 which became known as Black Week are complex and far-reaching and are by no means confined to the misjudgements of the individuals who led the British Army in South Africa at that time.

One of the reasons that prompted me to write this account was after considering the brilliant essay by John Gooch on 'Britain and the Boer War' in *The Aftermath of Defeat*, edited by George J. Andreopoulos and Harold E. Selesky, in which he analysed thoroughly, not only the factors which led to the British defeats but also the process of reform which ultimately, they prompted.[1] The Boer War led in due course, to the introduction of many organisational, tactical and command doctrines which stood the British Army in good stead when it came to fight the First World War. The process of modernisation was complicated; it had already – if slowly and erratically – begun, but the Boer War compelled the abandonment of many of the attitudes which had obstructed that process.

I had not realised, when I first contemplated writing about the events of December 1899, what a vast literature there was on the subject of the Boer War. I am very conscious that my research in it fails to do justice to the work that has been done by so many over the years.

Outstanding among modern historians is of course Thomas Pakenham's book on the Boer War, which will never be surpassed.[2] Throughout the writing of this book, I have always had in mind, his penetrating explanation not only of the war itself but of its surrounding context. He identified the two major contemporary sources – the Official History, which studiously avoided criticism, and *The Times History*, which expressed a great deal.[3] Apart from these, I have naturally also spent a lot of time with the evidence taken by the Royal Commission on the War in South Africa which covered the subject in immense detail, but which generally allowed the participants to give their own point of view without serious challenge.[4] The members of the British Cabinet were to be disappointed in their hope that the Elgin Commission would plant the blame for what went wrong on the generals, but when it came to it, its members firmly declined to explore the conduct of operations. In fact, the government's own share of the responsibility stretched back many years.

1 George J. Andreopoulos and Harold E. Selesky, eds, *The Aftermath of Defeat* (New Haven and London: Yale University Press 1994).
2 Thomas Pakenham, *The Boer War* (London: Weidenfeld and Nicolson 1979).
3 Major General Sir Frederick Maurice, et al, *History of the War in South Africa 1899–1902* (4 vols) (London: Hurst and Blackett, 1906), passim; L.S. Amery, ed, *The Times History of the War in South Africa 1899-1902* (7 vols) (London: Sampson Low Marston and Co. 1905, 1910), passim.
4 *Report of the Royal Commission on the War in South Africa* (London: 1904), passim.

1

Approach to War

Leo Amery, the editor of *The Times History of the War in South Africa*, called the Boer War 'the greatest political event in the history of the British Empire since the conclusion of the Napoleonic Wars.' He justified British policy in South Africa in terms of the outward and visible reasons why the British government went to war: 'We have fought, not to maintain the white man's burden but to vindicate the white man's birthright – the right of all white men that come into a new country and join in the work of developing and making it, to claim their share of its political privileges.'[1]

That was one way of putting it; in fact, Great Britain went to war to assert her supremacy over southern Africa, which was seen as facing a serious challenge from the Boer republics. In any case, even if Amery's formulation of Britain's war aims was right, it was the way in which the so-called birthright was to be maintained, that led to war. This, to the imperialists who in the end dictated British policy, could only be achieved by ensuring British paramountcy over southern Africa, by whatever means necessary. This objective was wholly inconsistent with the political independence of the republics of Transvaal and the Orange Free State and that, however Cabinet ministers might find themselves able to ignore this reality, ultimately meant war. In presiding over the gradual drift to war, the Cabinet did so without making the kind of preparation for it that was so obviously necessary to the military advisers.

Responsibility for the outbreak of war is usually ascribed to the implacable imperialism of Sir Alfred Milner, the British High Commissioner in South Africa. This was certainly one of several influences which led to it; his relentless ambition to extend British power over southern Africa meant that unless the Transvaal – and President Paul Kruger – were prepared to take an altogether improbably flexible approach, war was always on the cards. Before he left in the spring of 1897 to assume his duties as Governor of the Cape Colony and High Commissioner in South Africa, Milner exchanged letters with his close friend Lord Selborne, Under Secretary of State at the Colonial Office. Milner was already looking ahead to the consequences of the policy which he intended to pursue, and made his opinion plain:

> Where I differ from you is in thinking that our being compelled to have recourse to war is very improbable ... It is next door to inconceivable that the Transvaal should prefer war

1 *Times History*, vol. I, p. 2.

> to such a moderate concession as that of discussing an immigration bill with us instead of forcing down our throats an act concocted independently of us. But the question will not be dealt with apart, on its own merits, or in cool blood.[2]

Milner's conviction that the South African problem could only be solved in one way had been firmly held from the outset; in February 1898, he expressed himself candidly to Percy Fitzpatrick, the Uitlander leader who had been involved in plotting the Jameson Raid. Assuring him that he had the support of the British government, Milner told him that 'there is only one possible settlement – war! It has got to come.'[3]

It was already clear to Selborne and to Milner, and also to Joseph Chamberlain as Colonial Secretary and Lord Salisbury as Prime Minister, that the growing economic strength of the Transvaal made it the hub of South African politics and would, sooner or later, form the centre of a union of the separate states of South Africa. The key issue was, therefore, whether that union would be achieved 'inside or outside the British Empire,' as Selborne had pointed out to Chamberlain in 1896 soon after taking up his post. It was Milner's absolute determination to ensure that this took place within the British Empire. However determined he was on carrying through his policy, the buck did not stop with him, or even with Joseph Chamberlain. The responsibility lay with the Cabinet as a whole, though ultimately it was Lord Salisbury's call as Prime Minister.

He had watched, with some detachment, Chamberlain's conduct of British policy. He sympathised with the Colonial Secretary's desire to re-establish British suzerainty over the Transvaal, nominally existent since the convention that had ended the First Boer War, as being essential to the assertion of British paramountcy. However, Salisbury was equivocal when it came to consideration of the brutal probability that this policy would lead to war. He wrote to Chamberlain in 1897 that he would 'look with something like dismay to a Transvaal war;' he had hoped that ultimately the Transvaal would come to 'be mainly governed by English men' but that this would not be as a result of external aggression but as the 'result of the action of internal forces.'[4] Nonetheless, he agreed at that time to grant Chamberlain's request for a doubling of troop strengths in the Cape, albeit from a very low base. Thereafter, it must be said that Salisbury, Chamberlain and the Cabinet, if they had eyes to see, were acquiescing in the drift to war. As it became more likely, Salisbury came to accept its inevitability.

As war became imminent, Salisbury, in his famous letter to Lord Lansdowne, the Secretary of State for War, of 30 August 1899, seemed to be suggesting that he was a prisoner of events. Commenting on Milner's recent appeal for the sending of 10,000 troops to South Africa, with which he had some sympathy, he nevertheless wrote:

> His view is too heated, if you consider the intrinsic significance and importance of the things which are in controversy. But it recks little to think that now. What he has done cannot be effaced. We have to act upon a moral field prepared by him and his jingo supporters. And therefore I see before us the need for considerable military effort – and all for people whom we despise, and for territory which will bring no profit and no power to England.[5]

2 D. George Boyce, ed, *The Crisis of British Power* (London: The Historians Press, 1990), p. 47.
3 A. N. Porter, *The Origins of the South African War* (Manchester: Manchester University Press,1980), p. 146.
4 Robert Taylor, *Lord Salisbury* (London: Allen Lane, 1975), p. 177.
5 Andrew Roberts, *Salisbury: Victorian Titan* (London: Weidenfeld and Nicholson 1999), p. 732.

Andrew Roberts, Salisbury's biographer, reckoned that in dealing with his Cabinet colleagues, the Prime Minister 'was playing something of a double game, letting some ministers such as Balfour, Hicks Beach and Lansdowne think that he was against the war, whilst letting Chamberlain reject the Smuts proposals in such a way as almost to encourage one.'[6] As Roberts pointed out, policy was ultimately made in London, and Salisbury had personally approved all the despatches sent to Kruger, often making amendments of his own and the phrase in his letter referring to the Uitlanders, was a candid admission of the ulterior imperialist motives of the British government.

The extent to which Salisbury was in effective control, appears with particular clarity in a letter of 27 July which his son-in-law Lord Selborne wrote to Milner. Selborne was heart and soul in support of Milner's forward policy and like him, readily accepted the prospect that it could lead to war; he kept the High Commissioner closely informed of opinions in London. Now, he wrote:

> The Cabinet is all right. I do not say there are no mugwumps in it. You could name them. But they are out of it. This is not based on what our chief has told me alone, but I know other Cabinet ministers and I draw them and above all I talk periodically to AJB (Balfour) to assure myself he is sound and last Sunday I had it all out with the Prime Minister at Walmer. I was wholly pleased with the result. He said he meant to secure full effective (as distinct from pedantic) compliance with your Bloemfontein demands as a minimum, and he added 'of course the real point to be made good to South Africa is that we and not the Dutch are Boss.'[7]

Salisbury had added, though, that he would not be hurried, but Selborne noted with satisfaction that he was 'altogether in favour of continuing steadily the military preparations.'

The next day, Salisbury, in the House of Lords, spoke in terms which showed that Selborne had correctly assessed the Prime Minister's belligerent determination. In his speech, he severely criticised the 1884 Convention, saying that he had resisted it to the utmost of his power and said that only if the Afrikaners showed 'a real desire to eliminate the racial inequality' between Briton and Boer could there be peace. He went on: 'If this country has to make exertions in order to secure the most elementary justice for British subjects, I am quite sure we will not reinstate a state of things which will bring back the old difficulties ... I do not think President Kruger has sufficiently considered this.'[8] The blunt threat of ultimate annexation was made to intimidate Kruger; but it was a clear indication of the way that Salisbury's mind was working and must have greatly encouraged Selborne and Milner.

The Cabinet considered Milner's request for a reinforcement of 10,000 men on 1 August, and a clear majority supported it. Hicks Beach and Arthur Balfour had made clear their reservations, but Salisbury told the Chancellor of the Exchequer that the moment had passed when Chamberlain could be restrained, ingenuously adding that even if he had wanted to, he did not know enough of the details of his game.[9] He was, though, anxious to avoid being hustled, since he wished to develop a more favourable public opinion. As it was, the Cabinet's acceptance

6 Ibid.
7 Boyce, *Crisis*, pp. 91-92.
8 Roberts, *Salisbury*, p. 726.
9 Ibid., p. 728.

of a hawkish policy was in part explained by a belief that when push came to shove, Kruger, obstinate until the last moment, would then cave in.

Nevertheless, the sending of reinforcements was an expensive business and the cost troubled not a few members of the Cabinet. They were still more troubled to learn on 12 August, that to send out a complete army corps would cost nearly £1 million. Salisbury had a low opinion of the War Office but told Chamberlain that it would be 'uncivil' to criticise it when on the brink of a war. He was himself now becoming aware of the extent of Britain's military unpreparedness, but he still thought it best not to incur substantial expenditure 'until it is quite clear that we *are* going to war.'[10] He thought that it might add slightly to the initial delay in beginning operations, but that the slight addition would not 'increase materially the scandal which will certainly be created by the conditions of our military preparations.' He knew that Hicks Beach, for one, was profoundly opposed to hostilities; the Chancellor had written to him to express the hope that Milner and the Uitlanders would not draw the country into war.

On 19 August, Milner received what was for him, the worst possible news, which was that Jan Christian Smuts, the youthful State Attorney of the Transvaal, had put forward to Conyngham Greene, the British agent in Pretoria, a proposal to concede a five-year residence qualification for the Uitlanders, together with 10 seats in the Raad. Milner was fearful that such a concession might be seen in London as acceptable; his reaction was to cable Chamberlain to warn him that the proposal was full of traps and pitfalls and to his relief, this had the desired effect. Chamberlain made a speech at a garden party in the grounds of his home, saying that he could not truly say the crisis had passed. Kruger, he said, procrastinated in his replies: 'he dribbles out reforms like water from a squeezed sponge, and he either accompanies his offers with conditions which he knows to be impossible or he refuses to allow us to make a satisfactory investigation of the nature and the character of those reforms … The sands are running down in the glass.'[11]

Salisbury and Chamberlain met on 28 August to agree the terms of the British response. They did not find it necessary to call a Cabinet meeting to discuss it. It amounted to a grudging acceptance of the franchise proposal, while calling for the establishment of a joint enquiry. It warned that if the Transvaal did not promptly send a satisfactory response, and it became necessary to send out further troops, Britain would withdraw previous compromise suggestions and submit its own demands for a settlement. Milner's cable, it would seem, had seriously shaken Chamberlain in his hopes for a negotiated settlement.

Leo Amery, whose history of the war was based on a belief in the absolute rectitude of the British bargaining position during the years leading up to its outbreak, claimed that 'nothing could have been milder than the reply' that was sent. Chamberlain, he argued, had accepted the new Transvaal proposal while refusing the rider that had been added two days later, and had abstained 'from directly pressing for any of the concessions agreed to informally by Mr Smuts.'[12] Amery went on to assert that instead of engaging with the points made in the despatch, the Transvaal were 'determined, in their folly, to treat Mr Chamberlain's qualified acceptance as a flat refusal, and to make this an excuse for directly breaking off all negotiations.' All that need be said of this piece of sophistry is that Milner will have read, with profound relief, the terms of the British response.

10 Ibid.
11 *Times History*, vol. I, p. 333.
12 Ibid., I p. 335.

When the Transvaal government sent a reply, it was to withdraw the offer of a five-year franchise qualification and the 10 seats in the Raad, reverting to a seven-year qualification and four seats in the Raad, and denying any claim to British suzerainty. There was no longer much doubt in Pretoria as to what the future held; on 4 September, Smuts sent a secret memorandum to the executive recording the position:

> South Africa stands on the eve of a frightful bloodbath out of which our Volk shall come … Either as … hewers of wood and drawers of water for a hated race, or as victorious, founders of a united South Africa, of one of the great empires of the world … An Afrikaans Republic in South Africa stretching from Table Bay to the Zambesi.[13]

It could not have been put more plainly.

Chamberlain told Selborne on 30 August, that he hoped the Transvaal would reject Britain's last offer: 'It is plain to me that mere menace will not now, whatever might have been the case if British opinion had been united at first, get a really satisfactory settlement out of them, and that, if it is not really satisfactory, we shall be worse off than ever.'[14] He knew that the government would shrink from the cost of a military expedition and from fighting, possibly heavy fighting; but in his view it would be worth millions to settle for ever, the South African question. The plunge, he thought, must be taken at once; if not, it would be too late.

In Pretoria, the position was now seen perfectly plainly. The diplomatic situation had so far deteriorated that Smuts could write candidly in August to the Cape Afrikaner bondsman Jan Hofmeyr that the dispute was not over the basis of the franchise law, but 'about possession of this land of gold.'[15] Even moderates like Smuts, who had done all they could to persuade Kruger of the benefits of an agreed solution, were coming to accept that they might be obliged to fight. Smuts himself had been given an earlier indication of British thinking in the course of a discussion with Edmund Fraser, the acting British agent in Pretoria at that time, on 23 December 1898. In an astonishingly frank expression of opinion, Fraser said that the time had come to take action, and that England had 'to show who's the boss in South Africa.' Thus:

> England is fed up with the maladministration in this country, and especially with the ill-treatment of British subjects. This is the point on which England will take action. I know perfectly well that England won't go to war over abstract subjects like suzerainty – that means nothing to the man in the street. She'll go to war about things that everyone can understand.[16]

This was the sort of language that, without realising it, Salisbury was to echo in his conversation with Selborne in July 1899; and it demonstrated clearly to Smuts that whatever negotiations thereafter took place between the parties, war had already become a matter of probability.

Fraser's suggestion that England was 'fed up' was made in terms that implied that this was the view of the man in the street, which is something that could not be assessed then and certainly, not even more than a century later. The members the Cabinet could, of course, read

13 Roberts, *Salisbury*, pp. 733-734.
14 Boyce, *Crisis*, p. 93.
15 Bill Nasson, *The Boer War: The Struggle for South Africa* (Stroud: The History Press, 2011), p. 54.
16 Thomas Pakenham, *The Boer War* (London: Weidenfeld and Nicholson, 1979) p. 45.

the newspapers, and from them derive some comfort that the general public might appear to support their policy. They would, for instance, have been reassured by the way in which *The Times* responded to the Transvaal's reaction on 2 September to Chamberlain's despatch of 28 August. It noted that the Cabinet had an onerous task, but that it was 'for Lord Salisbury and his colleagues to face it in a broad and statesmanlike spirit, without exaggeration and without illusions:'

> All that the Empire and the nation ask from their rulers is that there shall be no hesitation and no looking back. The government have put their hands to the plough, in the words of the Premier, and they are bound in duty and in honour to drive the furrow straight. When they formulate their own proposals, the one condition expected of them will be that they shall be of such a nature and of such a scope as must indeed lead to a settlement which shall be 'final.' With nothing less will England or her colonies be content.[17]

Selborne and Milner could not have asked for more.

When the Cabinet met on 8 September, they had before them Milner's call for 10,000 troops to be sent out. Chamberlain put forward a powerful case. Kruger, he said, was merely playing for time. He argued that the sending of the troops requested would not precipitate war. He cited the widely held view that 'the best way to avoid war was to make preparations for it' and that Kruger would 'bluff up to the cannon's mouth.'[18] Salisbury supported the Colonial Secretary; he accepted that Kruger was impossible to deal with, and that a hard line must be taken. Not only the political but also the military arguments were strong; Salisbury had received confirmation of that, if he needed it, in the shape of the memorandum of 5 September which he had received from General Buller, referred to in the following chapter. There was still however, not a unanimous acceptance of the need to send the 10,000 men. Lansdowne, who was a friend of Major General Penn Symons, presently in command in Natal, accepted the latter's view that 5,000 men would suffice to defend the colony, and he was, in any case, 'profoundly incredulous' about the suggestion from Wolseley that a Boer army of 10,000 men could invade Natal although, he was prepared to go along with the Prime Minister. Hicks Beach was still not persuaded of the political case and was deeply concerned about the cost involved in sending troops, which were now put at £350,000 for the first 10,000 men and over £5 million if the entire army corps was sent. Balfour, Salisbury's nephew and his deputy, also had reservations, putting forward the case against intervention, but as Thomas Pakenham puts it, 'Balfour was not the man to press home an attack. The 'divine Arthur,' as his friends called him, was too much the philosopher; he saw every side of the case and chose none. In the case of Chamberlain's South African policy he was no more of an obstacle than a beam of sunlight.'[19]

In the end, the Cabinet accepted that Milner should have his 10,000 men. Salisbury, who did not share the view that Kruger would, at the last, cave in, was grimly aware of what the decision actually meant. If Britain was to assert and maintain her paramountcy in southern Africa, war was almost certainly unavoidable. In his heart, he had never doubted that, sooner or later, the decisions taken as a result of the battle of Majuba Hill would have to be reversed, and now, in September 1899, the time for that had arrived. It has to be said, that in taking a

17 *The Times*, 2 September 1899.
18 Pakenham, *Boer War*, p. 93 .
19 Ibid., p. 94.

decision that might very well lead to war, the Cabinet does not appear to have considered any moral implications.

When considering the sending of the reinforcements, the Cabinet had also discussed the despatch of an ultimatum to the Transvaal government but chose not to do so. Salisbury did not want to be hustled immediately into war, believing that British public opinion was not in favour; and it would be much better if the final step to war was taken by the Transvaal.

By early September, the leadership on both sides had become convinced that war could no longer be avoided. On each side, there was a complete and crippling mistrust of the other, yet even then, the tragic reality was that war was not inevitable. Thomas Pakenham thought not:

> Inevitable? It would have been easy, Milner later confessed to his intimates, to patch things up with Kruger, and settle those difficulties with the Uitlanders in a Great Deal that could have lasted five, ten or fifteen years. He had resisted the temptation, and 'precipitated' a war before it was too late. The truth was that Milner believed in 'the clean slate,' and the 'big things in life.' He had long been determined to burst the mould of Kruger's Transvaal. War was the only means.[20]

Pakenham concluded that if Kruger had taken the advice of his allies in the Cape and in the Orange Free State, and maintained an unqualified five-year offer, a settlement must have followed; Salisbury, Hicks Beach and Balfour would, he considered, have led the Cabinet to accept such a deal, and Chamberlain would have gone along with it. That Kruger rejected such advice to seize the opportunity for such a compromise was explained by the fact that he did not believe it existed; the mutual distrust entirely obscured the possibility. The Boer leaders failed to realise that behind Milner, whose aims they perfectly grasped, stood the final decision makers whose aims were not so brutally resolute: 'Had they realised Chamberlain's capacity for compromise – and, still more, the British government's – they would have heeded the advice of their Afrikaner and Boer allies … They knew only the political masks of the opponent. They had never once met face-to-face.'[21]

Thus the stage was finally set for the curtain to go up on the tragedy. When it did, Michael Davitt, an Irish member of Parliament, resigned his seat and travelled to South Africa to be with the Boer armies. In 1902, he published *The Boer Fight for Freedom*, a book that was banned in Britain. In it, he called the Boer War 'the most dishonourable and unChristian war which has ever disgraced a civilised age,' describing it as the 'greatest infamy of the nineteenth century.'[22] Allowing for the passionate emotions of a man with no reason to admire the British government, it is hard not to feel that this was a proper view of an unnecessary conflict.

In his history of the war, Rayne Kruger noted, by way of explanation of, rather than excuse for, the events leading up to the outbreak of war, 'the importance which nations attached to upholding their prestige by the assertion of rights wherever rights were believed to exist, and by never relinquishing even the shadow of a claim without the substance of compensation. This must be remembered when Chamberlain's policy of British paramountcy in S. A, is impeached.'[23]

20 Ibid., p. 118.
21 Ibid., pp. 101–102.
22 Owen Coetzer, *The Anglo-Boer War: The Road to Infamy* (London: Arms and Armour Press, 1996) p. 40.
23 Rayne Kruger, *Goodbye Dolly Gray* (London: Cassell, 1967) p. 41.

The final steps down into the abyss were, however, still to be taken. In early September, there were factors on both sides which delayed the final outbreak of war, even though on both sides there was now little doubt that it would come. In London, Salisbury wanted to delay the event as long as he could because of his concern about public opinion and because it was much in his mind that it would be some time before the reinforcements which had been ordered would be in place. However, in the course of the Cabinet discussion, Salisbury had been at pains to spell out to his colleagues the character of the war that was about to break out. It was, he realised, not going to be an entirely straightforward task to overcome the Boers. He was reported by Edward Ashbourne as having remarked: 'We must remember that this is the first occasion we have gone to war with people of Teutonic race.'[24]

On the day after the Cabinet meeting, Salisbury wrote to Chamberlain to emphasise the importance of public opinion. He was particularly concerned with the choice of a *casus belli*; he wanted to get away from the franchise issue and take a stand on the alleged breach of the 1884 Convention: A proposal to revise it would of course be refused by the Boers, and it might then be formally denounced.'[25]

The possibility of sending an ultimatum to the Boers was again before the Cabinet on 22 September. It was still considered premature, but the despatch to the Transvaal government that was agreed at this meeting, further increased the pressure. In it, it was said that it was useless to pursue a discussion on the lines hitherto followed: 'Her Majesty's government are now compelled to consider the situation afresh and formulate their own proposals for a final settlement of the issues which have been created in South Africa by the policy constantly followed for many years by the government of the South African Republic. They will communicate to you the result of their deliberations in a later despatch.'[26]

Of immediate significance was the decision at last taken to send the whole of the army corps to South Africa. This sent a message to the Transvaal that war was now regarded in London as unavoidable, but this had already been taken for granted in Pretoria since the news of the first reinforcements had reached there on 9 September. Wolseley continued to rage against the government's handling of the situation. He was totally out of sympathy with the concern for public opinion, and the policy which the government had been following. He wrote to Major General Sir John Ardagh, the Chief of the Intelligence Department, on 23 September , immediately after receiving authorisation to spend the necessary money for the transport of the army corps: 'We have lost two months through the absolute folly of our Cabinet and the incapacity of its members to take in the requirements and the difficulties of war ... It is no wonder we never achieved much in war and have to struggle through obstacles created by the folly and war ignorance of civilian ministers and War Office clerks.'[27]

Selborne, like the rest of the government, was concerned with the state of public opinion, which was not easy to assess. However, no doubt buoyed up by generally supportive Press comment, he felt able to write to Milner on 7 October: 'You cannot realise the enormous difficulty we have had with public opinion at home. We have only now got 4/5 of the nation behind us because of our hesitancy (militarily almost universal) in making adequate preparations early

24 Roberts, *Salisbury*, p. 735.
25 Ibid., p. 736.
26 *Times History*, vol. I, p. 350.
27 Keith Terence Surridge, *Managing the South African War 1899–1902* (Woodbridge: Royal Historical Society/Boydell Press 1998) p. 52.

enough, and because they believe that there is now *no more opening for negotiation*.'[28] He was of course only guessing that 80 percent of the public supported the government. He was very conscious, though, of the possibility that war might not after all now break out, admitting to Milner that if President Steyn had persuaded Kruger to accept Milner's Bloemfontein terms, 'we could not have rejected them.' As it was, Selborne felt considerable satisfaction with the way that that things were turning out: 'Far the best thing given the home point of view is that the Boers should this last week or the coming week, and before they receive our proposals, commence the war by invading our territory.'

The British public might have been slow to catch on to the sense of their government's imperial mission in South Africa, but by the autumn of 1899, stoked by the fiercely patriotic Press, public support for the war, if still by no means unanimous, was rapidly increasing and the decision to despatch Buller and the army corps to South Africa had caught the imagination of the arch imperialist Rudyard Kipling, who wrote in his poem 'The Absent Minded Beggar,' reflecting the huge upsurge in the making of charitable donations:

When you've shouted 'Rule Britannia,' when you've sung 'God save the Queen,'
When you've finished killing Kruger with your mouth,
Will you kindly drop a shilling in my little tambourine
For a gentleman in khaki ordered South? …
Duke's son – cook's son – son of a hundred kings –
(Fifty thousand horse and foot going to Table Bay!)
Each of 'em doing his country's work
(and who's to look after their things?)
Pass the hat for your credit's sake, and pay – pay – pay!

Meantime, in Pretoria, Smuts was charged with drafting the Transvaal ultimatum, but it was still not to be sent at once, as President Steyn still believed that war was not inevitable, even after news of the decision to send the complete army corps. Whereas in London, military reasons dictated the need for delay, the opposite was true in Pretoria. Each week that passed reduced the opportunity for the Boers to take advantage of the pronounced numerical superiority which, for the moment, they enjoyed. To Steyn, Kruger sent a desperate appeal: 'You still seem to think of peace but that seems to be impossible … You think Chamberlain is leading us into a trap, but if we wait longer the position may become hopeless, and that would be our trap.'[29] With time passing, the Transvaal mobilised on 28 September without waiting for the Orange Free State; several more days would pass before Steyn was finally persuaded, and it was not until the afternoon of 9 October, that Francis Reitz, the Transvaal State Secretary, called on Greene in Pretoria to deliver the ultimatum.

As finally drafted, it accused Britain of a breach of the 1884 Convention and demanded a positive assurance on four points. First, that Britain would agree to arbitration. Secondly, that the British troops on the Transvaal border should be at once withdrawn. Thirdly, that troops arriving in South Africa after 1 June should be withdrawn and finally, that the troops en route should not be landed in South Africa. In the absence of these assurances being given within 48 hours, the Transvaal would with great regret, regard this as a declaration of war.[30]

28 Boyce, *Crisis*, p. 95.
29 Pakenham, *Boer War*, p. 103.
30 Ibid.

Amery would write of this ultimatum that 'a briefer or more arrogant ultimatum has rarely been penned in the course of history.'[31] Andrew Roberts, on the other hand, described it in more charitable terms as 'one of the bravest, if most foolhardy, documents of the nineteenth century.'[32] For the Boers, having seen for some time that war was inevitable, its only failing was that it had not been sent sooner; there was no reason for them to care about being seen as the aggressors, and the precious time wasted had cost them a significant part of their temporary advantage.

Thus Salisbury, Chamberlain and Milner had their war. The Colonial Secretary had been struggling to draft the British ultimatum, which was no longer required; Salisbury was entitled to regard the delay in the outbreak of war as a considerable success. For Milner, the arrival of the Transvaal ultimatum represented the achievement of all that he had been striving for. He realised, though, that all would not be plain sailing, writing to Selborne on 11 October: 'We have a bad time before us, and the Empire is about to support the greatest strain put upon it since the Mutiny. Who can say, what may befall us before that Army Corps arrives?'[33]

31 *Times History*, vol. I, p. 354.
32 Roberts, *Salisbury*, p. 739.
33 Boyce, *Crisis*, p. 96.

2

Preparations

Simply put, it may be said that the country's military readiness did not keep pace with the Cabinet's political ambition. There were a number of reasons for this, of which one of the most compelling was financial. The dawning realisation of the cost of even modest reinforcements for South Africa had given the Cabinet pause; the cost of full-scale mobilisation appears to have come as a particularly unpleasant surprise.

At the outset of the first chapter of the official history of the war, published in 1906, General Maurice addressed the question of British military unpreparedness. He wrote of a 'misunderstanding' between the government and the War Office as to the extent to which reinforcements sent to South Africa 'were sufficient for the temporary protection of our interests on the subcontinent.' Maurice went on to observe:

> It is remarkable that in the evidence subsequently given by the soldiers, not only do they admit that they anticipated beforehand that for this purpose the strength would be adequate, but they assume, at the end of the war that it had as a matter of fact proved so. This can only be understood in the sense that the numbers then in South Africa were able to retard the Boer operations until a large army was thrown into the country.[1]

Events were to demonstrate that in fact, even in the limited sense suggested by Maurice, the forces were utterly inadequate. He noted the comment of Lord Lansdowne on the point: 'I am not a soldier, but I never heard of sending out reinforcements to a country which might become the theatre of war merely in order that the reinforcements might successfully defend themselves against attack; they are sent there, I imagine, for the purpose of securing something or somebody.'[2] Since Lansdowne had persistently opposed the suggestions by Wolseley, as commander-in-chief, that urgent steps should be taken to strengthen the forces in South Africa in the face of increasing indications that war was extremely likely, his comments were extraordinary.

During the three years that followed the Jameson Raid in 1896, there were two principal reasons which led the British Cabinet to maintain wholly inadequate forces in South Africa. As mentioned, the first of these was the cost. The Chancellor of the Exchequer, Sir Michael Hicks

1 *Official History of the War in South Africa*, vol. I, p. 4.
2 Ibid., p. 5.

Beach, constantly resisted the notion of spending the substantial sums that would be involved in strengthening the army there. The other crucial reason, which was in the Cabinet's mind, was a desire to avoid taking steps which might in fact, make war more likely. The possible effect on the Transvaal's neighbour was considered important; there was a reluctance on the part of many of its members to believe that the Orange Free State would, in the event of Britain going to war with the Transvaal, renounce the neutral stance she had hitherto adopted and would take up arms alongside her neighbour.

In the spring of 1897, as Milner sailed to take up his post in South Africa, there had been vigorous discussions on the question of the forces available there should serious trouble arise. From the ship taking him on his 17 day journey to Cape Town, he wrote to his friend and tireless supporter Lord Selborne, to say that when he left England, 'the position of the reinforcements question was in a most unsatisfactory state.' The most that he had been able to obtain by way of reinforcements had been an infantry regiment and three batteries of artillery. A limit of £200,000 had been imposed by the Treasury on what could be spent. Milner was convinced, as he said, that 'we might be turned out of Natal tomorrow.' To Selborne he wrote:

> What I beg you to do is to hang on like grim death to the decision to send reinforcements and not let the government slip out of it on any account. I am sure the Secretary of State is bent upon it, but you know the sort of way in which sometimes tacit opposition, the making of difficulties of detail et cetera gets round even strong resolutions on the part of a busy man, and there is no one in England, who feels quite so strongly about this question of reinforcements, as I do.[3]

The assumption that a purely token force was all that was necessary in South Africa, was widely held, based on a belief that reinforcements, if ever needed, could be rushed there in time. This assumption largely accounted for the Cabinet's acceptance of the penny-pinching arguments of Hicks Beach and the Treasury, and Lansdowne's rejection of his military advice. Chamberlain, whose position made him the central figure in any Cabinet discussion of South Africa, was equivocal, notwithstanding the hawkish attitude of his key subordinates like Selborne and Milner. He had been, however, sufficiently concerned in the spring of 1897, to request the doubling of troop strengths in the Cape, a request which Salisbury had granted, although warning Chamberlain that he would personally 'look with something like dismay to a Transvaal war.' The Prime Minister explained his decision: 'I came to the conclusion that as Chamberlain based his demand principally on the effect of inaction upon colonial opinion it was hardly possible for us, who have not had his opportunities for watching that opinion, to refuse him the reinforcements he requires.'[4]

Sympathetic though Salisbury was to the idea of a South African Federation within the British Empire, he feared the growth of jingoistic public opinion. In the debate on the Queen's speech on 8 February 1898, he warned of the military consequence:

> I have a strong belief that there is a danger of the public opinion of this country undergoing a reaction from the Cobdenic principles of thirty or forty years ago, and believing that it

3 Boyce, *Crisis*, p. 49.
4 Robert Taylor, *Lord Salisbury* (London: Allen Lane 1975) p. 177.

> is our duty to take everything we can, to fight everybody, and to make a quarrel of every dispute. That seems to me a very dangerous doctrine, not merely because it might incite other nations against us … But there is a more serious danger, that is lest we overtax our strength.[5]

Accordingly, so far as the Transvaal was concerned, in 1898 Salisbury was not prepared to leave developments solely in Chamberlain's hands, intervening to take action effectively to shut off the Transvaal's access to the importation of arms through the Portuguese port of Delegoa Bay in Mozambique. He achieved this by concluding an Anglo-German convention in August, with a secret clause in which the parties agreed to oppose the intervention of any third power in the Portuguese colonies.[6] Beyond this, Salisbury saw no reason necessary to antagonise the Transvaal, and certainly not to send out substantial reinforcements. He aimed to control matters by ensuring that British relations with the South African Republic should be determined by the Cabinet and the Colonial Office rather than the powerful business interests that were concerned with maximising profits.

In 1899, after the shooting dead of Tom Edgar, a British subject, by a Boer policeman, and the sending of a petition to Queen Victoria signed by 21,684 Uitlanders in the Transvaal, the Cabinet faced the need to respond. A draft despatch prepared by Chamberlain protesting about the treatment of the Uitlanders was delayed. On 4 May, two days after the Cabinet discussion, Milner sent to Chamberlain a despatch couched in extravagant terms. It became known as the 'Helot Despatch' and was written with the sole intention of increasing the political temperature to a striking extent. In this, he claimed that the case for intervention was overwhelming,and referred to 'the spectacle of thousands of British subjects kept permanently in the position of helots constantly chafing under undoubted grievances and calling vainly to Her Majesty's Government for redress.' There was, he said, a 'ceaseless stream of malignant lies about the intentions of the British government.'[7]

This was written at a time when there had been no increase in troop strengths in South Africa since the reinforcements sent in the spring of 1897. Milner was playing with fire, and well knew it, but in his determination to maintain the pressure on Kruger and the Transvaal, he was prepared to increase his forward policy notwithstanding the obvious military risks. His intention was to raise the stakes so that a call for additional troops could not then be resisted. In the short term, his cabled despatch achieved the desired result, in leading to the Cabinet's approval of Chamberlain's draft despatch to the Transvaal, and thereby creating the climate in which it was seen as necessary to send reinforcements.

It was a crucial step along the road to conflict. Next, though, came the Bloemfontein Conference, when Milner met Kruger in a meeting that might have avoided war. That it did not was Milner's responsibility; his object was not to reach a compromise but, as he put it, to 'screw' Kruger, by rebuffing the Transvaal President's offer of a reform bill which marked a significant advance on his previous offers. Instead, Milner put forward proposals which he knew would not be accepted; and on Tuesday, 6 June he closed the conference, saying: 'This conference is absolutely at an end, and there is no obligation on either side arising from it.' Kruger, with tears

5 Roberts, *Salisbury*, p. 687.
6 Ibid., p. 695.
7 Pakenham, *Boer War*, p. 59.

in his eyes, stood repeating the words which absolutely expressed what was in Milner's mind: 'It is our country you want.'[8]

Events were moving inexorably towards a military solution to the difficulties. Milner left Bloemfontein under no illusion as to where all this was leading. He had in fact, broken off the conference before receiving a telegram from Chamberlain urging him not to do so hastily; at this time the Colonial Secretary cherished the hope that the offer Kruger had made and which Milner had spurned, was not his last offer. However, Milner knew what he was doing; he had written to Selborne on 17 May to say that if he failed to get an acceptable deal from Kruger, it would be necessary to raise the ante to a significant extent: 'If I fail, it will then be *your* turn … assume at once the diplomatic offensive and back it with a strong show of military force.' He considered that absolute determination and a large temporary increase of force could force a climbdown, and if it did not, it would be better to fight at once than in five or 10 years' time.[9] In his heart, he had always known that war must come.

In considering the demand for a major reinforcement, those at the War Office – and beyond them, the members of the Cabinet – had available an accurate assessment of Boer strength. This was a document entitled 'Military Notes on the Dutch Republics of South Africa.' Prepared by the War Office Intelligence Department, headed by Major General Sir John Ardagh, it placed the total (based on the correct assumption that the Orange Free State would join the Transvaal) at 54,000 men. Of these, it was calculated that 20,000 would be held back to meet any threat from the Uitlanders and the Kaffirs. However, the Intelligence Department went on to draw the conclusion that the remaining Boer forces would confine themselves to raids by units of the strength of 2,000 or 3,000 men.

This serious misjudgement was based on a belief that the Boers were, man for man, not the equal of those that had won the battle of Majuba Hill; that their leaders had no experience of managing large forces; that they would be hampered by problems of transport and supply; and that they would lack discipline. Additionally, it was believed that the Boer artillery, acquired from Krupp and Creusot after Jameson's raid, would prove inferior to the British field artillery, while it was thought that they had a dread of regular cavalry. Thomas Pakenham summed up the conclusions of the Intelligence Department:

> In short, far from the Boers being able to invade successfully, an 'adequate' force of British infantry, supported by cavalry and artillery, would have no difficulty in invading the republics. They would easily beat the Boers in the open plains of the Free State or the Transvaal (though they might have trouble in the broken country of the Natal frontier).[10]

Pakenham ended his summary of the Intelligence Department's assessment by quoting its final sentence: 'It appears certain that after [one] serious defeat, they would be too deficient in discipline and organisation to make any further real stand.'

However, though the Intelligence Department's speculation about Boer strategy proved so wide of the mark, the work that it had done in assessing Boer strength was remarkable in its accuracy, and its performance must be judged against its lamentably small budget. That it had done so well, apart from its final conclusion, reflected great credit on Ardagh and his small staff,

8 Ibid., p. 68.
9 Boyce, *Crisis*, p. 80.
10 Pakenham, *Boer War*, p. 77.

and also on his three immediate predecessors as Director of Military Intelligence. The first of these was Sir Henry Brackenbury, who was now Director General of Ordnance, having taken up his latest post early in 1899 in time to make a start on the reform of a grossly inefficient department.

The War Office should have been, therefore, under no illusion as to the scale of the task that would face a British Army in a war with the Boers. Regrettably, when the general unreadiness of the army had later become apparent, both Lansdowne and Wolseley sought to pass as much of the blame as possible to the Intelligence Department; but after the war, the Elgin Commission would emphatically clear Ardagh and his staff, concluding that the foresight they had shown was remarkable.

The War Office was fitful in the use which it made of the intelligence reports available to it, but it was prompted on 21 December 1898 to send a letter to Lieutenant-General Sir William Butler to ask him as commander-in-chief in South Africa to report his proposals for the distribution of troops which he would make in the event of war with the two Dutch republics. In sending this letter, the War Office had before it, the Intelligence Department's earlier assessment of the strength of the potential enemy, in which the figure of Boer troops available for offensive operations was put at 27,000; this was subsequently increased to the figure of 54,000.

The War Office letter reviewed the strategic situation, observing that the total of the British forces in South Africa at that time 'would be inadequate to any other than a defensive attitude, pending the arrival of reinforcements from England.'[11] The letter went on to say that it was Wolseley's opinion as commander-in-chief that 'the plan for offensive operations must depend upon the political and military situation of the moment, and cannot now be fixed.' Butler was referred to the Intelligence Department's report, and to its conclusion that apart from an attack on Kimberley and the northern strip of Natal, it was unlikely that more would be attempted than raids of 2,000 to 3,000 men

Butler did not reply, and the War Office found it necessary in June 1899 to send telegrams pressing him to do so. By telegraph and a letter dated 12 June, he finally replied, having previously had a frosty exchange with Milner, who wanted to see if Kruger could be intimidated by moving British troops to Laing's Nek, just inside the Natal frontier. It was a proposal which Butler firmly rejected. In his view, to compel the Boer republics to submit would require a minimum of 40,000 men. His proposals for a defensive strategy with the very limited number of troops that were available, continued a forward policy that was intended to bluff the enemy by posting small detachments close to the frontier. Butler did not advocate, however, the occupation of the passes through the Drakensberg or the bridge over the Orange River which had been proposed by his predecessor.

As commander-in-chief, Butler was proving absolutely unacceptable to Alfred Milner. For his purposes, he required a general of a much more belligerent demeanour and he was determined to see him replaced. Butler, who had been Acting High Commissioner during Milner's visit to England in the winter of 1898–1899, had seriously angered him by declining to forward the first petition from the Uitlanders to the British government. In Milner's eyes, Butler was dangerously pro-Boer and he began doing all he could to engineer his removal.

In a letter to Selborne of 24 May, before the Bloemfontein Conference, Milner had suggested that in order to take up a strong position on the frontier, a force of an additional 10,000 men

11 *Official History*, vol. I pp. 35–36.

might be required. He dealt with the obvious suggestion that might be made in opposition to such a strong reinforcement, which was that it would lead the Boers to feel that they should at once seize the strong positions of the Biggarsberg and Laing's Nek: 'I don't so much mind their seizing them though I should greatly prefer to get there first. By seizing them they put themselves in the wrong and become the aggressors. What I do fear is their seizing these positions without our being able at once to hit back.'[12] Milner was quite sure that a small reinforcement was not good – it excited without quelling.

As for Butler, Milner conveyed in strong terms to Selborne his belief that he must at once be replaced and of course, received a sympathetic response: 'I have just spent two hours deciphering your telegram about Butler – you are quite right, you cannot do yourself justice with him at your elbow. I presume it will go before the Cabinet on Tuesday.'[13] To Chamberlain, Milner had expressed himself in equally outspoken terms, adding to his report about the Bloemfontein Conference:

> One word in conclusion. The general. He is too awful. He has, I believe, made his military preparations all right, but beyond that I cannot get him to make the least move or take the slightest interest ... His sympathy is wholly with the other side. At the same time there is nothing to lay hold of. He never interferes with my business and is perfectly polite. But he is absolutely no use, unless indeed we mean to knuckle down, in which case he had better be made High Commissioner.[14]

At the War Office, Lansdowne was quick to send a rebuke to Butler for saying that he deprecated the sending of reinforcements: 'You cannot understand too clearly that, whatever your private opinions, it is your duty to be guided in all questions of policy by those who are fully aware of our views, and whom you will, of course, loyally support.'[15]

Butler had only been in post since the previous year, but he had made no secret of his sympathy with the Boers and his belief that war could be avoided. Milner's insistence on his removal would soon bear fruit and in August, Butler was ordered home to take up a post in command of the Western District. His effective replacement was to be Lieutenant-General Sir George White, currently Quartermaster General at the War Office, but he was appointed only as commander-in-chief of the troops in Natal. Before his arrival, the command there remained in the hands of Major General Sir William Penn Symons, who had been previously appointed to command the troops in Natal in July. White's appointment was made only after prolonged discussion between Chamberlain, Lansdowne and Wolseley. The Colonial Secretary had urged that General Sir Redvers Buller should go; Lansdowne was keen on White, who was a member of the so-called 'Roberts Ring' because, as he told Chamberlain, he was 'not one of the old gang,' a reference to those who comprised the 'Wolseley Ring.' Buller, of course, was much the most prominent member of this, and had previously been earmarked by Wolseley as his successor as commander-in-chief. During the second week of June, Buller was told that if war came – he would be in command. Nothing more was done at that point to prepare for the sending of reinforcements, while Buller himself was decidedly unenthusiastic about the prospect of the chief command.

12 Boyce, *Crisis*, p. 82.
13 Ibid., p. 85.
14 Julian Symons, *Buller's Campaign* (London: The Cresset Press 1963) p. 89.
15 Symons, *Campaign*, p. 83.

The scope for a mutual failure of understanding between Wolseley and Lansdowne was considerable. The commander-in-chief had long held politicians in contempt. As early as 1890 he wrote:

> Party government nowadays does not mean the leading or the endeavour to lead public opinion so much as the following of public opinion and the giving effect to it. The worst side of it is the controlling of public opinion, directing it into side issues so as to avoid expenditure which would be inconvenient from a party standpoint. In the army and navy affairs no great measure is ever taken up by any government until public opinion forces its consideration upon the ministers in a way that to neglect it would injure the party then in power – take the recent additions to the navy as an instance.[16]

In this, Wolseley identified the two great obstacles to what he considered the proper freedom of the War Office to do what it considered necessary – the party system and the penny-pinching of the Treasury.

As to this, White would subsequently give evidence to the Elgin Commission of his experiences as Quartermaster General: 'I think we were unnecessarily restricted in the question of expenditure for certain things we asked for. We were met more than once by their saying that there had been no provision in the Budget … It was the Chancellor of the Exchequer who put so heavy a check on the Secretary of State for War.'[17]

The question of reinforcements for South Africa was the subject of an illuminating exchange of correspondence between Wolseley and Lansdowne. In addition to Wolseley's distaste for party politics, there existed between them – on Wolseley's part in particular – a fundamental personal lack of sympathy. Wolseley often referred to Lansdowne in letters to his wife in terms of profound personal dislike and contempt, describing him in one of these as 'an obstinate little fellow, very conceited, and his obstinacy is born of ignorance.' In another, he said that he spent his day 'struggling with my little gentleman … Such a small mind it would be difficult to imagine. I am sure some little Jew must have "overtaken" his mother before he was conceived.'[18] It was a remark which reflected little credit on Wolseley and was scarcely an encouraging basis on which the leadership of the British Army must depend; it certainly contributed to its unpreparedness for war in 1899. As early as 1896, Wolseley chafed at the limits of his power as commander-in-chief, writing in his diary of having had a distressing day: 'I am vice-chairman of a debating society. The Secretary of State is the Commander-in-Chief as far as we have one.'[19]

The fifth Marquess of Lansdowne had occupied a central position in British politics for many years. He had held office first under Gladstone before, in 1883, becoming Governor General of Canada, a post which was followed by appointment as Viceroy of India in 1888. Lansdowne was a Liberal Unionist, but in June 1895, on returning from India, he entered the Conservative Cabinet. He was one of the richest men in England but had been brought up with the Victorian ideals of public service; Pakenham describes him as an 'epitome of the mid-Victorian virtues

16 W. S. Hamer, *The British Army: Civil-Military relations 1885–1905* (Oxford: Clarendon Press 1970), p. 219.
17 *Report of the Royal Commission on the War in South Africa*, Vol. II, p. 143.
18 Pakenham, *Boer War*, p. 75.
19 Major General Sir Frederick Maurice and Sir George Arthur, *The Life of Lord Wolseley* (New York: Doubleday Page 1924), p. 293.

– the victory of education over breeding, and of character over both (of priggery, so to speak, over Whiggery),'[20] though too conscientious and lacking fire and steel and above all, imagination.

Lansdowne was instinctively hostile to Wolseley and 'the old gang,' so that the latter's attempts to get the government to face the reality of the military situation in South Africa fell on stony ground. On 8 June 1899, Wolseley wrote to Lansdowne pointing out that at that point, there were about 10,000 fighting men all told in South Africa: 'In the event of war with the Transvaal we should require, in addition to the force now in South Africa, one complete army corps, one cavalry division, and one battalion of mounted infantry. For the line of communications we should require four battalions.'[21] He went on to call for the immediate mobilisation of the army corps and the cavalry division 'under the general whom it is intended should command in South Africa in the event of war.' The expense of this, he pointed out, would be 'an extremely small matter when compared with the cost of a war.' He recommended that the Majuba position and Laing's Nek should be suddenly occupied, whenever it appeared expedient to do so.

Buller took a somewhat different view to that of Wolseley, writing a memorandum of 6 July to say that he did not 'like the idea of commencing operations in South Africa by sending out four generals and a force of 10,000 men.' He deprecated sending out any troops until it was necessary to put a force into the field, hostilities having so far been decided upon. He was especially concerned to point out that the supply difficulties were so great that they should be faced from the outset, 'and that even 10,000 men for a week, if they are not wanted to fight, are better anywhere than on a frontier across which they are not intended to be sent.'[22] Forwarding this to Lansdowne, Wolseley reiterated his call for the mobilisation of the complete army corps and cavalry division.

Buller had known since early June that he would be in command in South Africa if war came. This was at an extremely uncomfortable meeting with Lansdowne, who liked Buller no more than he liked Wolseley. His feelings were reciprocated by Buller, who later complained that Lansdowne had treated him 'in a most ungracious manner.' During the course of this meeting, Buller reminded the Secretary of State that he had never held an independent command and told him that a better plan would be for Wolseley to be sent as commander-in-chief, with him as his Adjutant-General.

Although Buller's record and his seniority made him an obvious candidate, another option would have been Sir Evelyn Wood, who was also one of Queen Victoria's most successful generals, and of whom she held a particularly high opinion. Wood had had an uncomfortable time in South Africa during the First Boer War when sent out with reinforcements for Colley before Majuba Hill, becoming involved in the peace talks which ultimately, ended the war on terms which were widely disapproved of in the army. Subsequently, he was to earn Wolseley's extreme disapproval during the abortive attempt to relieve Khartoum. Wolseley wrote of Wood that his 'vanity and self-seeking and the detriment of everyone but himself would be positively disgusting if one did not view it from the ridiculous side and laugh at it and him instead of being angry over it.'[23]

20 Pakenham, *Boer War*, p. 72.
21 *Elgin Commission Report*, vol. IV, Appendix D, p. 262.
22 Ibid., p. 263.
23 Stephen Manning, 'Evelyn Wood' in Steven J. Corvi and Ian F. W. Beckett, eds, *Victoria's Generals* (Barnsley: Pen and Sword Books, 2009) p. 40.

Thereafter, in spite of his previous dislike of him, Wolseley promoted Wood's career as a military administrator and he became responsible for important army reforms. In due course, Wood became Quartermaster General and then Adjutant-General. In the latter capacity, he was to be responsible for overseeing the successful mobilisation of the army corps for South Africa in 1899. He was, though, disappointed not to have been chosen for the command there. Buller acknowledged that he might have been a suitable candidate when remarking to a friend just before he sailed for South Africa: 'I have always looked upon this as Evelyn's journey, and had been wondering whether when it came off I should have a look in … I think he would have done it better than I shall, but I shall try my best.'[24] From the moment of his first conversation with Lansdowne, it is apparent that Buller's lack of self-confidence never left him.

On 18 July, in the course of a meeting in Lansdowne's room, Wolseley asked Buller if he was quite satisfied that the present position in the Cape Colony and in Natal was altogether safe. Buller replied that he had complete confidence in Butler's ability and forethought, and that as long as clever men like Butler and Symons, on the spot, did not say there was danger, he saw no necessity for sending out troops in advance of the army corps. This, according to Wolseley, was the essence of Buller's opinion as explained to him and Lansdowne, and it must have had a considerable influence on the latter's mind.

When, at the beginning of August, the Cabinet came to consider Milner's call for reinforcements of 10,000 men, it was not prepared to go further than making 'some addition to the strength of the forces now in that colony;' the government, as Lansdowne told Wolseley, was not prepared to accept responsibility for the 'complete protection' of Natal. The additional troops would, however, be intended to strengthen the position there, and reassure the colonists and above all to strengthen the British hand in the ongoing diplomatic discussions. 2,000 men or thereabouts should suffice. It was a futile and lamentable decision; but Wolseley was prepared to accept it as strengthening the position north of the Tugela River and at Ladysmith, though not rendering Natal entirely free from external danger.

In rebutting the later accusation that Wolseley contributed to the British unpreparedness for war, his biographers cite his important memorandum of 24 August; but he had already, on 18 August, spelt out the real danger to Natal that presently existed. There, with the forces currently available, it would not be possible to put more than 4,000 men into the field near Colenso, since it was essential not to leave the line of communication and the base at Pietermaritzburg unprotected. He begged the government 'to consider the advisability of sending to Natal, with the least possible delay, one infantry division, one regiment of cavalry, two brigade divisions of artillery and some Royal Engineers – altogether about 10,000 men.' He calculated that he could put such a reinforcement into Ladysmith within nine weeks of receiving the order to do so.[25] It would, he said, be unsafe and unwise to delay further action of this kind.

Responding to this on 20 August, Lansdowne told Wolseley that the outlook in South Africa had improved and that Chamberlain had written to him to say that 'while he wished to avoid relaxing the pressure, he saw no occasion for reinforcements.' Lansdowne said that he was rather sorry that Wolseley had not put forward his views earlier, when the situation was more critical; it is hard to see how he could justify such an observation, since Wolseley's minute of 7 July, had been explicit in his call for the mobilisation of an army corps. In reply, on 24 August, Wolseley

24 Geoffrey Powell, *Buller: A Scapegoat?* (London: Leo Cooper 1994), p. 119.
25 *Elgin Commission Report*, vol. IV Appendix D, p. 266.

told Lansdowne that the Transvaal could be made to see that Britain meant business 'by such a display of force as that I have recommended from the first in this matter, and which on a smaller scale I strongly advocated in my note to you of the 17th instant … At this moment we are *not* locally prepared for war in South Africa.'[26] This meant, as he pointed out, that if war came, the initiative would be surrendered to the enemy.

Wolseley was also at odds with his political master over the selection of units to send reinforcements. He had no doubt that troops from home and from the Mediterranean would be a better fighting body than those from India: 'The battalions etc would have a larger proportion of young men, but they would have better health and go than those coming from India.'[27] Wolseley had not forgotten that the battalion that lost Majuba was from India. He would, he said, infinitely prefer to lead any of those which he had selected for the force of 10,000 men for Natal than most of the battalions in India. Lansdowne, replying three days later from his estate in Ireland, was not convinced; he was sure that the government of India would send good battalions, and could supply the force more cheaply and more expeditiously than could be done with a force from home. In addition, Lansdowne was not persuaded that reinforcements should be sent yet, anyway, at least until the Transvaal's latest proposals had been finally rejected.

As the prospect of military action became increasingly likely, Lord Salisbury took a hand, asking Buller for his ideas, which the general incorporated in a memorandum dated 5 September. He was without up-to-date information as to the number of troops already in South Africa; he estimated that it would take five weeks to send 5,000 men from India, 10,000 men from England in 11 weeks, and the full army corps from England in 16 to 20 weeks. In Buller's opinion, if the Transvaal was to be invaded from Natal, 20,000 men would be required for the advance, 10,000 for the lines of communication, 10,000 as a reserve in Natal and 10,000 for the defence of Cape Colony – 50,000 men in all. He also pointed out that the attacking force and that in Cape Colony, would require transport and must be mobile; until then, there could be no advance, so that if an ultimatum was sent to the Boers before this, the two colonies would be liable to invasion.[28]

Buller sent a minute to Wolseley on the same day; hitherto he had, since he had been told that he would be in command, refrained from doing so in order not to hamper those conducting the negotiations. Now, however, he felt obliged to point out the huge risks that were being run. He was not concerned about the possibility of an invasion of Cape Colony, but thought that hostile acts against Natal were probable, and that the existing force there was strong enough to protect itself but not nearly strong enough to protect Natal. Buller concluded his analysis by asking Wolseley to put forward, once more, these considerations as the view of the officer who would be expected to organise the force to be sent out.

Thinking it over, Buller decided to tackle Lansdowne directly. On 8 September, he went to London to have a personal meeting with him. This went badly. Buller had become increasingly angry at being kept in the dark, as he saw it, and being denied the right to choose most of his own staff, while still uncertain of what arrangements would be made for the transport of the army corps. Above all, he was concerned that nothing had been agreed with White and Symons as to the strategy to be pursued for the defence of Natal.

26 Maurice and Arthur, *Life of Lord Wolseley*, p. 317.
27 *Elgin Commission Report*, vol. IV, appendix D, p. 207.
28 Ibid., p. 268.

On the next day, when he returned to his headquarters at Aldershot, Buller sat down to write a letter to Lansdowne which Pakenham has justly described as of particular importance. In this, he implored Lansdowne to send a further force to Natal at once, additional to the 10,000 which the Cabinet had authorised: 'We have let things drift until we are now in a very uncomfortable military position – if the Boers are bold … They now have the chance of inflicting a serious reverse upon us in Natal – should they do that every day saved in the sending of reinforcements would be worth its weight in gold.'[29]

The gulf that thus existed between political master and commanding general could not fail to cast a shadow over the conduct of the coming campaign. Buller was in no doubt that White should not take up too forward a position, but rather should stand on the defensive behind the Tugela River. The garrisoning of Ladysmith and the advance on the Biggarsberg was in his view, extremely hazardous.

As has been seen, throughout the months leading up to the situation that had been so clearly pointed out by the military, the politicians had been heavily influenced by cost; the position of Hicks Beach and the Treasury was that account must be taken of this by the War Office, and this had been obliged to limit its recommendations in the face of Lansdowne's insistence that cost was a supreme factor. This reluctance to pay the price for its imperialism also heavily inclined Lansdowne – and through him – the Cabinet, to pay insufficient regard to the warnings from Wolseley and the War Office. The Cabinet was accordingly all the more ready to accept Chamberlain's assessment of the improbability of a pre-emptive strike by the Boers.

Nevertheless, when it came to it, Wolseley was proud of what was achieved in sending the army to fight in South Africa, telling his wife that the war was the most important since the Crimean War, adding: 'But in the present case we shall send out a much larger force from these shores and it will be one under the very ablest soldiers and thoroughly equipped for war – a very different condition of things from that which existed in the army sent out to the Crimea in 1854'[30] However, it would not be long before Wolseley's confidence would be seen to have been misplaced and the British Army would have to pay the price for the Cabinet's desire to conduct an aggressive imperialist policy on the cheap.

29 Pakenham, *Boer War*, p. 97.
30 Dennis Judd and Keith Surridge, *The Boer War* (London: John Murray 2002) p. 58.

3

The Opposing Armies

A great deal has been written about the readiness of the British Army in 1899 to fight a war such as confronted it in South Africa. There were a large number of contemporary accounts, many of them written by war correspondents who accompanied the army. When the war ended, a Royal Commission examined in minute detail, the preparations for war and heard a large amount of evidence relating to the early stages of the war. The four volume *Official History* edited by Major General Sir Frederick Maurice and others, delivered an authoritative – if extremely restrained – account, while avoiding controversial judgements. *The Times History of the War in South Africa*, which ran to six volumes, edited by L.S. Amery, was very much less restrained. All these were followed by very many historians who examined the British Army, its officers and men, and its culture and organisation as it stood in 1899.

Fundamentally, the British Army was far too small for the responsibilities that it might, at any time, have to face. The British Empire was enormous, and the army was scattered across the globe. It was a volunteer army, so that its size was determined not by numbers of population but by the amount which politicians were prepared to spend on it. In considering the figures of troop numbers bandied about between politicians and the military, as war in South Africa became increasingly likely, the total size of the army must be kept in mind. Aanother key factor was the announcement by Lord Salisbury on 28 July 1899, that only white troops would be employed in any operations that became necessary there. The Official History records that in October 1899, the grand total of all ranks of white troops, exclusive of reserves, amounted to 227,159, of which, on the day that the war began, 27,054 were in South Africa. Of the grand total of the British Army, only 108,098 were based in the United Kingdom; of white soldiers, 67,921 of the rest were in India, 3,699 in Egypt, 7,496 in Malta and 5,104 in Gibraltar, with smaller forces in many other locations. In 1888, as part of a process of reform, it had been decided that 'though it was highly unlikely that so large a force would ever be required, two army corps, with a cavalry division, or a total of 81,952 men, were to be available for the purposes of action beyond the seas.'[1] In addition to the standing army, there were theoretically, 81,134 reservists available.

The decision that was taken in September 1899 to mobilise an army corps and cavalry division, represented therefore, the commitment of a large part of the available troops. Limiting the expeditionary force to white troops meant that the huge Indian regular army, and its ancillary

1 *Official History*. vol. I, pp. 89–90.

units, amounting to nearly 300,000 men, could make no contribution. There were, however, a number of locally raised units in South Africa, based on police forces and volunteers; Cape Colony had 9,200 men under arms, and Natal 3,500. There were also 2,500 locally raised troops in Rhodesia.

The quality of the British private soldier in 1899 was considerably affected by the fact that he was generally recruited from the lowest class of society, unskilled, frequently illiterate and coming from a social background which left him in poor physical condition. Additionally, he was often of below average intelligence. These characteristics arose directly from the very low pay earned by the British private soldier, who was described by Wolseley as 'the worst paid labourer in England.' *The Times History* noted, though:

> Once in the army, however, the raw material was considerably improved. Good food and an admired system of gymnastic training rapidly developed the physique of the recruits. The habits of discipline and neatness, and the influence of their officers and non-commissioned officers had an equally good effect on the character of the majority. The social and moral conditions of the soldier's life had been greatly raised in recent years by the efforts of officers, among whom no more prominent example can be quoted than Lord Roberts, to provide them with reasonable comforts and amusements in their barracks, and to keep them from drink and debauchery.[2]

Little effort was made, however, to develop the soldier's intelligence, and the low level of literacy increased the difficulty of improving his military efficiency. It was calculated that only two months in the year was devoted to military training; the rest of his time was spent in a range of relatively menial duties: 'In fact, as a school of military training, the army was nothing more or less than a gigantic Dotheboys Hall,' a circumstance ascribed to the whole army system.[3]

The training of officers had certainly improved since the departure of the Duke of Cambridge as commander-in-chief in 1895, but it was still regarded as a profession for the sons of officers and gentlemen. Throughout the army, there remained a marked resistance to the concept of promotion by selection, and a majority of young officers still did not take their duties very seriously, nor did they make much effort to advance their military knowledge. Sandhurst was the means by which their education might be promoted but in practice, the teaching there was indifferent. Material wealth was important; it was calculated that to be an officer in the British Army, a young man in the infantry should have a private income of £150 a year, and in the cavalry £500.

Organisationally, the British Army lagged some way behind those on the continent of Europe. Recommendations by Edward Cardwell and by the Hartington Commission, that the office of commander-in-chief should be replaced by the establishment of a general staff, were not popular in the army. It had been opposed not only by the Duke of Cambridge, but also by Wolseley as his successor. Outside the army, the Queen did what she could to scupper the proposal, since it was her hope that her son, the Duke of Connaught, might in due course succeed the Duke of Cambridge. The Liberal government which took office in 1893 was instinctively opposed to anything that smacked of militarism and the proposal was abandoned. Although Wolseley duly became commander-in-chief in 1895, the suggestion by the Hartington Commission that

2 *The Times History*, vol. II, p. 33.
3 Ibid.

instead there should be a chief of staff, had led to a coolness between him and Brackenbury, whom he suspected of aspiring to such a post.

Fortunately for the army, Brackenbury's upward career in the army continued and in 1899, he became Director General of the Ordnance, embarking on a wholesale reform of the supply system, although too late for the commencement of the war in South Africa. Brackenbury would, in due course, produce a report in December 1899 in which he described 'a situation as regards armaments, and reserves of guns, ammunition, stores and clothing, and as regards the power of output of material of war in emergency which is, in my opinion, full of peril to the Empire.'[4] He had already, in September, drawn attention to the difficulties and delays which the financial system produced. In the following year, Lansdowne produced a memorandum looking back at the situation at the start of the war which emphatically confirmed Brackenbury's view, describing the resources available as 'absolutely and miserably inadequate.'

The army's practical unreadiness for war in terms of personnel and organisation was bad enough. It was even more serious when it came to collecting the arms and equipment necessary to fight such a difficult campaign as was now to be required of it. The closing decades of the nineteenth century had seen remarkable advances in the development of both artillery weapons and small arms, but military thought as to their employment had not kept up with the pace of change. Tactical thought remained stuck in the past: 'In the minds of the majority of officers the parade ground theory of war, which looked upon all irregularities of the ground as disturbing and incalculable elements interfering with the normal evolution of tactical operations, was still deeply rooted.'[5]

The German General Staff history of the war observed that 'very little weight was laid upon the preparation of the attack by fire, there being a strong emphasis on the use of the bayonet.' Reviewing the army's training methods, it noted:

> The tactical training of the British infantry suffered from the disadvantage of being carried out on training grounds which were too small and afforded too little variety, while the laws practically prohibited training elsewhere than on government property. The apprehension lest troops should get out of hand and shoot badly had led to an excessive preference for volley firing, nor did the instruction in musketry and utilising cover correspond to present-day requirements.[6]

Another weakness of the British Army in 1899, was the failure to grasp how far the changes of modern warfare had made the traditional cavalryman almost irrelevant. In this, of course, the British Army was no different from the armies of Europe, which had forgotten the bloody and largely ineffective cavalry charges of 1870–1871. Brian Bond has written:

> A combination of factors, however, gave the cavalry national as well as service prestige out of all proportion to its size. Over its real historical achievements there had accumulated an aura of glamour and romance, epitomised by the half serious boast that the cavalry's role in battle was to add tone to what would otherwise be an unseemly brawl.[7]

4 *Official History*, vol. I, p. 32.
5 *The Times History*, vol. II, p. 32.
6 German General Staff, *The War in South Africa* (Nashville: Battery Press 1998) vol. I, p. 28.
7 Brian Bond, 'Doctrine and Training in the British Cavalry 1870–1914' in Michael Howard (ed.), *The Theory and Practice of War* (London: Cassell 1965) p. 100.

However, there had been some developments in the use of irregular cavalry, from which some serious lessons might have been learnt. In the Kaffir War of 1878, Buller had commanded an unorthodox mounted force which operated to considerable effect, and in the following year in the war against the Zulus, he led a larger force, which also did well. He commented on the use of the carbine and made clear that he had no use for the sabre. The inspirational military writer Colonel G. F. R. Henderson had, during the 1890s, come increasingly to the view that it was firepower which had enabled the unorthodox cavalry tactics of the American Civil War to be successful. The actual training of mounted infantry had made little progress in the years leading to the Boer War.[8]

The British Army of the nineteenth century had conducted a large number of expeditions overseas in all climates in every quarter of the globe, fighting against a wide range of very different opponents. None of the wars it had fought, however, had provided the army with the sort of experience relevant to fighting the Boers, with the exception of the disastrous campaign of 1881 which ended with the defeat of Sir George Colley's red coated infantry at Majuba Hill. The army's campaigns were largely fought by ad hoc units assembled at short notice for the particular purpose, and it thus gained no experience of the management of large bodies of men. In particular, the staff had to be put together on a makeshift basis, which meant that the links between commanding generals and their individual units were frequently inadequate due to mutual unfamiliarity: 'It was no fault of theirs, but a consequence of that past history which had built up the British Empire, that they had neither previously worked together, nor practised in peacetime their special part in an organisation which had, in fact, to be created anew for the immediate task in hand.'[9]

However, in one respect, the army's history of frequently conducting operations overseas had provided valuable experience. The navy had often had to make arrangements for shipping considerable forces overseas at short notice, although certainly not on the scale required for the war in South Africa. The possibility that shipping might be required for as many as 50,000 men and 8,000 horses was first put to the Admiralty in August 1899. In the following month, the task of assembling the necessary shipping began, although the official requisition for the transport of the army corps was not issued until October. The first units were embarked on 20 October and between that date and 30 November, a total of 58,000 men and 9,000 horses left England. The Elgin Commission observed that the exercise 'affords a remarkable illustration not only of the greatness of British maritime resources, but also of what can be done when careful forethought and preparation is applied to the object of utilising rapidly in war instruments which are in peace solely engaged in the purposes of civil life.' The Commission added the telling comment that if the same forethought had been applied throughout, 'there would have been little criticism to make with regard to the South African war.'[10]

Wolseley, the War Office and the Admiralty could therefore congratulate themselves at least on the arrangements for mobilisation, transport and the calling out of the reserve. The despatch of the army corps and cavalry division to South Africa had gone entirely smoothly. Wolseley, who went to Southampton to watch the first ships to leave, wrote to the Queen: 'I never saw five finer Batns., not *one man* under the influence of drink.'[11] This will certainly have confirmed

8 Bond, 'Doctrine and Training', p. 105.
9 *Official History*, vol. I, pp. 88-89.
10 *Elgin Commission Report*, vol. I, pp. 125–126.
11 Symons, *Campaign*, p. 93.

Wolseley's belief that the army was in good shape to fight what he knew would be a difficult campaign, but the successful despatch of troops to South Africa, and the patriotic sentiment that it inspired, masked the extent of the underlying problems that would soon become apparent.

When he came later to review the remarkable success which the Boer army enjoyed, particularly in the early stages of the war, General Maurice reflected on a number of historical examples of seasoned troops being checked by an enemy inferior in numbers, discipline and armament. In spite of these deficiencies, such a soldier had nevertheless enjoyed some advantages, 'due either to the nature of his country, to his own natural characteristics, or to a combination of both.'[12] This, he observed, certainly applied to the Boers, whose self-reliance and individuality were of the greatest importance in the particular circumstances of the South African War. These included the wide dispersion of the combatants, the distances between commanders and commanded, the availability of weapons of greater range and accuracy, the open terrain and the clear atmosphere.

The independent spirit of the individual Boer fighters made them an extremely unusual opponent for the British Army. The Official History went on to analyse their characteristics in considerable detail, noting their particular value in the conditions of modern warfare. It observed that South Africa was 'a country which gave the freest play to the deadly properties of small-bore rifles.' These enabled the Boer soldier to conduct operations at long-range, making it difficult for their enemy to close with him:

> He had an antipathy to fighting at close quarters, but he knew the value and necessity of striking; the Mauser enabled him to strike at the extreme limit of vision, multiplying tenfold the losses and difficulties of the enemy who attempted to close with him. The portability of the ammunition, the accuracy of the sighting, the absence of betraying smoke, all these increased the Boer's already great trust in himself.[13]

These characteristics were not, or should not have been, unknown to their opponents: 'The British War Office could not have been in the dark respecting the peculiarities of the theatre of war and of its adversaries. Englishmen and Boers had frequently fought shoulder to shoulder against the native populations and had also been opposed to each other.'[14] Nor should the British commanders have been surprised by the Boer's tactical nous; his ability to fight stubbornly on the defensive was matched by a willingness at once to abandon a position, however strong, if it ceased to be the best means to his immediate end, and his mobility enabled him swiftly to take up a new position. The Boers were extremely skilful in their choice of ground, and in its preparation for defence. One weakness, however, of their great mobility was a marked reluctance ever to launch a counter-attack.

Moreover, in attack, their individuality meant that it was rarely made in full strength, or pushed home, due to their reluctance to engage at close quarters. The Official History reflected on the uniqueness of these military characteristics:

> No fighting men have been more ready for war, yet so indifferent to military glory, more imbued with patriotism, yet so prone to fight for themselves alone, more courageous, yet

12 *Official History*, vol. I, p. 68.
13 Ibid, p. 70.
14 *German Staff History*, vol. I, p. 11.

> so careful of their lives, more lethargic, or even languid by nature, and yet so capable of the most strenuous activity. Such were the Boers of the veld. In one particular they had never been surpassed by any troops. No Boer but was a bold horseman and a skilled horse master, who kept his mount ready at any moment for the longest march or the swiftest gallop, in darkness or over the roughest aground ... The unrivalled mobility of the Boer armies, therefore, and the vastness of its theatre of action, gave to them strength out of all proportion to their numbers.[15]

The military system of the Boers was based on the commandos, which consisted of the entire male population organised in three groups: youths under the age of 18 and men over the age of 50, men between 18 and 34, and men between 34 and 50. The second of these groups was the first liable to service, and then the third. The country was divided into wards; the leaders of these, known as field cornets, were elected for a term of three years, and would be responsible for leading the men of the ward to the assembly of the commando, which would elect a commandant. It was a system which, in terms of enrolment and mobilisation, worked extremely well; but the election of an officer was frequently not for solely military reasons, which meant that he was not necessarily the man best fitted to discharge his duties. The size of a commando varied considerably according to the population of its district and might be anything from 300 to 3,000 men strong.

In addition to this citizen army, the principal element of the regular army was the very efficient and well organised state artillery. The field artillery of the Transvaal consisted of six Creusot quick firing 75mm guns, four Krupp howitzers of 120mm, eight Krupp quick firing 75mm guns, 21 Vickers-Maxims (pom-poms), four Vickers mountain guns, four Nordenfeldt 75mm guns, an Armstrong 15-pdr and an Armstrong 12-pdr. Excluding the Maxims, therefore the Transvaal possessed 28 field pieces; there were also a number of obsolete weapons and a dozen pieces of fortress artillery; the peacetime complement was 406 officers and men. The Orange Free State could contribute a further 23 field pieces: 14 Krupp 75mm guns, six Armstrong 9-pdrs, one Krupp quick firing 37mm gun and three Armstrong mountain guns. There were also three Maxims. The Free State artillery, with a total complement of 375 officers and men, was rather less well-organised than that of the Transvaal.[16]

The total number of troops that the Boers would put into the field during the course of the war has never been precisely ascertained, but the best estimate suggests an overall total of 87,365, a total which included the commandos, the regular forces, foreign volunteers and rebel Afrikaners from Natal and Cape Colony. In terms of weaponry, the commandos were extremely well provided; it is estimated that the two republics had over 108,000 rifles of various makes in stock. They had ample ammunition; actual figures are quite uncertain, but it has been suggested that the total stock was probably of the order of 1 million rounds.[17]

Unlike the British Intelligence Department, its Boer counterpart was provided with lavish funds, spending over £286,000 on information gathering between 1896 and 1898. It has been suggested that their intelligence work was directed not so much in determining the likely British strategy, which was considered to be more or less self-evident, but rather on obtaining a picture

15 *Official History*, vol. I, p. 74.
16 Ibid., pp. 82–85
17 Ibid., p. 79.

of British preparations and morale. In October 1899, the Boers knew with some accuracy, the strength of the enemy forces which they would immediately face.

There was no permanent command structure or staff system, which had to be improvised from scratch. The chain of authority was, therefore, imperfect from the start, and was never really fully effective. Nor, of course, was there a pool of professional commanders on which to draw, but there were a considerable number of gifted amateurs. Bill Nasson has pointed out that, contrary what to what has been suggested, they included many who had studied military history with some care:

> Indeed, Boer generals were fond of the didactic study of foreign wars, with professional knowledge of the conduct of not only the 1870–71 conflict, but also the Napoleonic wars, the American Civil War and, by no means least, because of its inspirational legacy as a struggle for national independence, the American War of Independence.[18]

The theatre of war which these armies would contest was remarkable, both in its terrain and its climate, which made considerable demands on the troops which fought there:

> All natural features are on a large scale; the endless plains, as well as the bare rugged mountains, while the gloomy grandeur and the death-like silence of the wilderness overpower the mind of the spectator. Scattered settlements and cultivated oases are to be found there, but only where there is a plentiful supply of water.[19]

The climate also varies considerably. Warm winds blow from the east and cold winds from the west. Summer runs from October to March, and it is during this period in the eastern region that the rain chiefly falls; on the other hand, in the western region the rainy season tends to occur during the winter months from April to September. The temperature varies enormously, and in the summer months marches by day became intensely fatiguing. Not surprisingly, the Boer soldiers were far more used to both to rain and weather and enjoyed thereby a considerable advantage. In one respect, though, South Africa had an outstanding merit as a theatre of war; it was for the most part extremely healthy:

> The purity of the air, the geniality of the temperature, the cool nights, the brilliant sunshine, and the hard dry soil were palliatives of evils inseparable from all campaigning. Otherwise, for regular armies of invasion, South Africa was unfavourable. The railways were so few that the business of supply and movement was always arduous; spaces so vast that large forces were swallowed up; the enormous distances from one strategical point to another, intensified in difficulty by the almost entire lack of good roads, the scarcity of substantial bridges … All these complicated every military problem to a degree not readily intelligible to the student of European warfare alone.[20]

Reference has already been made to the unusual clarity of the atmosphere, 'which makes it possible to detect the very smallest object miles away, and, in the absence of all distinguishing

18 Nasson, *Boer War*, p. 78.
19 *German Staff History*, vol. I., p. 5.
20 *Official History* vol. I, p. 65.

points, such as trees or fields, to guide the eye, renders all judgement of distances difficult for a stranger.'[21]

The physical features of the country are also unusual. South Africa is a tableland:

> To the Indian Ocean on the east it shows a face of scarped mountains. Following the coastline at a distance inland of from 70 to 100 miles, these sweep around from north to south: then stretch straight across the extreme south-west of the continent through Cape Colony, dwindling as they once more turn northward into the sandhills of Namaqualand, and rising again to the eminences above Mossamedes in Portuguese territory.[22]

Back in England, Buller had drawn attention to the huge importance of mobility. The lack of any good road system, and the inadequacy of the rail network for the supply of fighting armies meant that it was essential that the armies be provided with the necessary transport, and in the early stages of the war, the shortage of this would exercise an almost crippling effect on the movement of the British troops, dependent as they were on its vulnerable lines of communication.

21 *The Times History*, vol. II, p. 51.
22 *Official History*, vol. I, p. 55.

4

Talana Hill and Elandslaagte

Milner was entirely justified in feeling the anxiety which he expressed to Selborne about the military situation. It was beginning to get complicated. By 11 October, when the ultimatum expired, Lieutenant-General Sir George White and his staff had already reached South Africa, having arrived in Natal to assume overall command on 7 October. His intention had been to concentrate the available forces there just in front of Ladysmith, on the slopes of the Biggarsberg range. He did not accept the suggestion that he should move up to Laing's Nek, on the Transvaal border but at the same time, he also ignored Buller's warning not to go beyond the Tugela River. When he arrived in South Africa, however, he discovered that Major General Penn Symons had taken the decision to push part of the force available to him up to Dundee, 70 miles north of Ladysmith.

White's reaction was that this was a mistake; it would be better to keep the British force concentrated and he resolved to withdraw the advanced force to Ladysmith. This, however, aroused strong objections on the part of the governor of Natal, Sir William Hely-Hutchinson, who feared that it would prompt the Boers living in Natal to rise in revolt, with the possibility that this might spread to Cape Colony.

The question was discussed at a meeting with the governor, attended by White and Symons, and by Major General Archibald Hunter, who had been designated by Buller as his chief of staff, but who for the moment was accompanying White, and by the latter's military secretary Beauchamp Duff. White expressed his view that Symons' force should be withdrawn from Glencoe and Dundee. In this he was supported by Hunter and Duff, but Symons took the opposite view. Hely-Hutchinson pressed his argument that it was important to protect the coal supplies at Glencoe and that withdrawal might encourage Zulus to rise. Asked for his opinion, Hunter said that it was a case of balancing drawbacks and on reflection, agreed with Symons and the governor. In the face of this, White backed down, and decided to acquiesce in the existing deployment. Symons set off for Dundee on 10 October and White travelled next day to Ladysmith. Nothing that he had seen and heard since he arrived in South Africa thus far had encouraged him; the size of his force compared with that of the enemy was constantly on his mind. He wrote to his wife to say that there should be 20,000 more troops in South Africa than there were: 'The Cabinet have only themselves to thank if they have to reconquer South Africa from the sea.'[1]

1 Pakenham, *Boer War*, p. 99.

As previously mentioned, Butler – when pressed by the War Office to outline his proposals for the defence of Natal and Cape Colony – had maintained the policy of seeking to bluff the Boers by taking up a forward position, both in Natal and along the border with the Orange Free State. General Sir Frederick Forestier-Walker, who took up his post as commander of the forces in Cape Colony on 6 September, decided that he should continue this policy. Posts were established along the border of the Orange Free State at Kimberley, Orange River Station, De Aar, Naauwpoort and Stormberg, each garrisoned by a half battalion of infantry and some engineers, with a number of guns; at each of Orange River Station, Naauwpoort and Stormberg there was also a company of mounted infantry. Buller, when these arrangements were reported to him, approved by a telegram on 29 September, in which he told Forestier-Walker of the decision to despatch the army corps, a cavalry division and seven battalions for the lines of communication, and ordered him to prepare for their disembarkation in due course.[2] Pending their arrival, the British forces for the defence of Cape Colony were very thinly scattered indeed.

In Natal, White and Symons had to do the best they could with the forces which they had available. Neither before White left England, nor when Buller followed him on 14 October, had any sort of plan of campaign been devised at the War Office; it was to be left to the generals on the spot to make up strategic policy as they went along. As a commentator writing in January 1900 observed: 'It is pretty clear that, though this war had been pending for years, no English Moltke has thought out a general plan of campaign and provided for all possible contingencies.'[3]

Meanwhile, the Boer forces were on the move. Joubert reached Volksrust on the evening of 12 October, with General Johannes Kock at Botha's Pass and General Lukas Meyer 40 miles to the east. The next day, Joubert occupied Laing's Nek. Moving cautiously forward, he reached Newcastle where on 18 October, he held a council of war. He planned to isolate the British force at Dundee while his right wing made contact with the Free State commandos advancing through the passes of the Drakensberg. On his left, Lukas Meyer was slow to concentrate, but on 19 October prepared to move on Dundee from the east, while General Daniel Erasmus, with 5,000 men, advanced on the town from the north.

White's situation was unenviable. His 8,000 men at Ladysmith and just under 4,000 at Dundee under Symons, both risked being cut off by superior forces not only from the rest of Natal but from each other. White had been disturbed to learn on 15 October from one of his staff who had visited Dundee that, contrary to his orders, Symons had taken no steps to put the place in a state of defence. It took White three days to telegraph Symons ordering him to retreat from Dundee if he did not comply with his instructions. Symons replied that he could not do so and would accordingly retire but would need all the available rolling stock to bring away his military stores and the non-combatant inhabitants of Dundee. This alarmed White, who asked Symons if, in view of the risks to which an evacuation by rail would be subject, he thought it better to remain. Symons, a more assertive character, replied that he could and must stay at Dundee; in no doubt that this was right, he cancelled the orders to retire. To this, White now telegraphed that he supported Symons' decision.[4]

Symons and White, debating by telegraph the wisdom or otherwise of standing fast at Dundee, seem to have given little thought to the appropriate tactical response to a Boer movement on the town. For what was in White's mind, it is necessary to look at his evidence to the

2 *Official History* I, pp. 42-43.
3 'The War in South Africa,' *Quarterly Review*, January 1900, p. 282.
4 *Official History*, Vol. I, p. 127.

Elgin Commission three years later. Lord Elgin asked what was actually intended at Dundee: 'But in the local schemes of defence, I think in all of them there were provisions for holding Dundee?' To this, White merely offered a flippant reply: 'Yes, there were provisions, but it was provisions in the eating sense.' He was pressed further by a member of the Commission to agree that 'it was only a weak detachment, which could not have resisted the Boer army?' To this, White offered the feeble and evasive answer: 'I cannot stand cross-examination on that scheme. I do not pretend to have attached any weight to it.'

He went on to recapitulate the sequence of events which led to Symons remaining at Dundee, remarking that in the course of their telegraphic discussion, he had told Symons that the governor of Natal's insistence on the garrisoning of Dundee had decreased. He thought that Symons' failure to investigate the water supply there 'was part of the grand confidence of the man;' presumably, he also attributed to this confidence, the failure to put in hand proper defences of the place.[5]

White went on to claim, unconvincingly, that the holding of the advanced position at Glencoe and Dundee had had a very beneficial effect. All in all, his evidence reflected little credit on either his strength of character or his military judgement. In any case, he was quite content to leave it to Symons, whose ability he much admired, to take his own decisions.

Full of confidence, Symons awaited the appearance of the enemy with no anxiety about his position, but apparently with no clear plan in his mind as to what he should do when they arrived. Apart from posting pickets to give him early news of this, he took no action to forestall an advance on Talana Hill, even though it commanded both the town of Dundee and the British camp to the west. It would have been a straightforward matter to post a force on the hill. His apparent insouciance almost certainly derived from a pronounced under-estimate of the quality of the Boer army, an opinion which appears to have been shared at first by a number of other British commanders. Symons' reason for not posting more cavalry pickets in advance of his position at Dundee appears to have been due to a wish to keep his cavalry fresh.[6]

On 19 October the situation deteriorated, when a party from Kock's force seized Elandslaagte, cutting all communication between Dundee and Ladysmith. Symons was by now well informed of the enemy movements and of an intended attack on Dundee. This was to be carried out by Meyer's force, advancing from Doornberg at dusk on 19 October towards Talana Hill, three miles to the west of which lay the British camp. The advance was to be supported by Erasmus's force advancing from the north to take up a position on Impati mountain, north-west of Dundee. At 2:30 a.m., Meyer's leading troops clashed with a picket of British mounted infantry, which alerted Symons to the Boer advance. Meyer pushed on, and by dawn on 20 October, had occupied Talana Hill and also Lennox Hill, linked to Talana by Smith's Nek. The position was a very strong one.

Symons had turned out two companies of the Dublin Fusiliers to support the picket, which had taken up a position in the Sandspruit. He left the rest of his force to sleep until standing to at the normal time of 5.00 a.m. At 5.30 a.m., the mist which had shrouded Talana Hill lifted, and the Boers could be seen silhouetted along the skyline. Ten minutes later, Meyer's artillery, which included three 75mm guns from the Transvaal State Artillery, opened fire. Symons at once determined to assault Talana Hill. One battery of field artillery opened fire on the Boer

5 Elgin Commission, *Minutes of Evidence*, vol. II, pp. 149-150.
6 Erskine Childers, *War and the Arme Blanche* (London: Edward Arnold 1910), p. 62.

position from the camp, while two more advanced to a position just east of the town. Within 10 minutes they had silenced the Boer guns for the moment, while the Royal Dublin Fusiliers and Royal Irish Rifles, with the King's Royal Rifles, moved around Dundee to take up a position along the Sandspruit, preparatory to an advance on the hill.

The 1st Leicestershire Regiment, with one battery, was to defend the camp, which was expected to face a Boer advance by Erasmus from Impati, which was still hidden by a thick mist. The cavalry and mounted infantry, under Colonel Möller, were to wait under cover until ordered to advance, unless he saw a good opportunity to do so. Symons put Colonel Yule in command of the assault, which was to be in three phases; first the artillery preparation, then the infantry attack, and finally a charge by the cavalry to cut off the enemy's retreat.[7]

By 7.00 a.m., all of the infantry had assembled in the Sandspruit under cover, and 20 minutes later began their advance, breaking into a run as they gained the edge of the wood below Talana Hill. On its farther side was a stone wall, then a gap and then a hedge. As the advancing infantry emerged from the wood, they were assailed by heavy rifle fire from the hill and were pinned down; Yule was unable to get the attack moving again. At 9.00 a.m., Symons, increasingly impatient at the lack of progress, rode up, to hear from Yule of the tremendous fire from Talana. The latter's suggestion was to delay the infantry advance until the artillery had weakened the Boer resistance, but Symons would have none of this. Dismounting, and ignoring the protests of his staff, he walked forward to the front of the infantry, accompanied by his ADC with a scarlet pennant, calling on the Royal Irish Fusiliers to 'push on.' Within minutes, he was shot in the stomach; he walked slowly to the rear and remounted, riding to the stretcher bearers, who carried him to the dressing station; at 9.35 a.m., the surgeon pronounced his wound to be fatal.[8]

Meanwhile, the British infantry had begun to advance along the right side of the wall, coming under fire from Lennox Hill. As they advanced, they crossed to the left side of the wall, finding as they did so that the upper terrace was unoccupied. The Dublin Fusiliers were, however, pinned down and for a while the advance was halted again. It took two hours to collect sufficient men for an advance on the upper slopes of Talana Hill and during this period, British casualties mounted. At 11.00 a.m., the artillery were ordered to cease fire to enable the further advance to begin but it was shortly found necessary for the bombardment to resume. At 11.30 a.m., it ceased again, and the batteries galloped forward, attracting heavy fire from the Boer line before taking up a position to open fire once more. Soon after this, the Boer fire began to slacken and the infantry attempted an advance, which was only partially successful. Once more, the artillery opened up in support, but the opposing lines were now so close that many British infantrymen fell under friendly fire.

Nevertheless, a final assault cleared first Talana Hill and then Lennox Hill, from which the Boers streamed back to collect their ponies with which to make a rapid retreat. It was the moment for which Möller's cavalry should have been waiting, but they were nowhere to be seen. Pickwood, the artillery commander, misunderstanding the situation, held his fire and the Boer forces melted into the distance.[9] Yule, who was still fearful of a Boer advance by Erasmus from Impati, ordered his men back to camp.

A considerable opportunity had been lost, as a result of Symons' imprudent suggestion to Möller that he need not wait under cover if he saw a good opportunity to advance. Möller

7 Pakenham, *Boer War*, p. 128.
8 *Official History*, vol. I, p. 134.
9 Ibid., p. 137.

had needed no encouragement. As early as 5.45 a.m. he had sent a squadron of hussars under Major Knox, to reconnoitre the northern flank of Talana Hill, in the hope that it might be possible to threaten a Boer retreat. Knox reported that this might well be so, and Möller sent him another squadron and a section of mounted infantry; and then, learning from Symons that the enemy's artillery had fallen silent and might be withdrawing, Möller followed with the rest of his force. When he joined Knox, he had a chance to fire on the Boer ponies behind Talana, but instead took up a position two and a half miles in rear of the centre of the Boer position.[10] He had sent Knox towards the rear of Smith's Nek, who had a successful encounter with a Boer patrol before moving to a point in rear of Lennox Hill. Möller, with the rest of his force, remained in the open behind Talana Hill, where he soon became threatened by large numbers of Boers who were falling back from the hill. To escape, Möller attempted to ride around the northern flank of Impati, but soon found that his retreat there was cut off by Boers descending the hill. He now attempted to make a stand at the Adelaide farm, but increasing numbers of enemy troops surrounded him, and at 4.00 p.m., he surrendered his force to Commandant Trickardt.

Knox, meanwhile, with his two squadrons of hussars, had been more fortunate, moving swiftly towards Malungeni, and thence westwards to safety. Möller had surrendered with 214 men, having suffered 31 killed and wounded. Total British casualties during the day's fighting amounted to 500, of whom 51 were killed and 203 wounded, the remainder being taken prisoner. Total Boer casualties were approximately 142.[11]

In taking the hill, the British had won a victory of a sort, but it had scarcely increased the security of a force which should not have been at Dundee in the first place. A recent historian has noted that 'great damage had been done to British confidence.'[12] On the other hand, Amery, in *The Times History*, put a different face on it; although it was a battle which cost the British force about four times as many casualties as the Boers, he felt able to write that it had 'created a respect for British valour,' and that 'from the British point of view, Talana was a splendid example of the bravery of the British soldier.'[13] What the battle had done, however, was to demonstrate to the troops on each side that their opponents were more to be reckoned with than they had supposed.

Brigadier General Yule had now taken command of the force at Dundee. His first move was to shift the position of his camp further to the south, in the hope (which in the event was unrealised) of getting it out of range of the Boer artillery on Impati. It was becoming clear to him that his position was critical; the water supply, which came from Impati, was in enemy hands, while the Boer occupation of Elandslaagte meant that his force could no longer retreat direct to Ladysmith.

Back in Ladysmith, White sent his cavalry commander Major General John French, to investigate the situation at Elandslaagte. He had with him the 5th Lancers, the Natal Mounted Rifles, the Natal Carbineers and a battery of field artillery, while an infantry brigade under Colonel Ian Hamilton was ready to move in support. Kock had arrived with the bulk of his force at Elandslaagte at dawn on 20 October. French set off on his reconnaissance at 11.00 a.m., but while he was on the march, Boer activity from the west began to assume such a

10 Ibid., p. 139.
11 Ibid., p. 462.
12 Nasson, *Boer War*, p. 103.
13 *Times History*, vol. II, p. 173.

threatening aspect that White recalled him; he returned to Ladysmith at sunset, having made contact only with the small German corps under Schiel which was acting as a screen covering Kock's main body.

That evening, news came in of the battle of Talana Hill, which suggested that it was a more complete victory that was in fact the case. Emboldened by this, White resolved now to attack Kock's force in some strength, and at 4.00 a.m. on 21 October, French pulled out from Ladysmith with five squadrons of Imperial Light Horse and the Natal field artillery with orders to clear the Boers from the area and to restore the railway. He was followed by rail two hours later, by a half battalion of the 1st Manchester Regiment together with some railway and Royal Engineer detachments.[14] By 8.00 a.m., French was in sight of the station and colliery buildings at Elandslaagte and his artillery opened fire on the parties of Boer troops that were seen. A squadron of Imperial Light Horse rushed the railway station by galloping forward in open order, releasing a number of British troops taken prisoner on the previous day. It soon became clear to French that to deal with Kock's force he must have reinforcements, and he reported accordingly to White. The Boers now had two guns in action, outranging the British artillery, which fell back. In his message, French asked for three infantry battalions, two batteries of artillery and additional cavalry. White put this reinforcement in hand, replying to French: 'The enemy must be beaten and driven off. This is of great importance.'[15]

The position which Kock had taken up consisted of four kopjes in the form of a ridge, running for some 4,000 yards south-east of Elandslaagte railway station. The principal feature was a steep hill, the summit of which was more or less flat, which was 400 yards long by 200 yards wide. At its northern end it fell steeply towards the line of the railway, but at the southern end, sloped gradually to the plain. Six miles to the north-west of the main position beyond the railway, lay Jonono's Kop, from which descended long spurs towards Elandslaagte. On one of these was posted the German corps under Schiel, who had been reinforced by about 100 Free Staters. The Hollander corps under Commandant Lombard and the Johannesburg commando under Ben Viljoen, were in the main position together with part of the Vrede commando under de Jager. There were 850 men in all, with two 75mm field guns and one Maxim.[16]

Having examined the Boer position, French had resolved in the first instance to wait for his reinforcements, the first of which to arrive being a squadron of lancers, a squadron of dragoons and the 42nd Field Artillery Battery. With these, he fell back to the Modder Spruit. After his exchange of messages with White, French decided next that he should wait no longer but move forward, advancing towards the line of kopjes at about 1:30 p.m. The lancers were the first in touch with the enemy, held up by pickets from the Johannesburg commando in advance of the line of kopjes. However, an advance by four squadrons of Imperial Light Horse, supported by the lancers, stormed the ridge.

Meanwhile, French's infantry reinforcements under Hamilton had begun to arrive in trains from Ladysmith. It had been White's original intention that he should put Hunter in command of the operation against the Boer position at Elandslaagte, but the latter felt that it would be unfair to deprive French of the command and White accepted this.[17] The infantry began to detrain at 2:20 p..m about three miles south-west of Elandslaagte, first the four companies of

14 *Official History*, vol. I p. 160.
15 Pam McFadden, *The Battle of Elandslaagte* (Randburg: Rava Press 1999), p. 10.
16 Ibid., p. 40.
17 Archie Hunter, *Kitchener's Sword-Arm* (Staplehurst: Spellmount, 1996), p. 123.

the Manchester Regiment, then seven companies of the Devonshire Regiment and finally five companies of Gordon Highlanders. French and Hamilton conferred briefly, agreeing on the plan to be adopted, which was to hold the enemy in front with one battalion and to attack his left flank with nine companies and the dismounted Imperial Light Horse.

As the infantry began to move on the Boer position, the squadron of dragoons, which had been advancing on the far side of the railway, encountered Schiel's position on the lower spurs of Jonono's Kop. The dragoons met with such a fierce resistance that French switched his two field artillery batteries together with the lancer squadron to support them. The artillery was soon able to silence the enemy riflemen; as it happened, at about 3.30 p.m., Schiel was ordered by Kock to rejoin the main Boer position. He and his men found time to drink the health of the Kaiser before retiring by a circuitous route as instructed, taking post on a low rise near the main Boer position, where they suffered numerous casualties, including Schiel himself who was wounded in the leg.[18]

The advance of the British infantry continued in the face of heavy Mauser fire from the Boers who were, however, steadily forced back. Their two 75mm guns did their best; but when the British field artillery changed position, moving forward by about 1,650 yards, they were quickly silenced.

As the force making the turning movement on the Boer left flank pressed forward, its advance was aided by the bursting of the thunderstorm which had hung over the battlefield all day. At close range, casualties mounted on both sides. The Manchester companies, in the Boer front, paused to allow the turning movement to take effect. By now, the British were fighting under the eyes of their commander-in-chief, White having ridden up from Ladysmith to watch the progress of the battle. When he arrived, French offered to hand over its conduct to him, but White insisted that he should continue in command.

Hamilton had ordered that the infantry advance should be in widely extended order, a decision that greatly reduced the casualties suffered by his troops as they pushed forward over open ground. Although the various units became intermingled as they closed the enemy, their advance was irresistible until practically the whole of the Boer position was overrun. In a final attempt at a last stand, Kock was fatally wounded. By 5:55 p.m., the infantry held the whole of the upper part of the Boer position.[19]

Well before this, many of the Boers had begun to abandon their position, streaming back down the reverse slope. However, as they did so, they passed within 500 yards of the British cavalry which had taken up a position at the foot of the lower slopes of Jonono's Kop. At 5:30 p.m. Major Gore, commanding the cavalry, advanced in an easterly direction. He was at first impeded by broken ground; then, as his men crossed a slight rise, they came in sight of about 300 Boers, riding slowly northwards. The charge was sounded, and the two squadrons, one of lancers and one of dragoons, riding in extended order, fell on the retreating Boers, scattering them in all directions. After about a mile and a half, the cavalry were rallied and reformed and returned, again charging those Boers still falling back from the high ground and inflicting heavy casualties with lance and sword.

It was an incident that was to attract strong allegations of atrocity; many Boers were cut down, it was said, while trying to surrender. The number of Boer casualties during this part of the battle is unknown. There were undoubtedly instances of reckless cruelty during the cavalry

18 McFadden, *Elandslaagte*, p. 22.
19 *Official History*, vol. I, p. 168.

charges; on the other hand, many British historians, such as Hugh Rethman, have denied vehemently the charge of atrocity.[20] In propaganda terms, the Boers certainly played up the allegations, pointing to the lancers with particular outrage. Gore's own account was straightforward:

> My two squadrons were formed in line at extended files, and charged right across the line of retreat which the enemy were taking. The latter were going away quietly at a trot, till our men's heads appeared over the crest of the hill; they then changed the direction and galloped straight away in front of us and in all directions. Their ponies, however, were no match for our horses, and we rapidly overhauled them. Those men who still tried to escape were attacked with the lance or pistol and made prisoners of.[21]

As the battle ended, it was immediately clear that it would be dangerous to attempt to remain in possession of Elandslaagte. By 11.00 that morning, indications of substantial Boer forces debouching to the west had already become apparent, and at 5.30 p.m., Hunter at Ladysmith sent a message to White reporting an advance on the place from Beeler's Station. French was accordingly instructed to return to Ladysmith at once, and at 11.00 p.m., he issued orders for a retreat on the following day. Total British casualties amounted to 50 killed and 213 wounded; the Boers lost 67 men killed and 108 wounded, with 188 taken prisoner.[22] The Boer casualties included practically all their senior commanders. Kock was treated on the battlefield and was then transported to Ladysmith, where he later died.

Although the prompt retirement from Elandslaagte meant that the British victory had been devoid of practical benefit, it had been a well conducted engagement. The German Staff History, which was particularly impressed by the cavalry action, noted:

> As regards tactics and training, the British force had shown itself quite on a par with its adversary. The Boers were pressed energetically in front and flank and succumbed to the power of concentric infantry fire at very short range, which was effectively supported by a superior number of guns.[23]

The success of the cavalry would be seized upon by the adherents of shock tactics by cavalry as having shown its continuing effectiveness on the modern battlefield. It was a claim which Erskine Childers firmly dismissed in a detailed analysis of the action, finding that the cavalry benefited from no less than six favourable conditions: the novelty of the cold steel, the lack of Boer reserves, bad light, open and smooth ground, fresh horses and men, and the ragged retreat of a beaten enemy. This, he thought, could be regarded as a rare combination of ideal conditions.[24]

Leo Amery was enthusiastic about the extent and manner of the British victory:

> The Boers had been driven out of a strong position of their own choosing, and their retreat converted into a demoralised rout. They had left 300 wounded and whole prisoners in British hands and all the equipment of about 1,000 men. Kock's force was completely

20 Hugh Rethman, *The Natal Campaign* (Stroud: Amberly Publishing, 2017, p. 129.
21 McFadden, *Elandslaagte*, p. 32.
22 *Official History*, vol. I, p. 464.
23 *German Staff History*, vol. I, p. 38.
24 Childers, *Arme Blanche*, pp. 66–67.

> broken up. The success was due to the bravery of the troops, to the admirable cooperation of the three arms throughout, and not least to the skill with which the infantry attack was developed ... Colonel Hamilton showed an insight into the changed conditions of warfare which many other generals were destined still to learn by bitter experience.[25]

Amery dismissed complaints about the conduct of the British cavalry, remarking that 'it must be clearly understood that charging cavalry are fully justified in not giving quarter to individuals (though it was done in a good many cases in this charge at Elandslaagte), unless the whole object of the charge is to be frustrated.' He was, of course not an entirely dispassionate commentator.

Back at Dundee, Yule was extremely reluctant to abandon the town and embark on a retreat to Ladysmith, even though he had always been doubtful of the strategical decision to hold it. He was an elderly regimental commander who now found himself unexpectedly with an extremely difficult command responsibility; he was already worn out with fatigue and not in the best of health. However, one immediate decision was necessary and that was the relocation of the British camp, which was well within the range of the Creusot 'Long Tom' which Erasmus had located at Impati. Yule found what appeared to be a suitable site on one of the northern spurs of Mount Indumeni, about a mile to the south of the camp's existing location and by 3.00 p.m. on 21 October, with heavy rain falling, the whole of the force was concentrated there.[26]

The withdrawal had been disturbed by the Boer artillery which had opened up; outranged, the British field artillery had been unable to respond. To Yule, it was apparent that his position was extremely exposed and he sent a telegram to Ladysmith appealing for reinforcements. He got no immediate reply to this, although at 4.00 p.m. he received news of his promotion to major general. At 5.00 p.m., Hunter responded to the request for reinforcements to explain that White was in the field at the battle at Elandslaagte, but that he could hold out little hope of Yule's request being met.

Still unwilling to retreat, Yule looked for a fresh site further from Impati, which he found in a flat topped foothill of Indumeni on its northern side, a further two miles to the south. By 5.00 a.m. on the following morning, the whole force had taken up its new position. Three hours later, two despatch riders brought news of the Boer defeat at Elandslaagte and it appeared to Yule that in his present position, he would be well placed to intercept the retreating Boers, and he fixed on Glencoe Junction as the place to do so.[27] He assembled an advanced guard consisting of the 69th Battery, the mounted infantry and the 18th Hussars, which set off at 10.00 a.m. and soon discovered scattered parties of the enemy. Meanwhile, the rest of the column crossed the lower spurs of Indumeni, and came under fire from Impati, as did the field hospital, where the red flag was too small for the Boer gunners to see. As the mounted troops pressed on towards Glencoe, they found the Boers showing a firm front, and it was clear now to Yule that his thrust was getting nowhere. The recall was sounded and the column returned to Indumeni.

Pondering his next step, Yule considered a plan to concentrate on the top of Talana Hill and establish a defensive position there. He was talked out of it by his senior officers, who pointed out that they would be surrounded by 10,000 Boers, whose artillery outranged theirs, would be

25 *Times History*, vol. II, pp. 193-194.
26 *Official History*, vol. I, p. 143.
27 Ibid., p. 145.

short of ammunition and have no defensible water supply.[28] Reluctantly, Yule drafted a message to White to tell him that he would attempt to retire by the Helpmakaar road. However, before it could be sent, a telegram arrived from White at 6:30 p.m.: 'I cannot reinforce you without sacrificing Ladysmith and the colony behind. You must try and fall back on Ladysmith. I will do what I may to help you when nearer.' White had at least now assumed responsibility for the retreat, but it was a painful demonstration of the folly of the original decision to hold Dundee, taken so recently on fallacious political grounds.[29]

In great secrecy, a convoy of 33 wagons was assembled to carry what stores could be collected and then, abandoning the townspeople of Dundee and the field hospital with the wounded, including the dying Penn Symons, the whole force moved out south eastwards. By 11:15 p.m. the last of it was clear of the mountain and a good pace was maintained so that by dawn on 23 October, the leading units had cleared the defile of Blesboklaagte, some 14 miles from Indumeni. As the morning wore on, it became so hot that the column halted at 12:30 p.m. to wait for darkness to fall. The most dangerous part of the journey lay immediately ahead; the column must now negotiate the difficult Van Tonders pass, six miles in length. Despite the steep and obstructed road and the profound darkness, good progress was still made and by dawn on 24 October, the column was able to debouch into the open veld.

As they halted at 10.00 a.m., artillery fire could be heard to the west, which indicated that White was in action near Elandslaagte or Modder Spruit. Yule, despite his fatigue and worsening health, rode out with his mounted troops and artillery, leaving the rest of his force between the Sunday's and Waschbank rivers. However, when they had gone nine miles, the sound of the firing died away,and Yule turned back to rejoin the main body. What he had heard was the engagement at Rietfontein, described in the following chapter.[30]

Back at Dundee, the Boers had descended from Impati to occupy the town, once it was realised that its garrison had departed. Deneys Reitz described how the Boer soldiers went 'whooping through the town and behaving in a very undisciplined manner. Officers tried to stem the rush, but we were not to be denied, and we plundered shops and dwelling houses ... The joy of ransacking other people's property is hard to resist, and we gave way to the impulse.'[31]

On the Waschbank, Yule rejoined the column as a cloudburst deluged it with rain, filling the dried up bed of the river within an hour. It was not until 4.00 a.m. on 25 October that the march was resumed, the advanced guard crossing Sunday's River at 8.30 a.m. Seven miles further on, the column again paused for a brief rest before pushing on to a high ridge north of Kankana mountain, which it reached at 3.45 p.m. where it was now planned to pass the night. At 5.00 p.m., however, a patrol from Ladysmith arrived with orders from White. A force under Colonel Coxhead was moving out from the town; Yule was to meet it and hurry back without delay. By 3:30 a.m. the following morning, the leading mounted units rode into Ladysmith, and by 10.00 p.m. all had reached safety. Yule's health had deteriorated to the point where the senior officers of his staff largely had to manage the conduct of the retreat, which all things considered, had been skilfully executed.[32]

28 Pakenham, *Boer War*, p. 144.
29 *Official History*, vol. I, p. 146.
30 Ibid., p. 149.
31 Rayne Kruger, *Goodbye Dolly Gray*, p. 87.
32 *Times History*, vol. II, p. 208.

The Boer pursuit had been ineffectual. The *Official History* observed that Erasmus, who had only set off after Yule on 24 October, had 'so little hope of overtaking the retreat that he chose the only route by which it was impossible for him to do so, the main road west of the railway.'[33] All the same, by nightfall on 25 October, Erasmus had already reached Elandslaagte and further delay on Yule's part would have risked disaster to his force.

33 *Official History*, vol. I, p. 151.

5

Rietfontein and Lombard's Kop

In Ladysmith, White was very conscious of the possible dangers to which Yule's column would be exposed in its retreat from Dundee. His anxiety had been sharpened by the arrival of Free State commandos on the heights north and west of the railway, and he decided to move against these to protect Yule's force from any Boer move from there to intercept it. At 5.00 a.m. on the morning of 24 August, he marched out from Ladysmith with a column some 5,300 strong, consisting of two regiments of cavalry and two of mounted infantry under French, and an infantry brigade of four battalions and three batteries under Hamilton.[1]

His objective was the six Free State commandos occupying the crest of a line of hills about seven miles north-east of Ladysmith, of which the key feature was the height of Intintanyoni. The Boers had about 6,000 men in position here, which had that morning come under the command of General Piet Cronje.

White's force moved up the Newcastle road. At about 7.00 a.m., its advanced cavalry screen came under fire when it had reached a point about six miles from Ladysmith. It quickly drove back the Boer pickets across the Modder Spruit east of Pepworth Hill. By 8.00 a.m., the infantry had reached Rietfontein Farm, at which time the Boer artillery on Intintanyoni opened fire. The British artillery, pulling out of line and taking up a position west of the main road facing the Boer position, replied. The infantry now deployed in front of the line of British guns, the 1st Gloucesters on the left, and the Liverpool Regiment on the right, with the 1st Devonshires in support. The 2nd King's Royal Rifles remained in reserve. The Boers, along the crest of Intintanyoni, now opened a heavy rifle fire, to which the British infantry responded. The artillery now changed position, moving to the left of the infantry, and continuing a brisk exchange with the Boer artillery. As the rifle fire intensified, the Devonshire battalion moved up to extend the British line to its left.

At this point, there occurred an inexplicable incident, when just before noon, the commanding officer of the Gloucesters, Colonel E. P. Wilford, suddenly broke cover and dashed down the open slope at the head of one company and with a Maxim gun, with the apparent intention of assaulting the Boer position. Whether this was a simple error by Wilford in assessing his immediate situation, or a confusion as to his orders is unclear, but it was an impossible move. Having advanced down the slope, he would then have had to push on uphill in a frontal assault in face

1 *Official History*, vol. I, p. 158.

of concentrated rifle fire. The Boers had, temporarily, fallen silent under the fire of the British artillery, but now at once opened fire on Wilford's men. He was killed and casualties quickly mounted. It was only with great difficulty that the British infantry, which included other units which had advanced in Wilford's support, could be withdrawn.

Meanwhile White, observing a Boer movement which appeared to be directed against his left, sent the Natal Mounted Rifles forward against the ridges of Nodashwana, due west of Intintanyoni. They were soon able, with the support of the 42nd Battery, to drive back the Boer riflemen at this point. Gradually, the Boer fire again subsided, ceasing by about 2:30 p.m. and half an hour later, White, considering that his objective had been accomplished, ordered a general retirement on Ladysmith.[2]

Total casualties during the course of this engagement had not been high. The British lost 14 men killed, and 98 wounded, two men being taken prisoner. Boer casualties amounted to 13 killed and 44 wounded.[3] *The Times History* remarked:

> As a sensational action the engagement at Rietfontein presents little of interest, though the casualties in the Gloucester Regiment afforded a striking proof of the deadliness of modern rifles at long ranges. The men were simply called upon to carry out the trying task of demonstrating against a position the defenders of which they could not see, and suffering casualties without the gratifying knowledge that the enemy were losing as heavily as themselves.[4]

The Times History went on to suggest that the objective, which was certainly attained, might have been equally well attained by shelling the enemy positions rather than bringing the infantry within rifle range, or even by watching the enemy from the safety of the Newcastle road. As it was, the Boers were sure that they had beaten off a determined attack.

By 26 October, it was apparent to White that the Free State commandos had joined forces with those of the Transvaal and next day, he sent out French at 4.00 a.m. with his cavalry to reconnoitre along the Newcastle and Helpmakaar roads. At dawn he was in contact with Lukas Meyer in laager about seven miles south of Elandslaagte. French reported to White at 10.35 a.m.; there were, he estimated, 4–5,000 men on Intintanyoni, with other substantial forces between Pepworth Hill and Rietfontein. There were two laagers; one, with about 2,000 men was five miles south-east of Modder Spruit Station and the other, much larger, about one mile from the station. Hamilton, with an infantry brigade, had marched out of Ladysmith to the Neks between Gun Hill, Lombard's Kop and Umbulwana, causing the Boers to fear an immediate attack. White did in fact toy with the idea of attacking the laagers, but after a conference with French and Hamilton. abandoned the plan and the troops all returned to Ladysmith.[5]

The next day, about 2,000 Boers with three guns under Lukas Meyer advanced to Modder Spruit behind Long Hill, on which Boer pickets had already taken post. Further east, the Free State commandos on Intintanyoni moved down to occupy Surprise Hill on the heights above the Bell Spruit. Still endeavouring to assess the positions and strength of the enemy, White sent out a further cavalry reconnaissance on 29 October, which reported that the Boer laagers

2 Ibid., p. 156.
3 Ibid., p. 463.
4 *Times History*, vol. II, p. 205.
5 *Official History*, vol. I, pp. 172–173.

were now to the east and south-east of Lombard's Kop; that Pepworth Hill and Long Hill were strongly occupied and that a large camp lay to the north-west of Pepworth.

Thomas Pakenham has written of what was in White's thinking once he had concentrated all his force at Ladysmith, where a huge volume of supplies had now been built up, sufficient to stand a siege of three months:

> Yet to allow himself to be besieged in Ladysmith was the very last thing White had in mind, that Thursday, 26 October, as the Dundee column staggered into the town. He had only to look out of the windows of the convent to see that Ladysmith was a most unsuitable town, set in a most unsuitable piece of country, in which to let his 13,000 men be locked up.[6]

The town was on the north-western edge of a sandy plain, hot, dusty and unhealthy, and was surrounded by a ring of ridges and hills, while the country to the south, through which any relief force must come, was similarly difficult and broken.

Thus getting out of this trap should certainly have been the dominant thought in White's mind as he planned his next move. He knew it must be his decision; Lansdowne had in a telegram of 27 October, explicitly told him so, and that he was expected to put military considerations before political; the Secretary of State added that White would be supported in taking what he regarded as militarily sound steps.[7] Some idea of White's thought process at this point can be gauged from the message he sent to the Natal governor to the effect that he hoped he had located a sufficiently strong force of the enemy with guns to make a good objective.

This suggests that at the least, he hoped to buy time by defeating the Boers and perhaps sufficiently decisively to halt the invasion of Natal in its tracks. Realistically, the most he could do would be to check them for a matter of days. The Boer forces directly in his front and closing in on Ladysmith, represented only part of the advancing Boer army. It was no doubt with the hope of inflicting a decisive defeat on Joubert that White now conceived a plan to send a force up the Bell Spruit towards Nicholson's Nek to smash into the Boer's flank as they fell back, beaten, from Pepworth Hill and Long Hill. It was a scheme which at the time, seriously alarmed his senior commanders; with the benefit of hindsight, it looks rash to the point of folly. Nevertheless, White was determined on what he called 'a knockout blow.'

When, however, he came to write his despatches, many months later, he put an entirely different slant on his thought process, suggesting that he had never any serious intention of abandoning Ladysmith and retreating south of the Tugela. Ladysmith, he wrote, was the most important town in northern Natal, and there was reason to believe that the Boers attached great, even undue, weight to capturing it, which might be a signal for the Cape Dutch to rise:

> Strategically, the town was important as being the junction of the railways which enter Natal from the Transvaal and the Orange Free State, and until the republics could gain possession of that junction their necessarily divergent lines of supply and communication prevented their enjoying to the full the advantages of combined action. Tactically the place was already partially prepared for defence and offered a natural position of some strength;

6 Pakenham, *Boer War*, p. 149.
7 Elgin Commission, *Minutes of Evidence*, vol. II, p. 158.

> and although the perimeter that must be occupied is very great for the number of troops available, yet it afforded a possibility of maintaining a protracted defence against superior numbers. On the other hand, the mere fact of a retirement behind the Tugela would have had a moral effect at least equal to a serious defeat.[8]

The line of the Tugela, White pointed out, was 80 miles long and could be crossed anywhere, and could not be held by his small force against an enemy double its size. His ultimate hopes, he said, of saving Natal were centred in holding Ladysmith.

It was, however, a fundamental error to ignore Buller's warning that he should not go north of the Tugela. At the end of October, he could have retreated to Colenso, beyond the river; if compelled to retreat further, he could have retired by stages down the railway line. On the other hand, staying put meant that the focus of the reinforcements arriving under Buller would have to be the relief of Ladysmith. Pakenham is severe, observing that there was more to White's misjudgement than inexperience of modern war:

> He was also a weak man. He knew that his force was inferior in many ways to Joubert's. He believed that if he failed to beat Joubert in the field and he was locked up in Ladysmith, nothing could save Natal. Yet he lacked the moral strength to follow the logic of this and make a fighting retreat.[9]

The German Staff History is somewhat kinder, noting that to abandon Ladysmith 'could not fail to produce an unfavourable impression upon the wavering population of South Africa,' and that if White was able to hold strong enemy forces in check, the advance of reinforcements would be considerably facilitated: 'As events turned out, it was decidedly disadvantageous for Sir George White to remain in Ladysmith, but he could not have foreseen this.'[10] This perhaps is wrong; information before him should have led him to anticipate what would be the result of his decision, or lack of it.

Certainly Wolseley, at any rate, was in no doubt that White was gravely at fault. He was later to tell the Elgin Commission that he had never heard of anybody proposing to hold Ladysmith. He explained that the district in front of the town, the Biggarsberg, was a very strong position, while Ladysmith, in a hollow, was 'no position at all.' He said that if unable to hold the Biggarsberg he would have fallen back to the next position, which was not Ladysmith but Colenso. He developed this further:

> If I was in command of such a force as was then in Natal and having at that time realised (because they did) that there was a large force of the enemy coming for me, nothing would have induced me to stay in Ladysmith; I would have burnt my supplies sooner than stayed there ... If you are not strong enough to hold the Biggarsberg, you must fall back behind Colenso.[11]

8 Coetzer, *The Anglo Boer War*, p. 58.
9 Pakenham, *Boer War*, p. 151.
10 *German Staff History*, vol. I, pp, 39-40
11 Elgin Commission, *Minutes of Evidence*, vol. I, pp. 373–375.

Wolseley went on to tell the Commission of a telegram which he had sent to Buller saying that he had warned White before he left of what seemed to him to be the importance of Colenso, 'where I wish he was now, with the river rising from the rains.' Wolseley had watched the developing situation with mounting apprehension, noting on 31 October, that White's telegrams led him to fancy he meant to hold on and let himself be shut up in Ladysmith. In view of his strong feelings on the subject, the members of the Commission pressed him to explain why White had not been given any positive instructions. To this, Wolseley repeatedly affirmed that it would be wrong to hamper the commander on the spot with instructions from afar; he must be free to exercise his own judgement in the light of the situation which confronted him.

Sensitive to the implied criticism that no plan whatever had been made before White left for South Africa, Wolseley looked up overnight, a comment by Moltke in the German General Staff Official History of the Franco-Prussian war, and quoted it on the second day of his evidence:

> No plan of operations can with any safety include more than the first collision with the enemy's main body. It is only the laity who believe that they can trace throughout the course of the campaign the prosecution of the original plan arranged beforehand in all its details.[12]

Hearing this, Lord Elgin put to him: 'I should have imagined that General von Moltke as Chief of the Staff of the German army, in sending out a force, certainly would have sent it out with some general plan of operations from his office?' Wolseley's reply was to say that there was a great difference between sending an expeditionary force thousands of miles from merely invading a country like Bohemia.[13]

On the subject of planning, Buller did have 'a desultory conversation' with Lansdowne when they discussed possible plans of the campaign. He expressed the view that the best – even the only – way to attack the Boers was by advancing along the central railway through Bloemfontein, which meant war with the Orange Free State. Still hopeful of avoiding this, Lansdowne had told him that it was out of the question. Greatly disturbed by this, Buller went to see Wolseley, who shared his concern at the lack of serious consideration of what needed to be done.[14] Buller also, apparently, told Wolseley, as he had told Lansdowne, of the difficulty of combining his command at Aldershot with planning the campaign. In the event, nothing approaching a plan materialised.

Before the Elgin Commission, both Wolseley and Buller were severely critical of White, but Roberts let him down much more lightly. He agreed with the unsuitability of Ladysmith as a point to defend: 'It had a practically impassable river a few miles behind it, and was not in any way fortified for protection.' When the chairman asked him whether it would have been possible either not to put the supplies which had been accumulated into Ladysmith or have carried them back again, Roberts expressed (perhaps reluctantly) his view of White's situation at the end of October: 'Ladysmith was in existence with everything there, and had been approved of as a place to hold on to, and I do not see how he could have attempted to leave it. His one object would have been to get every supply he could into the place, so as to be able to defend it.'[15]

12 Ibid., p. 383.
13 Ibid., vol. II, p. 385.
14 Powell, *Buller*, p. 119.
15 Elgin Commission, *Minutes of Evidence*, vol. I, p. 375.

In Ladysmith, White finalised his immediate plan of action at 4.00 p.m. on 29 October. He intended to employ the whole of his force in an operation in which Long Hill was to be the primary and Pepworth Hill, the secondary objective. The remarkable feature of his plan, previously referred to, was the despatch of a force under Colonel Carleton, the commanding officer of the 1st Royal Irish Fusiliers, who was to take his battalion and the 1st Gloucester Regiment, with a mountain battery, in a night advance northwards up the valley of the Bell Spruit towards Nicholson's Nek. It was to set off at 10.00 p.m.; the movement would cover the left flank of the army and should be able to take up a position from which it would be possible to fall on the Boers retreating from their main positions. On the army's right flank, French was to take his cavalry brigade to the ridges north-east of Gun Hill and demonstrate against the enemy left.[16]

In the centre, the principal attack would be made by the 8th Brigade under Colonel Grimwood with five battalions, three field artillery batteries under Colonel Pickwood and the Natal Field Artillery. The general reserve was to be the 7th Brigade under Hamilton, with three battalions, and the 2nd Rifle Brigade which was due to arrive from Pietermaritzburg. Hamilton also had three cavalry regiments and two companies of mounted infantry, together with three batteries under Colonel Coxhead.

Grimwood set off at 12:30 a.m. His column was led by the two battalions of the King's Royal Rifles and the 1st Leicestershire Regiment, followed by Pickwood's artillery, and then the 1st Battalion of the Liverpool Regiment, the Natal Field Battery and finally the 2nd Battalion of the Royal Dublin Fusiliers. Soon after setting off, the column was joined by Coxhead's artillery which marched behind Pickwood's batteries. When reaching a point between Flag and Limit Hills, Coxhead's batteries pulled out of line as ordered and took post behind Flag Hill; the units following wrongly assumed that they should also do so. Grimwood, unaware of this, marched on to occupy some low kopjes 1,800 yards south-east of Long Hill, and waited for dawn to break.[17]

French rode out at 3.00 a.m. towards Lombard's Kop, dismounting his troops in a hollow between that point and Gun Hill, some 4,000 yards in rear of Grimwood's leading units. Hamilton left at 4.00 a.m. and marched to occupy Limit Hill, with White riding with him at the head of his column. As they went forward, a muleteer from Carleton's mountain battery was brought to Hamilton, with the news that the mules of the battery had stampeded and broken away. Further reports of this mishap arrived, followed by some of the errant mules, and a patrol which White sent out to get news of Carleton, although unable to reach him, met a gunner who confirmed that the battery's ammunition and most of its guns had been carried off. A note from Carleton then arrived to tell White the bad news.

Meantime, on Grimwood's front, at first light Pickwood's guns opened on what was presumed to be the Boer position on Long Hill; in fact, the Boers had abandoned it and had concentrated on Pepworth Hill, from where at 5.15 a.m. their artillery opened fire, shells bursting near the town and among Pickwood's batteries. Coxhead now opened fire in reply, but was far out ranged,and Colonel Downing, the overall artillery commander, moved them out into the open to a point 4,000 yards from Pepworth Hill. Here they came under heavy fire and Downing next shifted Pickwood to a point to the right of Coxhead. By 6.30 a.m., the British artillery here was getting on top in its exchanges with the Boer gunners, although after half an hour, fresh Boer guns opened fire.

16 *Official History*, vol. I, p. 174.
17 Ibid., p. 176.

Grimwood's three battalions in front of Long Hill had meanwhile, begun to experience raking rifle fire from the right along the Modder Spruit, while two guns opened up from a point near the Elandslaagte road. Grimwood was obliged to turn his line towards the east to face this developing attack, and his line was now prolonged by two companies of the missing Royal Dublin Fusiliers which joined hands with the cavalry on Lombard's Kop. There, French had attempted to advance around what had appeared to be the left flank of the Boer army, only to be forced back by the strength of the enemy riflemen along the Modder Spruit. French took up a position on the high ridges running northward and downward from the summit of Lombard's Kop, where he was reinforced by two squadrons of the 5th Dragoon Guards and by the 18th Hussars, under Major General J. F. Brocklehurst, newly arrived that morning in Ladysmith. In addition, Downing withdrew the 69th Battery from his gun line in front of Pepworth Hill and sent it to support French.[18]

From 9.00 a.m. until 11.00 a.m., the British artillery was constantly engaged in replying to the intense enemy artillery and rifle fire. During this period, there was little movement in the position of either side. On Limit Hill, Hamilton remained in reserve, although he had steadily been deprived of units of his brigade; first the artillery and then most of his cavalry were withdrawn, and at 10.00 a.m., the Manchester Battalion was sent, part of it to cover the artillery and part to strengthen the position on Lombard's Kop. With practically all his forces being committed to his planned operation for the day, White had left only a few companies of infantry to cover the town, under the command of Colonel Knox. During the morning, he was able to collect two of the guns that had been stampeded from Carleton's force, but the Boers facing him were closing in from the Bell Spruit and the nearby kopjes. Knox reported to White his anxiety that the town might shortly be coming under attack, which added to the concern which White was beginning to feel about the overall situation.

Sometime after this, White sent Hunter out to Farquhar's farm, behind Grimwood's position, in order to report on the situation there. It was at once clear to Hunter that Grimwood could make no progress and that he should be withdrawn; White, on receiving this report, accepted it and at 11.00 a.m., ordered Grimwood to fall back. Hunter remained with Grimwood to supervise the operation, which was conducted under cover of the fire of the 13th Battery, which unlimbered about half a mile behind the infantry.

At first the retirement was conducted in an orderly manner and the Boers made no effective attempt to hamper it, but the infantry units had become very intermingled. As they retreated across the open ground towards Ladysmith, they came under heavy fire and they soon lost all discipline. One war correspondent, Henry Nevins, described them as retreating 'slowly, tired, disheartened and sick with useless losses.'[19] As the infantry streamed back, they were only saved from greater destruction by the courage of the British artillerymen, particularly those of the 13th Battery, which took heavy losses as it sought to cover the retreat. Hunter had remained with the guns and stayed on in the outposts during the night to help bring in the stragglers.

The Boers were to some extent, taken by surprise by the British retreat; one wrote: 'Turning round, we saw the entire British force that had come out against us on the plain that morning in full retreat to Ladysmith. Great clouds of dust billowed over the veld as the troops withdrew, and the manner of their going had every appearance of a rout.'[20] Watching the disorderly retreat

18 Ibid., p 181.
19 Hunter, *Sword Arm*, p. 125.
20 Symons, *Buller*, p. 125.

of the British, Christian de Wet, from the heights north of Ladysmith, could see what an opportunity existed to turn a defeat into a total disaster. Frustrated, he watched as the British fell back, and is said to have muttered: 'Loose your horse men, loose your horse men,' but Joubert made no move to pursue.

The Times History did not disguise the seriousness of the setback:

> The covering of the retreat by the batteries was the one bright spot in one of the gloomiest days of the British Army. Rarely have British batteries behaved better; they fell back generally at a walk, never more hastily than at a trot; yet the only support which they had first received was the little which they could afford each other while covering the withdrawal of the whole.[21]

From Pepworth Hill, the Boers' Long Tom Creusot piece had during the morning, been shelling Ladysmith, hitting the station buildings in particular. Now, however, the British received a timely and effective reinforcement. White had appealed on 24 October to Admiral Harris, the naval commander at the Cape, to send a detachment of heavy guns up to Ladysmith to match those available to the Boers. Thanks to the ingenuity of Captain Percy Scott, of the *Terrible*, suitable gun carriages were devised, and within four days a naval brigade was on its way to Ladysmith, where it arrived under the command of Captain Hedworth Lambton on 30 October. It consisted of two 4.7 inch and three 12-pdr quick firing guns and was 283 men strong.[22] Lambton's guns came into action at once, quickly silencing the Boer artillery on Pepworth Hill. After conferring with Knox, Lambton moved forward to Limit Hill, but by now the retirement was under way and he was soon ordered back. As he withdrew, the guns on Pepworth Hill opened up again, hitting one of the naval guns, but the naval artillery soon regained the upper hand.

As Grimwood's retreat was well under way, French began to pull back from the crests of Lombard's Kop, covered in his retreat by the guns of the 21st and 69th batteries, and by 2.30 his troops were safely back in Ladysmith. The retirement of White's forces was now complete, save for four companies of the 1st Devonshire Battalion which remained on Limit Hill.

There remains only to be told the fate of Carleton's column and its advance along the Bell Spruit. The stampede which had cost him his artillery had occurred when the mule trains panicked as Carleton led the column up the steep hillside. The cause of the panic was never clearly established. It began with the mules of the ammunition column of the Royal Irish Fusiliers, which suddenly became terrified by a disturbance in front:

> Kicking and squealing they broke loose from the inexperienced soldiers who led them and stampeded right into the mules of the battery. In a moment, all the mules of the column were stampeding madly to the rear. The Gloucesters heard the turmoil coming towards them and fixed bayonets, while someone in the rear of the column fired off a wild shot. The next minute the crowd of frenzied animals charged through them.[23]

21 *Times History*, vol. II, pp. 234-235.
22 *Official History*, vol. I, p. 185.
23 *Times History*, vol. II, p. 210.

Carleton, whose column had made good progress up the valley to a point about two miles south of Nicholson's Nek, decided to take up a position on Tchrengula Hill, with the intention of being well established by daylight, and then moving on to Nicholson's Nek when it seemed safe to do so. Accordingly, he turned to his left and had almost reached the crest of the hill when the disaster to his mule trains occurred. After order had been restored, the force was assembled on the summit, but without any of its mountain guns or its reserve ammunition. It would have been wiser to have accepted that the venture had failed and to retreat to Ladysmith. As it was, Carleton and Major Adye, his chief staff officer, fixed upon the southern end of the hill as the point to hold. However, when the sun came up, it became clear that it was not as defensible as had been first thought. Nevertheless, Carleton organised it for defence, posting the Gloucesters on the western crest of the hill, with the Royal Irish Fusiliers on the eastern crest.[24] Carleton sent a message to White to tell him of his intentions.

The Boers soon discovered Carleton's presence and began a steady rifle fire on the position from Surprise Hill to the south-west. The nature of the ground was such that only the shallowest sangars could be constructed to protect the British infantry. By 7.00 the Boers were also in position on the heights opposite, on the other side of the valley, from which came a steady hail of Mauser bullets. A more serious threat was soon to develop, however.

At 2.00 a.m., Commandant van Dam, who had been behind Pepworth with his Johannesburg police, some 400 strong, was ordered to occupy the ridge above Nicholson's Nek. When he arrived there, he found about 150 Free Staters under Christiaan de Wet and Commandant Steenkamp. These he sent round the flank and rear of the British, while he advanced straight over the top of the mountain. By 10.00 a.m. the Free Staters had swung round the western side of the steep ground and had begun to climb the slope. Carleton's force was now effectively surrounded. The contours of the hill exposed his men to heavy rifle fire; the more advanced companies on his left were steadily forced back. Progressively, the Boers closed in; confusion and misunderstandings led to further retreats, and then one company, totally exposed, surrendered without Carleton's authority. Seeing this, Carleton and Adye had to decide whether to repudiate the surrender; but it soon became clear that even if he did so, the rest of his force would be overrun in any case within the hour. Ordering his bugler to sound the ceasefire, Carleton and Adye walked out to the Boers and Carleton handed Steenkamp his sword. At 1:30 954 British soldiers became prisoners of war.[25] Their captors treated them with decency and restraint: 'In the moment of their triumph the Boers behaved with the same courtesy and unaffected kind heartedness which they had shown at Majuba, and which they displayed after most of their victories. Though exultant, they were not insulting.'[26] Carleton had lost 46 men killed and 138 wounded; the Boer losses here were not separately recorded, but they were not substantial. When the news of the surrender reached him, Joubert sent a courteous message to White to tell him what had occurred.

With good reason, 30 October became known as 'Mournful Monday.' Thr losses of Carleton's column inclusive, the British had lost 69 killed and 249 wounded, with 954 taken prisoner. They had been outmanoeuvred and out fought; man for man, the Boers had proved superior. The defeat effectively broke White's spirit. At the very moment that he needed all his resolution to face the decision that must now be made, he lost heart completely.

24 *Official History*, vol. I, pp. 189-190.
25 Ibid., p 195.
26 *Times History*, vol. II, p. 233.

6

Ladysmith Besieged

On 31 October, as White gloomily contemplated the ruin of his offensive of the previous day, the Boers had still not surrounded Ladysmith. Although they had closed up to the town, it was theoretically still possible for White to put his defeated army in motion at once, and to commence a move southwards to the line of the Tugela. The risks associated with taking that course had increased dramatically during the 10 days that had elapsed since the battle of Talana Hill, and particularly so since Yule's arrival at Ladysmith with his column from Dundee.

As previously observed, to remain at Ladysmith, and therefore to allow himself to be besieged there, meant that White would utterly disrupt any other scheme that might have been adopted by the British. The need to relieve the besieged town would necessarily become the primary strategic objective. On the morrow of the battle of Lombard's Kop, however, it would have required a commander with a lot more courage and a much clearer understanding of the situation than White possessed, to take such a step. *The Times History* looked at a comparable historical instance from a century earlier:

> When one remembers how Napoleon deliberately sacrificed his siege train at Mantua in 1796 in order to retain the mobility of his force in the field, it is difficult to believe that a general of his insight and self-confidence would not have preferred to incur any sacrifices sooner than allow himself to be immured. If Sir G. White had fallen back, first on Colenso, and then, step-by-step if necessary even as far as Maritzburg, destroying the railway and clearing the country of stock and produce in front of him, he might well have kept the superior Boer forces engaged till Buller's main army had entered Bloemfontein.[1]

This, of course, was what Wolseley, looking back with hindsight at the campaign when giving evidence to the Elgin Commission, said that he would have done in White's place.

However, for White and for his exhausted and beaten army, it was much too late for such a bold course of action. It is possible that he was telling the simple truth when he told the Elgin Commission that he had not contemplated abandoning Ladysmith, its population and the stores that had been accumulated there. It was not a decision which a man of his character and abilities

1 Ibid., p. 262.

could have considered during the situation in which he found himself, and he had become resigned to the fact that his army must now face the siege that had become inevitable.

Even so, there were still urgent decisions that did have to be taken. One was to keep the road to the south open as long as possible and on the evening of Lombard's Kop, White roused himself from his abject gloom and ordered the Dublin Fusiliers, with a company of mounted infantry and the Natal Field Battery, down to Colenso. He did so reluctantly, to 'give some confidence to the governor and the people at Pietermaritzburg, and in attention to Lord Wolseley's call to me to take care of Colenso bridge.'[2] His objective was reasonable enough, but such a force was quite inadequate to prevent the Boers seizing the Tugela crossings. When he reached Colenso, Colonel Cooper, the commander of the Dublin Fusiliers, took command of the post, where he found a small force already in place. This consisted of a squadron of the Natal Carbineers, a squadron of Imperial Light Horse, a party of mounted police, the Durban Light Infantry (about 380 strong) and a detachment of 50 men of the Natal Naval Volunteers, with two 9-pdr guns. With these, Cooper had in all about 1,200 men under his command; 25 miles down the railway line, at Estcourt, there was a small force of the Natal Royal Rifles.[3]

A better option would have been for White to send down the whole of his cavalry to the Tugela. It was a course strongly urged on him by French and also by Hunter. The cavalry brigade would have been immensely useful in any subsequent operations to relieve Ladysmith, while penned up in the besieged town they would be of very limited value. *The Times History* wrote: 'Based on Colenso and Chievely the cavalry could have done invaluable work in preventing Boer raids across the river and have greatly facilitated the task of the relieving force. In Ladysmith they were far less use than outside.'[4] White, however, would have none of it. It was a subject that was explored when he gave evidence to the Elgin Commission. In the course of this he quoted a telegram which he sent on November 1:

> I think the cavalry could not get through without heavy loss so I have countermanded them. If roads clear will send one cavalry regiment across Tugela. I cannot reduce perimeter without yielding artillery positions that would make Ladysmith untenable. Their guns are better than our field guns. Do not ask me to detach another battalion. The enemy are in great force[5]

Nor did White accept the proposition that the cavalry would have been of limited use as part of the garrison of Ladysmith, insisting that they were an essential part of his defence. He acknowledged that Hunter did not agree with him but said that even if Hunter had suggested as an alternative, reducing the perimeter of the defence, which he did not, he would not have accepted it because it would mean leaving unoccupied positions on which the enemy would have had guns the next morning. As it was, he claimed that his cavalry represented the only mobile reserve he had which were able to gallop to any threatened point, citing an instance on 6 January when the cavalry were able to reach Wagon Hill and Caesar's Camp in time to prevent a disaster.

With the battle of Lombard's Kop, the initiative had passed firmly into the hands of the Boers. On 1 November, a council of war, attended by all the Boer generals and commandants,

2 Elgin Commission, *Minutes of Evidence*, vol. II, p. 153.
3 *Official History*, vol. I, p. 262.
4 *Times History*, vol. II, p. 262.
5 Elgin Commission, *Minutes of Evidence*, vol. II, p. 153.

assembled outside Ladysmith to consider their next course of action. It was to decide 'whether the main effort of the Boer army should be to concentrate on the attack of that town, or whether, leaving a detachment to hold Sir G. White's troops, they should at once advance on Maritzburg and Durban.'[6] The discussions brought out sharply differing views. Among the younger leaders, including Louis Botha, there was a strong preference to take the latter course. At that time, Botha was still only a commandant, but he had displayed great ability as second-in-command to Lukas Meyer, whose troops had fought so successfully against the right flank of the British Army during the battle of Lombard's Kop. The majority, however, led by Joubert, took a more cautious view, considering that in the face of White's 12,000 men in Ladysmith, they were not strong enough to mount an offensive against Pietermaritzburg and Durban. It was a decision which confirmed the dissatisfaction with which many of the younger Boer commanders viewed their elderly and overcautious superiors.

The 37-year-old Botha had first distinguished himself as one of Lukas Meyer's commandants at Talana Hill. He was a successful farmer and a member of the Raad, where he had been among the moderates in favouring a more conciliatory stance in dealings with Britain, and is said to have been one of those who voted against Kruger's proposal to bring about a war. He was soon to replace Meyer, when that commander was invalided home.

In the meantime, Joubert convened a further council of war. By then, the Boers had cut the railway line to the south of Ladysmith and the siege had begun. White and his senior commanders had put in hand defences on the long perimeter around the town, which was some 14 miles in length. White told the Elgin Commission that it was 'too big for any school rule to hold,' with the men he had, so that to a certain extent, he had to play 'a game of brag' with the positions he held.[7]

Even so, a number of positions had been abandoned which would have made it more difficult for the Boers to complete the investment of the town. One important example of this was the failure to prevent the enemy from occupying Bulwana, a flat topped mountain some 7,000 yards south-east of Ladysmith upon which the Boers soon posted one of their Long Toms.[8] The fortifications around the town consisted principally of separate groups of shelter trenches with overhead and shell cover. The Boer's line of investment ran about 2,800 yards from the British position on its north and south sides and about 4,500 yards on the east and west. The Boer artillery outranged the British, which could only be used effectively against a close attack. The German Staff History noted that the Boer policy of employing only direct fire, not firing at night on Sundays and sparing an agreed neutral zone, and not working to any system, meant that they made no effective use of their artillery superiority.[9] White had established a committee presided over by Hunter, including the commanders of his engineers and his artillery, together with Hamilton and some other officers, to draw up plans for the defensive works to be constructed.

In the telegram to the governor which he sent on 1 November, White explained what he planned to do: 'My intention is to hold Ladysmith, make attacks on the enemy's position wherever possible, and retain the greatest number of the enemy here.'[10] At the same time, he instructed Brigadier General Wolfe Murray, in command of the lines of communication, that

6 *Official History*, vol. I, p. 264.
7 Elgin Commission, *Minutes of Evidence*, vol. II, p. 152.
8 *Official History*, vol. I, p. 264.
9 *German Staff History*, vol. I, p. 41.
10 *Official History*, vol. I, p. 262.

he was 'to retain and defend Maritzburg to the last.' Three days later, Buller sent a telegram warning of the risk of 'losing Durban by over prolonged defence of Maritzburg but hold the latter as long as you safely can. I fear it will be at least ten days before I can send you substantial assistance.'[11]

Hunter had hoped to be among those who left Ladysmith before it was cut off, but White insisted on his remaining. He did, though, allow French and his chief staff officer, Major Douglas Haig, to leave on the last train out of Ladysmith at the particular request of Buller, who had arrived at Cape Town on the evening of 30 October. French and Haig had a hair-raising journey under fire from Boer patrols and they only escaped injury by lying flat on the trucks carrying them.

At the Boer council of war it was believed that an assault on the garrison of Ladysmith might meet with success and on 9 November, an attack was launched. It was however ill planned and proved abortive, achieving little except to establish that the garrison would not yield easily, and that a prolonged formal investment of the town would be necessary.[12] The Boers had opened fire at 5:20 a.m., shelling the campsites of the army and the town itself, before two hours later attacking first, King's Hill and then Caesar's Camp, at each point being repulsed.

That afternoon, Joubert convened another council of war to review the situation. On the one hand, the Boers had suffered defeats at both Talana Hill and Elandslaagte, due as much as anything to mistakes made by Lukas Meyer and Kock respectively; Joubert had been shaken by these setbacks, describing them as a 'total defeat.' On the other hand, they had penned up White in Ladysmith and soundly beaten his attempt to strike a major blow at the Boer army before it closed in on the town. There were, it appeared to Joubert, three options. One was to make another attempt to storm Ladysmith. Alternatively, they could invest the place, and dig in along the Tugela. Finally, they could advance deeper into Natal.'[13]

The conclusion that was drawn from the abortive attack on the town was that the bulk of the Boer army should settle down to besiege Ladysmith, but that Joubert, with Botha as his second-in-command, should take a force of 4,200 men across the Tugela. The first objective of this operation was to reconnoitre a British force, some 5,000 men strong, which was, incorrectly, believed to have been concentrated at Frere. The *Official History* suggests that Joubert took charge of this personally in order to restrain what was seen as the probable impetuosity of his second-in-command.

As Pakenham points out, Joubert's proposal to launch such a raid into southern Natal was surprising. He had been thoroughly dispirited after Lombard's Kop by the number of his men who, without authority, had left the army to return home, writing to Kruger: 'The officers themselves … set the example in going off home. Every morning I receive such serious complaints about the melting away of the burghers and disobeying my orders, that I shudder at the situation.'[14] The government responded at once, ordering the burghers to return to their duty, but Joubert remained extremely anxious.

The plan to raid deep into Natal was not without its risks, and many of the Free Staters in particular were opposed to it. They held their own council of war, following which Martinius Prinsloo, their Commandant General, notified Joubert on 11 November that they were not

11 Ibid., p. 264.
12 *Official History*, vol. I, p. 265.
13 Pakenham, *Boer War*, p. 170.
14 Ibid.

prepared to go south of the Tugela. Nevertheless, Joubert was still determined to go on with the operation, although with a smaller force than had been intended. With 1,500 Transvaalers and 500 of the more bullish Free Staters who did not share their leaders' fears, he crossed the river on 14 November at Colenso and set off southward down the railway line. By the evening, the force had ridden as far as Chieveley, some 20 miles north of Estcourt.

It had almost at once become clear to Wolfe Murray that Cooper's force at the bridge at Colenso was in serious danger, and he ordered him to fall back to Estcourt if he should consider his position untenable. Once the Boers appeared on the heights overlooking the river, with artillery which far outranged the guns of the Natal Field Artillery, it seemed to Cooper that it was time to go, and during the night of 2/3 November, he retreated to Estcourt, where Murray joined him with the 1st Battalion of the Border Regiment, bringing the total force to resist the Boer advance to about 2,300 men.

Back in Durban, a colourful personality was now lending some backbone to the defence of Natal. Captain Percy Scott of the *Terrible*, whose naval career had been frequently punctuated by controversial episodes, was now appointed military commandant of the town. Arriving on 6 November, he set about organising a further naval brigade under Commander Limpus, 458 strong with 30 guns. Thereafter, Scott personally supervised the bringing ashore from the fleet the longer range guns which were essential if the Boer artillery was to be matched. The first instalment of naval guns had been those which reached Ladysmith under Captain Lambton in time to take part in the battle of Lombard's Kop and which would thereafter, play a major part in the siege.

Scott, in response to appeals from the army, designed the gun carriages which would enable the naval guns to operate alongside the field artillery which was so badly out ranged. He deployed batteries to cover all the approaches to Durban by both road and rail, so that by 4.00 p.m. on 8 November, he was able to report to the governor and to the fleet commander Admiral Sir Robert Harris, that Durban was safe.[15] Subsequently, Scott much enjoyed his brief episode of military command, supervising the supply of guns and technical equipment to the army, and strictly enforcing martial law in the town.

Had the Boers moved sooner to cross the Tugela and push southwards, the opportunity would have been greater. As it was, the British made the most of the breathing space which they had been given. On 11 November, Murray handed over command of the Estcourt garrison to Colonel Charles Long and went back to Pietermaritzburg to supervise the arrangements for bringing up the reinforcements expected shortly to arrive at Durban. He had been told to expect three brigades and divisional troops under Lieutenant-General Sir Francis Clery. The latter had been commandant of the Staff College. When he came to face the Boers, he was to find that they did not fight at all in the way that they were expected to do : He complained: 'The worst of the Boers is that their tactics are never according to rule. You attack them in a position, and when you get there they have galloped off and are coming in on your rear.'[16] Clery's troops began to arrive on 11 November, and Murray sent the first units up to the line to Estcourt the next day with the commander of the 2nd Brigade, Major General Henry Hildyard. Clery himself arrived at Durban on 15 November and took command of all the troops south of the Tugela, which by then substantially outnumbered the Boer force under Joubert.

15 Admiral Sir Percy Scott, *Fifty Years in the Royal Navy* (London: John Murray, 1919), p. 107.
16 Symons, *Campaign*, p. 120.

This was not large enough to do more than conduct a reconnaissance in force to assess British strength and movements. No attempt was made to attack Estcourt, from where Long was unwisely sending out patrols in an armoured train, unescorted by mounted infantry. On 15 November, the train steamed north from Estcourt, with 150 men and a 7-pdr naval gun aboard, together with Winston Churchill in his capacity as a war correspondent. Botha, with 500 men, ambushed the train as it returned after crossing the Blaauw Krantz River, having scattered rocks on the line. As it approached a bend, the Boers opened fire, the train crashed into the rocks, and all three trucks were derailed. In the ensuing firefight, four British soldiers were killed, 14 wounded and 58 taken prisoner. The Boers had four men slightly wounded. The armoured engine in the end managed to escape, but Churchill was taken off as a prisoner to Pretoria.[17]

Joubert and Botha continued southward, in heavy rain, giving Estcourt a wide berth, with the intention of breaking up the railway, which they reached on 21 November. After tearing up the line, they camped on a kopje beside it near Willow Grange, several miles south of Estcourt. Without realising it, the Boers had taken up a position between two British brigades – that of Hildyard, at Estcourt, and that of Barton, 23 miles south at Mooi River. Together these amounted to a total of 9,700 men. Unable to communicate with each other, their attack on the 2,000 Boers was not coordinated. Rumour suggested that the Boers were 7,000 strong, so the British moved with caution. Hildyard launched an attack on the evening of 22 November against Brynbella Hill which the Boers were believed to have occupied as an advanced post. A heavy thunderstorm delayed the attack, which went forward under Colonel Walter Kitchener at about midnight, and the hill was duly occupied. The next day, however, Kitchener's force came under fire from the Boers holding a ridge to the south and he judged it wiser to retire. British losses were 11 killed, 67 wounded and eight taken prisoner. The Boers lost one man killed in the storm.[18]

On 25 November, before a council of war could be held, Joubert's horse stumbled and threw him; he suffered internal injuries, and it was at once clear that the 68-year-old Commandant General was no longer fit to exercise command. The council of war, held later that day, had no difficulty in deciding that the time had come to withdraw. Next day, taking with them 2,000 horses and cattle looted from the farms of Natal, the Boer column made its way back to the line of the Tugela which it reached on 28 November. Barton made an abortive attempt to intercept them, but the Boers were moving too fast. Once across the river, the railway bridge at Colenso was blown up, and under the temporary leadership of Louis Botha, they began at once the task of fortifying the line of the Tugela. The principal defences consisted of rifle pits and gun pits clawed out of the rocky hills, protected by dummy trenches and false gun emplacements, on a line some 10 miles in length.[19] The line would be manned by 5,000 men, with 10 field guns and would prove to be an obstacle far greater than the British could possibly have imagined.

17 Pakenham, *Boer War*, pp. 171–172.
18 *Official History*, vol. I, p. 272.
19 Pakenham, *Boer War*, p. 174

7

Buller

General Sir Redvers Henry Buller was born in 1839. He joined the army in 1858, and by the time he took command of the forces in South Africa in 1899, he had become one of the five most famous generals of Queen Victoria's reign, all of whom would to a greater or lesser extent play a part in the South African War. Wolseley was Commander-in-Chief of the army; Wood was Adjutant-General; Roberts, who would in due course take overall command in December 1899, was commander-in-chief in Ireland; and Kitchener, who would go out with Roberts as his chief of staff, was Governor-General of the Sudan following his victory at Omdurman. As has previously been noted, Buller accepted the command in South Africa with extreme reluctance, not concealing his lack of self-confidence and his personal conviction that he was past his best; but to the British public he was one of their great military heroes. His career was to end abruptly, in circumstances of some disgrace, and as a sympathetic biographer has pointed out, he was to be 'maligned for near on a century as the epitome of Victorian military ineptness.'[1] Geoffrey Powell went on to praise Buller, and Thomas Pakenham, whom he noted had in his landmark history of the Boer War, 'revealed that behind a caricatured facade lay an able and thoughtful soldier, one who had, as a French observer of the war judged, been given its toughest job.' Observing that another historian, Professor Robin Higham, had commented that 'this enigmatic man needs further assessment,' Powell concluded that Buller was not so much enigmatic, but was a mass of contradictions.

These contradictions have led modern historians to take diverging views about Buller's character. Julian Symons considered that the various aspects of his character were entirely relevant to his performance on the field, suggesting that Buller was 'overbearing, arrogant and unprepared to take the Boers seriously as opponents:'

> His basic shyness was hidden behind a blustering exterior. Always concerned for the welfare of his men, and deeply considerate of them, he was often brutally rude to the officers on his staff. Perhaps no combination of qualities could have led more certainly to failure.[2]

1 Powell, *Buller*, p. vii.
2 Symons, *Campaign*, p. 111.

It was Buller's misfortune that – lacking the essential temperamental elements for supreme command – he was in that position at the low point of Britain's war in South Africa.

Buller had had an energetic and successful battlefield career, taking part in many of the conflicts of Victoria's reign. He displayed outstanding bravery on many occasions, winning a Victoria Cross in the Zulu War in 1879. His last active service had been with the Gordon relief expedition in 1884–1885. Thereafter, he distinguished himself as a military administrator during his service in the War Office, first as Deputy Adjutant-General between November 1885 and August 1886, and then as Quartermaster General between October 1887 and October 1890, after which he became Adjutant-General for eight years. Then, after a year on half pay, he was posted to Aldershot as general officer commanding. It was in this position that he was chosen for the South African command. One of his considerable achievements as Adjutant-General had been the creation of the Army Service Corps to deal with the questions of supply and transport, which greatly improved these areas of staff service. Thereafter, every unit would be given Army Service Corps officers together with its own allocation of transport and supply.[3]

This innovation, which was greatly to improve the lot of soldiers in the field, was born out of Buller's concern for the welfare of his troops, a concern which never left him. As Adjutant-General, he improved the service conditions for enlisted men in respect of food, quarters and uniforms. He also drafted a new drill book and revised the manual of military law. Things did not go so well for him at Aldershot. Soon after taking command, and by now a full general, he took part in six days of manoeuvres, in which he failed to distinguish himself. He was overheard remarking at one point: 'I have been making a fool of myself all day.' As commander of an army corps, in this exercise he was surprisingly outperformed by his opponent, the Duke of Connaught.[4] After more than 10 years behind a desk, he was perhaps no longer as sharp as he was and his physical appearance testified to the effects of too much good living. Nevertheless, it was a remarkable fact that whatever may have been his personal uncertainties, his outward demeanour inspired great confidence in those around him, while his constant concern for the men who served under him ensured their personal devotion. He was, therefore, an obvious choice for the command in South Africa.

Buller sailed for South Africa on 14 October amid scenes of great popular enthusiasm, and arrived in Cape Town on a wet evening on 30 October. The next day he drove with Forestier-Walker through cheering crowds to the government house for a meeting with Milner. The High Commissioner despondently told him of the latest news from Ladysmith and expressed his acute anxiety about the possibility of a rising of the Dutch in Cape Colony. Buller exuded confidence, however, and in the following days this contributed considerably to a general improvement in morale. This was despite the bad news which continued to arrive, and which demonstrated just how difficult was the task which Buller faced. Privately, behind his cheerful exterior, Buller's self-confidence had not improved, although, as was shown by a remarkable letter which he wrote to his brother a few days after he reached Cape Town:

> I am in the tightest place I have ever been in, and the worst of it is that it is I think none of my creating. I don't know if I shall ever get out of it all right, and I think if I shall fail

3 Stephen M. Miller, 'Redvers Buller' in Stephen J. Corvi and Ian F. W. Beckett (eds.) *Victoria's Generals* (Barnsley: Pen and Sword 2009) pp. 60–61.

4 Powell, *Buller*, p. 114.

> that it is fair that my family should know afterwards what at any rate I had to say in my own defence.[5]

In this letter he explained how poor was his relationship with Lansdowne, and that he had been given no definite line of operations. He complained particularly of the failure to involve him in any of the discussions at the War Office, remarking that he had been wrong not to insist on attending the meetings which took place there, and about which he was not kept informed. Julian Symons has described this letter as 'one of the most curious documents ever penned by a British general before going into action,' considering it to be 'an attempted justification of his own position in relation to Lansdowne, an alibi constructed in advance to excuse defeat.'[6] Given his experiences in London before departing, however, it was scarcely unreasonable on his part to want to set down the difficulties which he had encountered.

The lack of any coherent plan of campaign troubled him particularly. He knew before he left that, contrary to the advice which he had given, troops had been sent forward into northern Natal, which he found disturbing, though this had not prevented him from reassuring the elderly and infirm Queen Victoria that it would 'not be a long business' and would not involve 'much hard fighting.'[7]

Whether or not this truly reflected his opinion, it was the lack of any planning for the campaign that was most in his mind. He was later to complain to the Elgin Commission that 'no Council of War was held; no campaign was adopted; no regular military preparations were undertaken.' He had, he considered, suffered a 'tremendous disadvantage by not having the smallest idea when I arrived at Cape Town of the course which negotiations had taken.'[8] When this was subsequently put to Lansdowne, he stoutly denied that anything was withheld from Buller: 'There was really nothing that we could have imparted to him which he could not derive from the ordinary sources of information.'[9] Lansdowne's evidence, of course, did not properly address Buller's complaint of a lack of instructions; if there was really nothing else that Lansdowne could have told him, it merely emphasised further the failure to consider the strategy that should inform the operations to be conducted by Buller when he arrived in South Africa.

Buller came with the intention that he should advance with his whole force up the line into the Orange Free State, with Bloemfontein as his objective. The situation which greeted him, however, was such that he soon thought better of this plan. There were essentially two alternative courses of action open to him. He might postpone any thrust towards Bloemfontein and, ignoring Kimberley, use his entire force to relieve Ladysmith; or he might split his force, with part going to relieve Kimberley, taking the rest to Natal to embark on the relief of Ladysmith. He chose the latter option, a decision of which Wolseley, at his desk in London, was unaware until Buller was on the point of departing himself for Natal. It was a decision with which Wolseley disagreed, still believing that the advance on Bloemfontein was the correct option. The German Staff History took a different view, believing it to have been 'more expedient to have renounced the relief of Kimberley for the time being, to have left the defence of Cape

5 Symons, *Campaign*, p. 135.
6 Ibid.
7 Powell, p. 132.
8 Elgin Commission, *Minutes of Evidence*, vol. II, p. 188.
9 Ibid., p. 515.

Colony to the troops already there, and to have concentrated the mass of the Army Corps in Natal for the decisive stroke.'[10]

Political considerations inevitably played a part in the evolution of Buller's strategy. For Milner, the most pressing concern was Kimberley, where Cecil Rhodes had allowed himself to be shut up and where he proved a fearful nuisance to Lieutenant-Colonel Robert Kekewich, the commander of the small garrison there. This consisted of half a battalion of regular infantry, amounting to 590 men, 352 police and a Town Guard of local volunteers 3,658 strong. The town had been invested by the Boers almost immediately after the outbreak of war and had been cut off from Cape Colony since 14 October. Three days later, the Boers occupied Belmont Station. Rhodes bombarded Milner with messages demanding that the town be relieved; he did not bother to keep Kekewich informed of his correspondence. In Cape Town, Milner and Buller felt some concern that implicit in Rhodes's telegrams, was a threat that unless relieved he would surrender the town, which would seriously increase the risk of a rising in Cape Colony. This therefore, was a contributory factor in Buller's decision to split his force. Given the pressing danger to both Kimberley and Ladysmith, Buller's abandonment of his plan for a direct advance on Bloemfontein was almost unavoidable, as even Leo Amery, his severest critic, conceded:

> It is difficult to see what other course he could have pursued. At the time when the first transports were sent on to Durban, there was really no question of relieving Natal by an immediate advance on Bloemfontein. In the first place the army would not have been ready to cross the Orange River for nearly a month. Before that the Boers might have captured Maritzburg, and overrun the whole of Natal, and Ladysmith might have fallen. From a military point of view alone, such a result would have been a terrible disaster. From the political standpoint it was unthinkable.[11]

On 4 November, Buller had telegraphed to Lansdowne that not only did he intend to reinforce Natal, but that he proposed to go there himself to take charge of the advance on Ladysmith: 'If under Providence we are successful there and at Kimberley, I think collapse of opposition possible. These proposals are subject to High Commissioner's views of state of Cape Colony, and to what may happen meantime anywhere else.'[12] Meanwhile, with two brigades, Lord Methuen would be in command of the advance on Kimberley. Buller had been asked whether a fresh division should come out from England; for the moment, he thought its preparation desirable, but he did not yet see the need for its despatch. Two days later, however, he thought he should have the additional division as soon as possible.

The Official History noted that the breakup of the divisions of the army corps as originally constituted 'would have been even more seriously detrimental had those divisions actually existed prior to the embarkation of the troops from England;' but in fact, the practice of the British Army in time of peace was not to develop higher troop organisations, so the individual brigades had not, in any case, had the advantage of working together or forming part of a division.[13] Apart from the reinforcements to be sent from England, the urgent need was for more mounted men. Buller, recognising that the advance on Ladysmith should have the priority in

10 *German Staff History*, vol. I, p. 40.
11 *Times History*, vol. II, p. 286.
12 *Official History*, vol. I, p. 200.
13 Ibid., p. 204.

the assignment of such additional mounted units as could be raised, sent to Natal the first such unit from Cape Town, the South African Light Horse.

Buller had kept to himself his decision to go to Natal, and neither the bulk of his staff, nor Milner, were told what he intended. When he finally left Cape Town on 22 November, he was accompanied only by his military secretary, Colonel Frederick Stopford, and several aides-de-camp. Amery thought that 'it was a strong and justifiable impulse' that sent Buller to Natal, but pointed out that it left no one in operational command in Cape Colony.[14] Forestier-Walker, whom he left behind as the senior officer in Cape Town, was principally responsible for the lines of communication, but the main commanders in the field, Methuen, Gatacre and French, were all directly responsible to Buller. Clearly, though, he envisaged that Forestier-Walker might well have to coordinate operations in Cape Colony and for his guidance, Buller left behind a memorandum dated 20 November setting out his appreciation of the situation:

> Ever since I have been here we have been like the man, who, with a long day's work before him, overslept himself and so was late for everything all day. In disposing the troops which arrived from England I have considered that it was of the first importance to keep Cape Colony from rebellion, even if by so doing I temporarily lost Maritzburg. I consequently have formed a strong column under Lord Methuen which is in a position to take the field, and I am forming a force of mounted men and horse artillery under General French, which will, I hope, be able to meet any commandos which may invade the colony. I have also done all I can to safeguard the western and eastern lines of railway. The state of Kimberley necessitated the first employment of Lord Methuen's force in that direction. He starts today. General French is at Naauwpoort, organising a column to attack Colesberg at the earliest possible date … As soon as they can be occupied General Gatacre's force should be advanced to Molteno or Stormberg, and any force at Burghersdorp should be attacked.[15]

After setting out some detailed instructions as to supplies, and as to the additional troops to be added to the forces in Cape Colony, Buller concluded on a hopeful note:

> In my opinion, so long as General White holds Ladysmith, the force able to attack you from the Orange Free State is not likely to be serious, but if Natal goes you will have to concentrate for defence, and you should make up your mind what positions to hold. Probably the best military positions about Queenstown, Middelburg, and Beaufort West will be found most convenient.[16]

In the three weeks before he left Cape Town for Natal, Buller and his improvised staff had been extremely busy with the redistribution of the army corps for the tasks to be undertaken, and Amery acknowledged that they had done 'good work:'

> The sending of troops to the front in Natal, and the despatch of Methuen's column, were in themselves considerable tasks. The troops were disembarked and entrained for the front with admirable despatch. Supply, transport and railway departments proved themselves

14 *Times History*, vol. II, pp. 286-287.
15 *Official History*, vol. I, pp. 209-210.
16 Ibid., p. 210.

> fully adequate to the task they were called upon to undertake, and at a later date managed to cope with remarkable success with the enormously increased burden thrust upon them.[17]

Buller travelled to Natal by sea, arriving at Durban on 25 November. While he had been en route, quite a lot had been happening in Natal and elsewhere, all tending to inspire the hope that the worst was passed, and that he could tackle the immediate problem of relieving Ladysmith, before he returned to execute his march on Bloemfontein. Therefore, he settled down at Pietermaritzburg to supervise the preparations for the offensive. Clery, as commander of the 2nd Division, was nominally in command of the whole force that would advance across the Tugela, and he went up to Frere to organise the force in readiness for its advance. He was a somewhat eccentric individual; Julian Symons described his term of office as commandant of the Staff College:

> He wore side whiskers dyed blue and dressed in a scarlet coat and wide trousers (he was unable to wear riding breeches because of his varicose veins), with buckskin ankle boots and gold spurs. Clery's strong brogue made it difficult for the students to understand what he was saying, but this was less important than it may appear, since he knew hardly one of them by sight.[18]

According to Pakenham, it had been at Clery's insistence that Buller came to Natal. His performance prior to Buller's arrival had not inspired confidence; he was thought to have retreated quite unnecessarily to Estcourt during Botha's raid into South Natal.[19] When Buller arrived, having left the bulk of his staff in Cape Town (part of the staff assigned to the army corps had been locked up in Ladysmith), he was obliged to issue orders through Clery's staff, which in due course, was to result in inevitable confusion.

By 10 December, an impressive field force had been concentrated at Frere, amounting in all to nearly 18,000 men. It consisted of four infantry brigades, under Hildyard (who had been Clery's successor at the Staff College), Barton, Lyttelton and Hart; a mounted brigade under Dundonald comprising the Royal Dragoons and 13th Hussars and 1,300 mounted infantry; five field batteries and two 4.7 inch and 14 12-pdr naval guns from Durban. The overall commander of the artillery was Colonel Long, who had been responsible for the unfortunate affair of the armoured train. The naval contingent was under Captain Jones of the *Forte*.[20]

There had been a significant change in the command structure of the Boer army. Joubert, suffering from shock after his fall from his horse, was so seriously ill that he was obliged to hand over command of the force on the Tugela to Louis Botha. This was to be of momentous consequence for the fortunes of the Boer army. Before he departed for Pretoria, Joubert convened a council of war on 1 December. At this meeting, it was agreed to send down 3,000 men from the lines around Ladysmith. This brought up Botha's strength to approximately 8,000 men with which to hold the line of the Tugela. This line was some hundred odd miles in length, but for the purpose of barring the route to Ladysmith, it was the 10 miles from the junction of the Little Tugela to the bridge at Colenso that was the key to the position. Before its strength could be tested, however, there had been important developments on the other fronts.

17 *Times History*, vol. II, p. 288.
18 Symons, *Campaign*, p. 108.
19 Pakenham, *Boer War*, p. 213.
20 *Official History*, vol. I, pp. 332–333.

8

Belmont and Graspan

Paul Sanford Methuen was born in 1845, the eldest of 10 children of the second Baron Methuen. He was educated at Eton and on leaving there, purchased a commission in 1864 as ensign and lieutenant in the Scots Guards. Three years later, he purchased the double rank of lieutenant and captain. The system of purchase, which created leaders by money rather than merit, was not finally abolished until 1871, though its damaging effects had been apparent for many years.

Methuen's first experience of war came during the Franco-Prussian war of 1870–1871, when he served as a runner for the British ambassador in France, carrying despatches between Paris and Bordeaux and on one occasion visiting Versailles, where he encountered Helmuth von Moltke.[1] It was a meeting which had a profound effect on the young Methuen's attitude to service. Many years later, he wrote in an introduction to a book about Moltke's home life: 'To soldiers he set the example of how to work through and for others, not to play for our own hand, and not to seek to enhance our own interest by means of self-advertisement.'[2] Methuen formed a very high opinion of the Prussian army, describing its officers as 'the finest built, best looking, most intelligent men I have ever seen;' he believed that they were the best role model for the British Army. Later, when serving as military attaché in Berlin, he had the opportunity to study the German army at close quarters, on which he became an expert.[3]

Methuen first saw active service as a captain in the second Ashanti war of 1873–1874, when he learnt a number of important lessons. In particular, he came to understand that transport, ordnance and medical departments all were important factors in the conduct of a campaign, while questions of terrain and climate must be considered in determining strategy. He became a member of Wolseley's 'Ashanti Ring' and formed a particular admiration for Redvers Buller, whom he considered as 'just perfect for a soldier.'[4]

Thereafter, Methuen held a number of administrative posts, including service on Wolseley's staff in Egypt in 1882. He served in South Africa in 1884 and again, by now a colonel, in 1888–1890. In 1897, he went to India to serve as a volunteer press censor on the staff of the Tirah expedition. Back in England, he became the army's youngest lieutenant-general in 1898 and

1 Stephen M. Miller, *Lord Methuen and the British Army* (London: Frank Cass, 1999) p. 14.
2 Friedrich August Dressler, *Moltke in his Home* (London: John Murray, 1907)., p. viii.
3 Miller, *Methuen*, p. 14.
4 Ibid., p. 15.

was then on half pay for 18 months before in October 1899, being appointed to the command of the 1st Division. Sailing for South Africa, he arrived in Cape Town on 8 November, in company with Lieutenant-Generals Clery and Gatacre. There, he met with Buller, who gave him an outline of the tasks he was to undertake. Two days later, he received his written orders. He was to take command of the troops at De Aar and Orange River Station, and with them to march to Kimberley as quickly as possible.

At this point, his troops comprised the 9th Brigade, in course of formation under Colonel Fetherstonhaugh, the 1st Brigade, under Major General Sir Henry Colville, the Highland Brigade under Major General Andrew Wauchope, the 9th Lancers (Colonel Hubert Gough) and two batteries of field artillery (Colonel Hall), together with divisional and supporting troops. He was to march from the Orange River to the Modder River, and communicate with Kimberley, bringing up stores and heavy guns for its protection. He was, however, to make it clear that he had not come to undertake its defence but to provide its garrison with better means of doing so.[5]

Methuen reached Orange River Station on 12 November. Two days later, Buller wrote him a letter with some suggestions as to how he should proceed, while being careful to emphasise that he did not want to tie Methuen's hands in any way. He added that he was sending a naval brigade with four 12-pdr guns, which were to be left for the defence of Kimberley. Buller went on in his letter: 'I have said in my instructions that you will proceed to Modder River. If you can from there get a clear road to Kimberley, so much the better, but you will act according to circumstances. The main object is to save time.'[6]

Before Methuen had arrived at Orange River Station, a number of reconnaissance missions had been undertaken in the direction of Belmont. These did not learn a great deal save that there appeared to be a force of 700–1,200 men at or near Belmont. The Boers, on the other hand, were very well informed of the British preparations for an advance and had a reasonably accurate idea of Methuen's strength. They had prepared defensive positions at Belmont and Graspan, which were to be held by the Orange Free State Commandant Jacobus Prinsloo with about 2,500 men.

By 20 November preparations for Methuen's advance had been completed, and on the following day at 4.00 a.m. they marched out from their bivouacs on the northern bank of the Orange River. The advance followed the line of the railway; the Boers, closely following the British movements, had had no doubt that this would be the case, and had made their preparations accordingly. Methuen had little choice but to stay close to the railway, due to the scarcity of water in the plain to the north of the Orange River. For this reason, he had kept his baggage trains to the minimum, intending to rely on the railway to bring up supplies. Protecting the lines of communication had necessarily, to be a key part of Methuen's thinking. Amery, writing a letter in December on the subject, was critical: 'We let the existence of the railroad completely paralyse our movements. [It] induces a mental paralysis on all our generals: it is so simple and obvious to stick to it – to improvise other transport requires thinking out afresh as it was not in the original programme and so it isn't done.'[7] As Miller observes, though, this criticism is unjust. The safety of the railway was of crucial importance to Methuen's problem of supply, and to enable him to carry out the task of evacuating the population of Kimberley to Cape Colony and then returning to take part in the proposed offensive towards Bloemfontein.

5 *Official History*, vol. I, pp. 212–213.
6 Ibid.
7 Miller, *Methuen*, p. 86.

The German Staff History noted the consequences for Methuen:

> The diminished mobility of his troops was bound to impede his operations greatly in face of an adversary who paid no heed to either baggage or trains; but Methuen's view, after the first fighting had taken place in Natal, was that an attempt to outmanoeuvre the enemy from his position promised to be less successful than would be an attack carried out with energy. He did not believe that the Boers would face a hand-to-hand struggle.[8]

The advance halted after four hours near Witteputs, about 12 miles north of the Orange River, and the 9th Lancers and the mounted infantry endeavoured to reconnoitre the Boer position, which they located in the hills to the east of Belmont Station. No worthwhile maps existed of the area, but Lieutenant-Colonel Willoughby Verner, on Methuen's staff, made a sketch of the Boer position from the low hills east of Thomas's Farm, which lay about a mile and a half south-west of Belmont Station. Methuen himself rode up to this point later in the day to see what he could of the Boers, before returning to the column.[9] The next morning, the mounted infantry occupied Thomas's Farm. Later that day, the entire column moved up to that point from Witteputs. Before it arrived, the Boers opened fire on the mounted infantry and engineers around Thomas's Farm, and Methuen sent forward the two batteries of field artillery to respond to this. By nightfall, his whole force was bivouacked there. To the south, the Highland Brigade under Wauchope was guarding the line of the railway. Meanwhile, 80 odd miles south-east of Orange River Station, Major General John French was assembling a mixed force intended to prevent any invasion of Cape Colony from the Orange Free State.

Methuen rode forward again on 22 November to have another look at the Boer position from the hills by Thomas's Farm and he then dictated his orders for the attack to be launched on the following day. He was seriously handicapped by being unable to determine the precise location of the Boer defences or indeed the actual topography of the hills on which they stood. Having only Verner's sketch to go on, Methuen had to give the various features of the battlefield his own names to make his orders clear. copies of Verner's sketch were delivered to the units undertaking the assault.

The Boer positions were in two lines of broken kopjes which ran roughly parallel to the railway. The southern end of the Boer line was based on Sugar Loaf Hill, which rose some 280 feet above the veld, two miles south-east of Belmont Station. About 1,200 yards north of this feature was a precipitous hill of roughly the same height, termed Razor Back, the northern side of which hung over a steep ravine 600 yards wide. Beyond this, was Mont Blanc, the most important feature of the range which stretched northward for about three miles; its average height was about 300 feet above the level of the plain. Between Mont Blanc and the railway, about a mile to the west, the second line of kopjes was about a mile and a half in length. Of these, the northernmost section was termed Table Mountain, while to the south of this, there was a series of heights known as Gun Hill, rising about 120 feet; all these hills were more or less steep sided.[10]

Methuen's plan for 23 November was entirely straightforward. He ruled out any attempt to outflank the enemy position as being entirely impracticable. In any case, he approached the

8 *German Staff History*, vol. I, p. 80.
9 *Official History*, vol. I, p. 216.
10 Ibid., pp. 218–219.

battle with every confidence that his troops could successfully execute a frontal attack; besides, as he is reported to have said before the battle, he intended 'to put the fear of God into these fellows.'[11]

In the first instance, Methuen proposed to attack Table Mountain and Gun Hill with the 9th Brigade and the Guards Brigade respectively. As soon as the 9th Brigade had taken Table Mountain, it was to swing its left round to attack Mont Blanc from the north, supported by the fire of the Guards Brigade from Gun Hill. The few mounted troops which he had were to guard the flanks. As for the artillery, the 75th Battery on the left and the naval guns and 18th battery on the right, were to shell the enemy positions with shrapnel. The troops were to move off at 3.00 a.m., advancing under cover of darkness, the aim being to get close to the Boer position before the sun came up.[12] It was Methuen's intention in this way to drive the Boers in an easterly direction, away from his line of advance.

Methuen was very conscious of the vulnerability of his officers to the accuracy of the Boer marksmanship. There had already been a number of instances in which the Boers had consistently picked out British officers and he was insistent that they should be indistinguishable from their men in appearance: 'Buttons, belts, and other marks of rank, once bright and shining, were dulled with mud or painted brown. Officers were ordered to carry rifles rather than swords. To confuse the Boers further, and conserve water, shaving was abandoned by most of the officers.' Methuen himself wrote home to say that he was 'in a Boer hat, a pair of Norwegian slippers, khaki trousers and short sleeves, looking the most disreputable man in camp.'[13]

A night march was always going to be hazardous at the best of times; without adequate maps the scope for error was greatly increased. In silence, the advance began. On the left, the 9th Brigade set off at the appointed time, with the Northamptons on the right, the Northumberland Fusiliers on the left, and the King's Own Yorkshire Light Infantry in reserve, following the other two battalions at about 1,000 yards. Crossing the railway line, they made for the western side of Table Mountain; the leading battalions extended to their left, and the Northumberland Fusiliers were ordered to move towards Belmont Station. By now, the Boers had opened fire, though not to any great effect at first; the Northamptons came under fire from Gun Hill. The advance of the Northumberland Fusiliers soon drove back the Boers from the south-west corner of Table Mountain, while the Northamptons successfully charged the Boer positions at the northern end of Gun Hill. Two companies of the Northumberland Fusiliers, which had been in reserve to the west of the railway, now moved up the line when their commander realised that as the sun came up, it shone straight into their eyes, and they were soon able to open fire on the main body of the Boers on Table Mountain.[14]

The Boers were, however, putting up a stubborn resistance; it was only when the efforts of the British troops combined that they were finally driven off the plateau. During the struggle Fetherstonhaugh, the 9th Brigade's commander, was severely wounded. Riding up and down at the head of his brigade, his courage perhaps exceeded his wisdom, as by so doing he had been hampering the fire of his men.[15] Lieutenant-Colonel Money, of the Northumberland Fusiliers, now assumed command of the brigade.

11 Miller, *Methuen*, p. 87.
12 *Official History*, vol. I, p. 220.
13 Miller, *Methuen*, p. 89.
14 *Official History*, vol. I, p. 224.
15 Kruger, *Dolly Gray*, p. 111.

Meanwhile, on the right, the Guards Brigade had set off somewhat later than intended to the attack of Gun Hill. It was to be launched by the Scots Guards and the 3rd Grenadier Guards, with the two battalions of Coldstream Guards in reserve. The leading units were delayed by the wire fences along the railway line, cutting their way through them with considerable difficulty. They then marched on in silence, conscious that any moment, the Boers would open fire. This they did at 4.00 a.m. as the sky began to lighten and the Guards soon began to suffer heavy losses. When the battalion of Scots Guards reached a position only 150 yards short of the first of the kopjes in their immediate front, they launched a charge which carried the position with relatively few casualties. Once there, however, they came under fire from a nearby kopje; turning against this, they soon drove its defenders back on Table Mountain.

The Grenadiers, meanwhile, had inclined towards a kopje to the west side of Gun Hill, which they assumed to be Gun Hill itself:

> By a mistake, only intelligible to those who know the extraordinary clearness of the South African atmosphere, the sketch map had underestimated the distance by fully a thousand yards. It was a serious error, for not only did it cause the attack to be delivered by day instead of by night, with all the disadvantages thereby entailed, but it probably prevented a complete surprise of the Boers.[16]

Nevertheless, another successful charge dislodged the defenders of the kopje after a bitter struggle, in the course of which the Grenadiers sustained considerable loss. Their commander, Colonel Crabb, was wounded within a few feet of the top of the kopje.[17]

At this point, Methuen had to consider whether to continue with his attack as planned. He was aware that his troops had suffered higher casualties than he had hoped; but he decided to press on, later explaining his decision:

> [Because of the misdirection] the brigades were leaving each other, the enemy were surprised and firing everywhere, and I was going straight for enormous precipices instead of going to A [the point of attack chosen from Gun Hill] … An awful movement, no retreat available, and a brave enemy ready to destroy us. I did not lose my head. I saw I was committed to a frontal attack, and sent one ADC to get the Guards straight, and another to the 9th Brigade … ; All was right in 10 minutes.[18]

The battle accordingly now moved into its second phase. At 4:50 a.m., the British artillery had begun to shell the Boer positions on Mont Blanc but had found it difficult to get into a good position on the higher ground of Table Mountain, due in large part to the exhaustion of the artillery horses. The original plan had been that the two Coldstream battalions should, once the Scots Guards and Grenadiers had taken Gun Hill, reinforce them and together with them, to advance for the attack on Mont Blanc. Seeing that Gun Hill appeared now to be in British hands, Colville ordered the Coldstreams to advance. As they did so, however they came under heavy fire from the Razor Back and Sugar Loaf Hill. Colville became concerned, because to deal with this meant the Coldstreams delivering a frontal attack over difficult ground under

16 *Times History*, vol. II, p. 327.
17 *Official History*, vol. I, pp. 222–223.
18 Miller, *Methuen*, p. 92.

heavy fire, and he tried to call off the assault. His brigade major managed to reach the 2nd Battalion and led them back to Gun Hill, from where Colville despatched them to link with the 9th Brigade. The rest of the Coldstreams, however, advanced to the attack of Razor Back and Sugar Loaf Hill.

Seeing this, Methuen determined to support them, and ordered the Grenadiers and Scots Guards down into the valley between the two ranges, advancing in extended order where they suffered from Boer plunging crossfire before reaching the base of the heights. The Coldstreams succeeded in taking the Razor Back and Sugar Loaf Hill and gradually, the combined effect of all the British troops engaged drove the Boers back off Mont Blanc.[19] The Boer defenders mounted their ponies and galloped off to the north-east under the fire of the British artillery. The gunners, however, could not see their target, and an attempt ordered by Methuen to get a naval gun to the top of Mont Blanc, proved unsuccessful.

By 10.00 a.m. the battle had ended. Methuen had won a sort of victory, although it was far short of the decisive outcome for which he had hoped. He had lost 54 men killed and 245 wounded. He had at least succeeded in driving the Boers away from the line of the railway and could continue his advance towards Kimberley. The Boer losses are uncertain but were probably between a total of 100 and 150 men killed and wounded.

Amery wrote of the battle:

> Originally planned with some tactical skill, it became, through no special fault of anyone concerned, a soldier's battle, the battalions going straight ahead at whatever height fronted them and marching up hill and down dale till the last Boer had been driven from the furthermost kopjes. A soldiers' battle in the best sense of the word, it exemplified the lasting value, even under the most novel conditions, of discipline and morale.[20]

Methuen's biographer is, however, critical of the decision to employ a night march to get close to the Boer position, noting that many military commentators believed that a night march was anachronistic under modern conditions. In the present case, Stephen Miller considers that two things had hampered its effectiveness: 'First, because of individual error, one of the brigades got lost and did not get to its assigned position. Second, the Boers were alerted as, just before the advance, the artillery conducted a barrage to clear the ground which effectively took away the element of surprise.'[21] Above all, the reason that the outcome was indecisive was that Methuen had insufficient mounted troops, impairing the effectiveness of his reconnaissance and his ability to pursue or cut off the retreating enemy.

On the day after the battle of Belmont, Methuen received a report that a party of Boers, believed to be about 400 strong, had taken up a position at Graspan with two guns. This was 11 miles further on along the railway line to Kimberley. The information was only partially correct. During 23 November, Koos de la Rey had arrived at the battlefield of Belmont too late to play any effective part there and thereafter, retired to take up the position at Graspan, from where he sent a message to Prinsloo asking him to join him there. This the latter duly did, leaving behind at Ramdan, to where he had retreated after the battle of 23 November, a force of 800 men under

19 *Official History*, vol. I, p. 226
20 *Times History*, vol. II, p. 332.
21 Miller, *Methuen*, p. 97.

Venter, and moving to Graspan with the rest of his men. On his arrival, the combined force there amounted to between 2,000–2,500 men, with five guns.

De la Rey, who would prove during the course of the war to be one of the most effective of the Boer generals, was born in 1847. A member of the Volksraad, he had opposed the war with Britain but once it had begun, he soon made his name as an effective commander. Initially, he led a force of 800 men operating in the Mafeking area but in mid-October, it was decided that he should take his force south to join that which was massing around Kimberley, in order to reinforce the Free Staters there.[22]

The position at Graspan was based on a cluster of small hills astride the railway line, and effectively barred the way north to Methuen's force. These hills rose abruptly from the level plain. The southern face of the position was about a mile long; at its eastern and western ends were two razor back kopjes rising to a height of about 150 feet, while in the centre, an oval kopje about 200 yards in length rose about 180 feet, connected to the others by re-entrant ridges. To the north, there lay two further clusters of hills.[23]

After the battle of 23 November, the British had remained that afternoon and night around Belmont. It was on the afternoon of the following day that Methuen sent forward all his mounted troops on a front of three miles either side of the railway to conduct a reconnaissance. This had produced the information previously referred to, and that afternoon, Methuen moved up the rest of his force to Swinkpan, about 7 miles south of the Boer positions, which they reached after dark. Methuen had accompanied his mounted troops in their reconnaissance and what he saw led him to conclude that the Boers could be driven from their position by a sufficiently heavy bombardment, and that his mounted troops advancing on either flank could cut off their retreat.[24] Accordingly, his plan was to bring forward his artillery units under the cover of darkness, so that they would be in a position to open fire with the dawn.

At 3:30 a.m. on 25 November, the mounted troops, the field artillery and the 9th Brigade (still under Money's command), moved out from Swinkpan. The Guards Brigade followed an hour later. The naval guns, aboard goods trucks, moved up the railway accompanied by three companies of engineers. The 9th Brigade now included a small naval battalion under the command of Captain Prothero. Methuen's orders to Gough were to take his lancers and go around the east of the enemy's position with two squadrons, taking with him a company of mounted infantry and Rimington's Guides. On the other flank, to the west, Milton was sent forward with the third squadron of lancers and two companies of mounted infantry. The 18th and 75th Field Artillery Batteries at first moved out with the 9th Brigade, but they were ordered forward at 5.00 a.m. when the sun rose, coming into action at 6:15 a.m. against the Boer position east of the railway.[25]

It soon became apparent to Methuen that he was in the presence of a much larger force then he had supposed. He ordered up the Guards Brigade to cover his right flank, which was threatened by the force of Boers under Venter which had come up from Ramdan. The assault on the main Boer position was launched by the 9th Brigade at the southern end of the easternmost kopje; the left flank of the brigade was covered by four companies of the Northampton battalion, while on their right came five companies of Northumberland Fusiliers, lying down

22 Peter Trew, *The Boer War Generals* (Stroud: Sutton Publishing, 1999), p. 214.
23 *Official History*, vol. I, p. 230.
24 Ibid., p. 233
25 Ibid.

about 2,000 yards from the enemy's position. Four more companies moved up to escort the naval guns and the 75th Battery. Further to the right, the 18th Battery took up a position more or less due east of Venter's force. The 9th Brigade's attacking line was prolonged by two companies of the North Lancashire Regiment, which had been added to the brigade. Next came the naval battalion, which was to assault the kopje forming the left of the enemy position; it was supported by two more Northampton companies and one of the King's Own Yorkshire Light Infantry (KOYLI). It is not immediately apparent why the companies of the various battalions of the 9th Brigade were so intermingled. Finally, extending the line around the left of the enemy position, supporting the 18th Battery, came six more companies of the KOYLI and three of the Northamptons.

In the first instance, the naval guns moved up to within 4,000 yards, and then shortened the range to 2,300 yards, remaining in action until the end of the battle. In the exchange of gunfire with the Boers, however, neither side's artillery succeeded in inflicting many casualties. The Boers had effectively extended their line so that what had been their left flank was now effectively part of their main front and as a result, the assault of the 9th Brigade was a straightforward frontal attack.

The scene as the infantry advanced was vividly described in an account written by Captain Mark Phillips, riding with Rimington's Guides out on the British right:

> A wide plain in front of me, four miles across, flat as the sea, and all along the farther side a line of kopjes and hills rising like reefs and detached islands out of it. You might think the plain was empty at first glance, but if you look hard you will see it crawling with little khaki clad figures dotted all over it; not packed anywhere but sprinkled all over the surface. Meantime, from three or four spots along the sides of those hills, locks and puffs of white smoke floated out, followed at long intervals by deep, sonorous reports; and if you look to the left, where our naval guns are at work, you will see the Boer shells bursting close to or even over them. The artillery duel goes on between the two, while still the infantry, unmolested as yet, crawls and crawls towards those hills.[26]

Two days earlier, the men of the naval battalion had been frustrated not to play a part in the battle of Belmont but were now elated to find that Methuen had selected them to be in the forefront of the assault. One of their officers later wrote: 'The news seemed almost too good to be true, and it was some short time before we could believe it and realise our luck.'[27]

At 9.00 a.m. Methuen gave the orders for the attack to commence. The men of the naval battalion advanced in a line at first extended to four paces, but as they approached the kopje, they had closed in, offering an easy target to the skilled Boer rifleman. It was, perhaps, due to their lack of experience in field exercises, but they paid a dreadful price; Colonel Verner recorded that the officers and men of the battalion 'were picked off like a deer, but they never flinched and fell with their faces to the hill and their officers walked ahead with their swords drawn.'[28] The Boers had held their fire until the sailors and marines were within 1,000 yards of their line. They made their advance in rushes of 50 to 60 yards, lying down to fire, and then rushing forward again, but it was impossible to escape the deadly fusillade. Neither the fire of

26 *Times History*, vol. II, p. 336.
27 Byron Farwell, *The Great Boer War* (London: Allen Lane, 1977) p. 94.
28 W. Baring Pemberton, *Battles of the Boer War* (London: B. T. Batsford Ltd. 1964), p. 54.

the artillery, nor the rifle fire of the companies on either flank of the naval battalion were able to suppress the Boer fire, which inflicted heavy casualties, especially among the officers, who had insisted on advancing at the head of their men and suffered accordingly. Prothero was among the first to fall, severely wounded.

In spite of the Boer fire, the sailors and marines pressed on, supported by the infantry on their right and left. As they approached the crest, most of the Boers briskly retreated along the whole of their line, and the surviving members of the naval battalion were able to see their enemy scrambling down the far side of the kopje, mounting their ponies, and riding off. The battalion's losses, however, were fearful. They had lost 13 killed and 79 wounded; the Marines had suffered particularly severely losing 44 percent of their strength. Methuen later recorded tersely in his despatch as the reason: 'The naval brigade attacked in too close formation.'[29]

The attack had taken little more than half an hour. The Boer troops on the right had taken little part in the fighting; the loss of the kopje to the 9th Brigade made their position untenable, and the whole of the force under both de la Rey and Prinsloo, fell back northwards. The two field artillery batteries advanced to the ridge between the two eastern kopjes, but by the time they took up a position there, the remaining Boers were out of range.

The mounted troops on each flank had advanced in accordance with Methuen's orders. On the British left, Milton had led his force well to the west of the railway, and then north before pushing eastwards to a point six miles in rear of the Boer positions, across the enemy's line of retreat. However, the large number of Boers falling back put Milton's detachment at serious risk; his lancer squadron fell back, covered by his mounted infantry who seized a kopje, after which Milton was able to effect his escape.

On the other flank, Gough had been engaged in holding back the Boer force from Ramdan. Once the main attack had succeeded, he advanced towards the Boer laager, but the escort there was too strong to attempt a charge, and he sent a message calling for artillery support. Ultimately, the 18th Battery was sent to join him, but the horses were too exhausted to move quickly and by the time the guns were in position, the Boer wagons were already 5,000 yards away.[30]

Methuen reported the outcome to Buller next day: 'The heights gained, I found I had taken the whole Boer force in flank and had entirely cut them off from their line of retreat. My guns played on the masses of horsemen, but my few cavalry, deadbeat, were powerless, and for the second time I longed for a Cavalry Brigade and a H[orse] A[rtillery] Battery to let me reap the fruits of a hard-fought action.'[31] It was perhaps a rather more upbeat report than was justified, but there is no question but that Methuen's lack of horsemen meant that his aim to cut off the retreating Boers had been much too optimistic. One mounted infantry officer wrote sadly: 'We saw them going away with a long train of wagons towards the Free State in the most perfect order in an absolutely open country, and yet as far as we were concerned so far from being able to do anything we were almost cut off ourselves.'[32]

Methuen was dissatisfied with the performance of his mounted troops, however, and he removed Gough from the command of the 9th Lancers, believing that an opportunity had been lost. He replaced him with Major Little. The decision was unjust; there was not much more that

29 T.T. Jeans, ed, *Naval Brigades in the South African War 1899–1900* (London: Sampson Low Marston and Co., 1902), p. 34.

30 *Official History*, vol. I, p. 241.

31 Miller, *Methuen*, p. 102.

32 Pemberton, *Battles*, p. 54.

Gough could have done. His dismissal had a tragic consequence; a few months later Gough took his own life.[33] Methuen's frustration is perhaps understandable; the terrain across which the Boers were retreating was, as the Official History pointed out, 'singularly favourable to cavalry action and had a satisfactory mounted brigade with a horse artillery battery been available, the Boers could not have effected their escape without suffering very heavy losses.'[34]

Methuen had won another victory, in that he had driven the Boers back from a strong position, but his losses had again, been not inconsiderable, totalling 188 killed and wounded. The total of Boer losses was probably between 80 and 90. The Official History concluded that Boer morale had if anything, been strengthened by the encounter by the realisation that their superior mobility enabled them to avoid a serious defeat. *The Times History*, on the other hand, reckoned that being obliged to abandon a strong position had left the Boers feeling profoundly dejected.[35] It does appear that the Free Staters were rather more cast down than the Transvaalers. Prinsloo had not particularly distinguished himself in the course of the fighting; but de la Rey's confidence remained high, as he was to demonstrate in the coming weeks. Although Piet Cronje had now arrived to take over the command, it was the conclusions that de la Rey had drawn, that were to prove of critical significance.

For his part, Methuen had come to some conclusions himself from the battles at Belmont and Graspan, which he embodied in his report to Buller of 26 November:

> There is far too great risk of failure in making flank and front attack in the case of a position such as lay before me at Belmont. The very first element of success is to keep touch between brigades from the first. Nor is there any question of taking the enemy in flank, as on horses he changes front in fifteen minutes as will be shown in the next fight. Shrapnel does not kill men in these kopjes, it only frightens, and I intend to get at my enemy.[36]

Methuen gravely doubted the wisdom of moving away from the railway. In 1902, he would tell the Elgin Commission that he had to keep to it because he could only carry a limited amount of supplies with the mule transport which he had; the remainder of his provisions came up by the railway, which followed him day by day. For this reason, Methuen was coming round to the view that he had no alternative but to rely on frontal assaults; these had, after all, been successful at to Talana Hill and Elandslaagte, and again at Belmont and Graspan. However, the generally held expectation that a heavy bombardment with shrapnel would suffice to drive the Boers out of prepared positions, had proved to be without foundation, as he had pointed out to Buller.

33 Miller, *Methuen,* p. 104n.
34 *Official History*, vol. I, p. 241.
35 Ibid., p. 242; *Times History*, vol. II, p. 341.
36 Miller, *Methuen*, p. 103.

9

Modder River

Following Graspan, de la Rey and Prinsloo met with others at Jacobsdal to decide their next course of action. De la Rey had realised that the Boer defeats had come about primarily as a result of the mistaken belief that occupying the crest of the steep sided kopjes was the best way to hold up the British advance. In fact, far from providing an impregnable defensive position, they offered a straightforward target for the British artillery, and their steep slopes provided cover to their attackers once they reached the base of the heights. Even more significantly, downward firing greatly reduced the effectiveness of the Boer rifle fire; the flat trajectory of the modern rifle was much better suited to firing on the level. With this in mind, de la Rey had already selected a position that would give its defenders a much better prospect of success.[1]

This was along the line of the Riet, which crossed the featureless plain on either side of the bridge over the River Modder, which joined the Riet just above it. Amery described the advantages of the position:

> It is essential to bear in mind that de la Rey's plan was not to dispute the passage of the river in the ordinary sense, by holding commanding points from which a heavy fire could be brought to bear on troops attempting to cross, but to utilise the bed of the river itself as a defensive position. For this purpose the Riet at Modder Bridge was admirably suited. Like most South African rivers, especially those that traversed the soft soil of the Free State, the Riet flowed some 30 feet below the level of the surrounding plain in a deep cutting or trough – an exaggerated donga or dwarf canyon.[2]

On either side of the river, a sloping space in places as much as 200 yards wide rose at its edge to meet the level of the veld in a steep cliff from six to 10 feet high. Along the river bank grew mimosas and willows, only the tops of which could be seen from the level of the veld. The river itself was quite invisible. It has been said that below the bridge for some two miles westward to the dam at Rosmead village, the Riet was at that time. comparable in width and depth to the upper Thames.

1 *Official History*, vol. I, p. 243.
2 *Times History*, vol. II, pp. 342–343.

With Cronje's troops about to arrive, de la Rey was able to persuade the Free Staters to make a stand in this position, and during the course of 26 November, the Boers began to concentrate along the line of the Riet. That afternoon and during the following day they spent in entrenching the position, building gun emplacements and marking off the ranges along the line up which the British were expected to advance. Cronje himself arrived on Monday, 27 November with a further 1,200 men, so that by the following day, the Boers had concentrated some 3,500 men in the position. They continued the digging of trenches on both sides of the river, according to the design of some German volunteers. From here, the Boers would be able to maximise the range of their Mausers, while effectively remaining invisible to the enemy.

There were few practical crossings of the rivers at this point. There was a ford across the Riet some three miles south-east of the Modder River bridge, at Bosman's Drift, but this was in any case, unknown to the British. A second ford crossed the river beside the bridge, on its eastern side at the confluence of the two rivers. To the west, at Rosmead, a mile downriver there was another ford, while the retaining wall of the weir which dammed the river there could also be crossed, though with some difficulty, by men in single file.[3]

The two hamlets, Rosmead and Modder River village consisted of farms and cottages with gardens, while on the tongue of land east of where the rivers joined, stood the Island Hotel. The area between the curving line of the Modder and that of the Riet was known as Twee River. As the Official History put it, ' the Riet and the Modder together formed not only a gigantic moat across the approaches to Kimberley from the south and south-east, but a covered way by which its defenders could move unseen to any part of the position.'[4] Beyond it, five miles north-east of Modder River village, the complex of heights around Magersfontein rose dark and threateningly, visible for miles around, and further to the north, astride the railway, rose the heights of Scholtz Nek and Spytfontein.

Although when Piet Cronje arrived he assumed overall command of the whole force, he did not interfere with the decisions which de la Rey had taken for the defence of the position. Cronje was not, however, an easy man to work with. Now aged 65, he had made his reputation in the First Boer War and he was known as the 'Lion of Potchefstroom.' He had been prominent in the politics of the Transvaal as a close associate of Paul Kruger and enjoyed considerable popularity, being seen as altogether more of a decisive leader than Piet Joubert. He was a natural choice to command the Boer forces in the west. De la Rey was officially described as an 'adviser' to Cronje, which was not a comfortable role, since Cronje was obstinate and opinionated and unenthusiastic about receiving advice. In any case, he disliked de la Rey; this feeling was mutual, not least since the latter had no high opinions of Cronje's military ability.[5]

Meanwhile, Methuen had been reviewing his options. Neither Belmont nor Graspan could be considered to have been major battles, but they had been much harder fought than he had expected. The casualties which he had incurred had somewhat shaken Methuen, who had originally been encouraged by Buller to believe that he would not encounter much resistance in his march to Kimberley.

Searchlight messages from the besieged town suggested that the Boers were preparing to take up a position to the north of the Modder River bridge at Spytfontein, which Methuen believed would be a very tough nut to crack. He had, on 26 November, sent Colonel Verner with

3 *Official History*, vol. I, p. 246.
4 Ibid., p. 244.
5 Trew, *Boer War Generals*, p. 215.

a mounted patrol to reconnoitre towards the Riet, but this returned without having gathered much information. When he got back, Verner, a key member of Methuen's staff, was seriously injured in a fall from his horse and had to be invalided home.

The next day, at 4.00 a.m., Methuen put his whole force into motion, advancing to Wittekop, about six miles south of the Modder River bridge. From here, his mounted troops did their best to reconnoitre on a six mile front, in the course of which they were able to observe some enemy movement from Jacobsdal, apparently in the direction of Modder River Station. Later in the day, Methuen himself rode forward with Major Little and a party of 9th Lancers towards the Riet, but saw nothing of significance; he was quite unaware that he had ridden within 300 yards of the Boer position.[6]

In spite of his reservations about the practicality of moving away from the railway line, Methuen's first thought as he considered his next move after Graspan, had been that he might undertake a flank march around the Boer left. Rather than face the difficulty of assaulting a strongly fortified position at Spytfontein, Methuen instead contemplated a move via Jacobsdal and Brown's Drift to strike at the Boer flank, masking whatever enemy forces were at Modder River bridge by a reconnaissance in force. He believed that when he reached Jacobsdal he would be able to seize a considerable stock of supplies there; it was understood that the town was only lightly defended.[7]

However, before dawn on 28 November, Methuen had received information that the Modder River bridge at least was strongly held. This was consistent with such intelligence as his cavalry had been able to acquire. It caused him to reconsider his plan for a flank march. Even if, as he supposed, the Boers at the river were merely occupying an advanced post to cover the main concentration at Spytfontein, he deemed it unwise to embark on his march to Jacobsdal, leaving the Boers at Modder River to threaten his line of communications. Amery, not an admirer of Methuen, considered this change of plan to have been a mistake:

> The soundness of the decision is open to doubt. If the Boers really were in force at the bridge, it was obvious that they expected him to march there and intended to dispute his passage. If so the march to Jacobsdal would surprise them, and by cutting them off from their base would create a state of alarm in which they were not likely to undertake active operations against his communications. If they were not in force the troops left at trailhead could be trusted to look after themselves.[8]

If Methuen had undertaken his flank March, it was Amery's view that he would have been able to fall unexpectedly on Cronje's convoys as they moved southwards.

However, this is to be wise after the event. Methuen decided to postpone his march on Jacobsdal until he had dealt with the enemy force on the river line. He was, though, seriously handicapped, to a greater extent than he realised, by his lack of any accurate maps of the area. The only map which he possessed was one which had been drawn by a Captain O'Meara on the outbreak of war and it was inaccurate in just about every particular. O'Meara had been instructed to report on the best way of defending the Modder River bridge with one or two companies of infantry: the task was executed under circumstances which, even had his instructions been more

6 Miller, *Methuen*, p. 104.
7 Ibid., p. 103.
8 *Times History*, vol. II, p. 346.

comprehensive, would have prevented him from effecting any extensive reconnaissance of the Riet and Modder Rivers.[9]

It was not until the night of 27/28 November that Methuen decided to postpone his flanking movement. Rimington had reported to him that the Boers expected reinforcements and that they were digging trenches on the south bank of the river near the bridge, while Little estimated the total number of Boers in the vicinity at 4,000. A loyal British subject sent a message that the Boers were in force and were 'digging themselves in like rabbits.'[10] All of this tended to confirm Methuen's view that he was merely facing an advanced post. He revised his orders, and by 4:30 a.m. on 28 November, his troops were on the march.

The cavalry preceded the infantry and were brought to a halt by enemy fire at 5.30 a.m. Little told Methuen, who for a while was riding with him, that all his information indicated that the river was strongly held from the bridge eastward to a clump of poplars. This, so far as it went, was correct; but what was quite unknown was that the concealed Boer trenches along the left bank of the river ran from Rosmead eastwards to the bend where the Riet turned sharply to the southward. Methuen was not impressed by Little's information, firmly believing that he was facing only a small force.

The left of the British advance consisted of the 9th Brigade, now commanded by Major General Reginald Pole-Carew, in succession to the temporary command of Lieutenant-Colonel Money. The brigade advanced on the west of the railway line; its left flank covered by Rimington's Guides. The Guards Brigade, under Colville, formed the right of the advance, moving up to the east of the railway line, its objective being what was taken to be the Boer position from the broken railway bridge to the clump of poplars on the Riet. As the two brigades advanced, Methuen sent a verbal message to the effect that he thought that there were no Boers along the river bank except possibly 400 men covering the bridge itself.[11] An officer described what was visible to the British troops as they advanced: 'We found ourselves at the top of a rise sloping very gently downwards for about three miles to a collection of houses and a clump of eucalyptus trees. There was a long line of bushes which we did not know at the time marked the line of the Modder River.'[12]

At the Island Hotel, Cronje breakfasted with de la Rey and Prinsloo. They were satisfied with the preparations that had been made but were very conscious that their forces were still no more than 3,000 strong. Cronje had become alarmed about the possibility that, as the British advanced, they might be planning to cross the Riet to the south at Bosman's Drift, and he despatched one of his guns and a pom-pom to support the parties of riflemen posted at the ford. During the day, the right rear of the British advance was in fact covered by Little and the 9th Lancers, but they had no intention of crossing the Riet.

De la Rey took up a position with his commandos close to the broken railway bridge, from where he could see the approaching lines of British infantry. Cronje was to his left, along the Riet, with the rest of the Transvaalers, while Prinsloo, with the Free Staters, extended westwards as far as Rosmead. The Boer artillery, carefully sited in positions prepared by the Prussian Major Albrecht, who had for the past 19 years been in command of the Free State artillery, had been located principally behind de la Rey's position, where four of the Krupp 75mm field guns

9 *Official History*, vol. I, p. 246
10 Ibid.
11 *Official History*, vol. I, p. 249.
12 Pemberton, *Battles*, p. 61.

were close to the railway line. The other two field guns and the 31-pdr Maxims were scattered eastward.[13]

It seemed to De la Rey to be a mistake on Cronje's part not to post any artillery in support of Prinsloo. As he watched the British advance, it was soon apparent to him that another mistake been made, when Cronje's men, in defiance of their orders, proved unable to resist the temptation to open fire on the lines of advancing infantry. De la Rey's intention had been that all along the defensive position the Boers should hold their fire as long as possible, but the premature fusillade simply alerted the British infantry to their danger, and they once took to the ground.

Colville had formed the Guards Brigade, advancing to the east of the railway, in two lines. The first consisted of the Scots Guards on the right, the Grenadiers in the centre and the 2nd Battalion of Coldstream Guards on the left, with the 1st Battalion of the Coldstreams in the second line in reserve. They had taken as their direction the tall clump of poplars. Methuen was riding with Colville at this time, and as they watched the Scots Guards deploying he remarked: 'They are not here,' to which Colville replied: 'They are sitting uncommonly tight if they are, Sir.' It was about 8:10 a.m. At that moment, just as the deployment was completed, the Boers opened fire with a blaze of musketry:

The whole British force had walked straight into the ambush so skilfully laid for it. Had but the Boers possessed the nerve to hold their fire a few minutes longer, the result would have been sheer massacre. Even as it was, in spite of the distance and the extended order, the casualties of those first few minutes were heavy enough. For a mile or more from the river, the air was full of bullets flying horizontally 'in solid streaks like telegraph wires.'[14]

The Scots Guards were at once pinned down; seeing this, Colville sent forward the 1st Coldstreams to prolong the line to the right, thereby hoping to overlap the enemy left. This advance, however, was unexpectedly stopped by the line of the Riet, the position of which was unknown to the British. Although an officer of the Coldstreams, with a handful of men, succeeded in wading across the river by a disused drift, they were soon ordered to return. The rest of the battalion took up a position along the left bank of the Riet where, entrenching itself as best it could, it remained until nightfall, suffering considerable losses.

By the time the advance of the British right had provoked the Boers to open fire, the sun was well up in the sky and the day was becoming extremely hot. For the soldiers, lying flat on their faces, the heat became almost intolerable; for the kilted Scottish troops, the sun burnt the backs of their knees so severely that some were scarcely able to walk and all the time they faced incessant sniper fire from the concealed Boer marksmen. As the day wore on, it became clear that it was impossible to get nearer to the Boer defences than about 1,100 yards:

> So long as the men lay flat on the ground they were little molested, as a growth of thistles hid them from the enemy's view, but any attempt to move brought upon them a shower of bullets, to which they were unable to reply with any effect, as the Boers, perfectly protected by their trenches or concealed by the vegetation which lined the riverbank, suffered little from the shrapnel of the supporting British guns, and could not be seen by the infantry.[15]

Pemberton described the ordeal of the Guards Brigade as it faced the fire of the Boer riflemen:

13 Pakenham, *Boer War*, p. 195.
14 *Times History*, vol. II p. 350.
15 *Official History*, vol. I, p. 251.

> Though the Boer tendency throughout the day was to fire too high, the raising of an arm, the showing of a helmet brought on a generally accurate fusillade. Even to attempt a little firing on one's own was to take a needless risk, for no Boer could be seen, not even a puff of smoke from his rifle. When Captain Heneage, grown desperate by boredom, worked up a little rush, four Grenadier sergeants fell dead.[16]

Pinned down in this way, the Guards Brigade could do little to threaten the unseen Boers in their positions and in this sector it was the artillery that played the greater part. The 12 field guns of the two batteries and the four naval 12 pounders, moved forward from one position to another until they were within 1,300 yards of the Boer trenches, firing just over the heads of the prone infantrymen. In reply, Albrecht's artillerymen moved from one to another of the emplacements which he had prepared the day before, firing at measured ranges at the markers that had been planted at intervals along the line of the railway. None of the Boer guns were knocked out; the British gunners, on the other hand, presented an easy target as they fought their guns on the open plain. Their heavy bombardment of the Boer position with shrapnel did not inflict many casualties but it did manage to keep down the Boer fire.

As the day wore on, the prostrate infantry suffered increasingly, not only from the blazing heat but also from ants that tormented them constantly; it was exceedingly difficult for stretcher bearers to crawl up to the firing line to evacuate the wounded or for fresh supplies of ammunition to reach the troops. As they lay there, lying upon their rifles to keep them cool enough to use when required, many men, overcome by heat and exhaustion, fell asleep. Those on the right of the Guards' position faced Boer rifle fire from in front and on their flank from the right bank of the Riet where it bent around to the southward.

Meanwhile the direction of the advance of the 9th Brigade was intended to be astride the railway line, the Northumberland Fusiliers to the east and the King's Own Yorkshire Light Infantry to the west, each supported by half a battalion of the Argyll and Sutherland Highlanders which had joined the force during the night. The half battalion of the Loyal North Lancashires was to come up on the left and if possible, to cross the river. It was soon apparent to Pole-Carew, however, that the line being taken by the Guards Brigade meant that it would extend almost as far as the railway and hence overlap his right, so he shifted his brigade westwards. Taking advantage of a slight swell in the ground, he came to within about 2,000 yards of the Boer positions; however, when the Northumberland Fusiliers began to cross the railway line from east to west, the Boer artillery opened fire, and a few minutes later, at about 7:30 am, the Boer infantry began an intense fusillade.[17]

It had been Pole-Carew's intention to turn the Boer right, but so fierce was the enemy's fire that he was obliged to push forward the Northumberland Fusiliers to cover his westward movement and later, to employ both the half battalion of the Argyll and Sutherland Highlanders and then the KOYLI similarly. This battalion succeeded in getting to within a few hundred yards of some farm buildings which lay about 300 yards south of the river, and which was strongly garrisoned as an advanced post by the Boers. From here in particular, they poured an incessant fire on the British infantry attempting to advance which were, as in the case of the Guards Brigade, several hundred yards from the Boer position.

16 Pemberton, *Battles*, p. 64.
17 *Official History*, vol. I, pp. 252-253.

Pole-Carew could see that these farm buildings represented the key to the Boer position in this sector of their front and prepared to advance upon them. He sent forward a small party of Argyll and Sutherland Highlanders into a donga running into the river between the farmhouse and the nearest Boer trench on the left bank. This detachment succeeded in reaching the river without loss. However, at 11.00 a.m., Methuen sent Pole-Carew an order that the 9th Brigade should, for the moment, cease fire, as the units of the Guards Brigade were about to make an attempt to cross the river and might become victims of friendly fire. When the 9th Brigade duly stopped firing, though, the Boer rifle fire increased in intensity to such an extent that in self-defence, Pole-Carew's infantry had to re-open fire. Soon after, Methuen joined Pole-Carew with the news that the Guards had not been able to effect a crossing; this gave the commander of the 9th Brigade the opportunity to discuss with Methuen his plan to launch an assault on the farm buildings.[18]

Methuen at once approved this, and personally led a small party of Argyll and Sutherland Highlanders to reinforce the captured donga. Throughout the day, Methuen was active in the support of his troops, constantly exposed to enemy. Conan Doyle, in his history of the war, wrote: 'It is but fair to Lord Methuen to say that his own personal and unflinchingly resolution set the most stimulating example to his troops. No general could have done more to put heart into his men.'[19] Later in the day, at about 4.00 p.m., Methuen was hit and seriously wounded in the thigh and he had to turn over the command to Colville. Those around him were similarly exposed; to Methuen's dismay, his key staff officer and close personal friend, Lieutenant-Colonel H. P. Northcott, had been killed while riding Methuen's horse with a message to Colville. It was a blow which hit Methuen hard; he wrote to his wife: 'My only staff officer, my one companion has gone in Northcott; I shall never get over his death. I am to blame, for each day he prayed me not to impose myself, and had I remained away from the firing line neither of us need have been hit.'[20]

Meanwhile, the capture of the donga had given Pole-Carew the opportunity which he sought. Covering fire from this position enabled the seizure of the Boer trench at this point, following which an assault by a patrol of the KOYLI supported by a detachment of Argyll and Sutherland Highlanders, was successful in capturing the farm and outbuildings. The Free Staters defending this position did not put up much resistance and retreated across the river, so that by about 11.30, Pole-Carew was able to make his next move. The Boers here had been badly shaken by the fire of two guns of the 18th Battery and had begun pulling out of Rosmead village.[21]

Although the rest of the 9th Brigade were still pinned down under intense Boer fire from both banks of the river, here was a real opportunity to break the deadlock and go forward. A body of troops drawn from various battalions began to cross the river by means of the weir, while a quarter of a mile downstream, two companies of the Loyal North Lancashire Battalion began to cross at the drift. Pole-Carew saw that the decisive moment had arrived and sent an urgent message to Methuen asking for reinforcements to exploit the advantage which he had gained; but none were available. Accordingly, he set about collecting together what troops he could – to the number of about 150 – and with these he dashed into the river at the weir; wading

18 Ibid., p. 254.
19 Conan Doyle, *The Great Boer War* (London: Smith Elder & Co., 1900), p. 146.
20 Miller, *Methuen*, p. 122n.
21 *Official History*, vol. I, p. 254.

up to their armpits, they gained the opposite bank, and stormed into Rosmead village from which the Free Staters hurriedly retreated:

> They had entered on the battle with a faint heart, shaken by their previous defeats and conscious of their general's incapacity; they had abandoned the south bank without a very serious struggle, and now the shellfire suddenly directed upon their crumbling defences and the sight of the advancing infantry completed their discomfiture. They abandoned Rosmead village and retreated in disorder on the centre of their position.[22]

Here, it had indeed been the British artillery that had been decisive in enabling this success to be achieved. In fact, all along the front it was the gunners that were bearing the principal burden of the battle, moving up by stages until they reached a point no more than 1,200 yards from the Boer position. They were strengthened by the arrival at about 2.00 of four guns from the 62nd Battery that had come up from the Orange River bridge, and which, learning of the fighting on the Riet, had proceeded by forced marches notwithstanding the intense heat, covering some 62 miles in 28 hours. These guns opened fire at 2:45, shelling the Boer positions on the left bank.[23]

With Rosmead village in his hands, Pole-Carew had now begun to organise a force to advance on Modder village, and by 1.00 had collected about 500 men from various battalions. With these, he pushed forward from Rosmead. At first, the advance encountered little opposition, but when they reached Fraser's Farm they found that the Boers were ready for them. A hail of rifle bullets and of shrapnel from Albrecht's guns, fell on the British infantry as they tried to cross long hedges of prickly pear and to clamber through strong wire fencing. The Official History noted: 'Major Albrecht fought his guns with great determination; his infantry escort, according to Boer accounts, retreated when they saw the advance of the British, and his ammunition was almost exhausted, but his gunners stood their ground.'[24]

Pole-Carew's advance was not helped by the fact that the Argyll and Sutherland Highlanders in the donga on the south bank, upon whose flanking fire he had depended on to keep the Boers in check, had mistakenly abandoned their position across the river to join in the advance. Pole-Carew found it impossible to get a message back to the troops still on the south bank of the river and the artillery was unable to target the Boer position effectively due to the thickness of the undergrowth. In the end, he was obliged to abandon the attempt to advance, and he fell back to Rosmead.

There, he found that his strength had been increased by the arrival of 300 Royal Engineers, and part of a company of Coldstream Guards. He sent a report to Methuen telling him of his failure to advance up the right bank and to seek support for a fresh attempt to do so. He then heard of the injury to Methuen and the death of Northcott. Soon after this, he learnt that Colville was preparing to launch an attack at dusk on the left of the Boer position, following a heavy bombardment. As darkness fell, there was a risk of his own action leading to enfilade fire hitting the Guards as they advanced, and he decided that realistically he could do no more than hold Rosmead.[25]

22 *Times History*, vol. II, p. 355.
23 *Official History*, vol. I, p. 258.
24 Ibid., p. 256n.
25 *Official History*, vol. I,. p. 257.

Colville had handed over command of the Guards Brigade to Colonel Arthur Pagett. The latter, mindful of the risks of attempting a night attack with the exhausted troops, advised against Colville's planned assault, and after due consideration it was abandoned. Colville instead proposed to launch an attack on the following morning, and he ordered Pagett to concentrate his brigade overnight at the southern reservoir on the bank of the Riet. He knew very little of the situation on the rest of the battlefield beyond the fact that Pole-Carew had succeeded in taking Rosmead.

There, all the available troops had been posted for the defence of the village against a Boer counter-attack and Pole-Carew ordered the rest of his brigade to cross to the north bank of the river during the night, with a view to launching a fresh attack on the following morning. This operation was completed by daybreak.

On the Boer side of the line, de la Rey had been shocked by the retreat of Prinsloo's men. He blamed Cronje for this, feeling that he was at fault in not ensuring that troops of doubtful constancy were properly supported. As the day drew to a close, he suffered a personal tragedy when his son Adriaen, was fatally wounded at his side. Accompanying the party taking Adriaen back to Jacobsdal, he encountered Cronje, who asked him how the battle had gone. Feeling as he did that Cronje had not done enough and understandably emotional, he furiously upbraided him, before Cronje rode off; Adriaen died in his father's arms later that night.[26]

De la Rey was not, therefore, involved in the discussions between Cronje and Prinsloo as their next course of action. Their decision was to pull back from the position on the Riet, and to retire in the first instance to Jacobsdal. Thus, when the British artillery commenced a barrage in the grey light of dawn of 29 November, they were shelling empty positions; the Boers, profiting by a breakdown in communication between Colville and Pole-Carew which resulted in a failure to realise that the Boers were retreating, were able to carry off their guns under the noses of their enemy.

The British were left in possession of the battlefield and on this basis, could claim that they had won a victory. However, it had been at a high cost; 71 officers and men were killed, and 389 wounded, with 18 missing.[27] Boer casualties were much lighter, probably of the order of 150 in total. From the Boer point of view, they could claim that they had at least succeeded in checking Methuen's advance and had bought precious time to prepare to resist his next move.

Methuen has been criticised for persisting in frontal attacks which, as the German Staff History pointed out, were fraught with difficulty in a flat region; and since he had evidently been ready to leave the line of the railway and consider a flank march before the battle of Modder River, it is not unfair to count against him his failure to attempt such a move. The German Staff History also criticises the decision to pause after the battle of 28 November: 'From our present knowledge of all circumstances such a course would probably have been advantageous to the British.'[28] Having regard to the exhaustion of his troops, however, the decision not to press on immediately was not unreasonable. In addition to this, reinforcements were on the way to Methuen, while it was also necessary to restore or replace the railway bridge which had been wrecked. In addition, the need to relieve Kimberley was not urgent; Methuen received a message that it could hold out for at least 40 days. Taking all these factors into account, Pemberton concluded that 'Methuen's case for resting and halting until he had received reinforcements cannot easily be refuted.'[29]

26 Trew, *Generals*, p. 216.
27 *Official History*, vol. I, p. 467.
28 *German Staff History*, vol. I, p. 85.
29 Pemberton, *Battles*, p. 78.

Lord Salisbury.

Joseph Chamberlain.

Lord Lansdowne.

A.J. Balfour.

From left: Alfred Milner, Field Marshal Viscount Wolseley, Lieutenant General Sir William Penn Symons.

From left: President Martinus Steyn, President Paul Kruger, Lieutenant General Sir George White.

From left: Lord Methuen, Piet Cronje.

Charge of the 5th Lancers at Elandslaagte by R. Caton Woodville.

Koos de la Rey.

Major General W.F. Gatacre.

Major General A.G. Wauchope.

Boers in position at Stormberg by F.J. Waugh.

Major General F. Clery.

Christiaan De Wet.

Boer trenches at Magersfontein.

General Sir Redvers Buller.

Major General F. Hart.

Major General N. Lyttleton.

Lieutenant General Lord Dundonald.

Louis Botha.

Colonel C.J. Long.

A BRUSH WITH THE ENEMY BEFORE COLENSO.

Cavalry under cover at Colenso.

General Sir Charles Warren.

Colonel A.W. Thorneycroft.

Winston Churchill.

Thorneycroft at Spion Kop by F. Craig. Based on a sketch by an officer eyewitness.

The Durham Light Infantry at Vaal Kranz.

Buller, Methuen and Gatacre: 'Greetings from the theatre of war. The play is over; the actors remove their masks.' A German satirical postcard.

Lord Roberts.

Lord Kitchener.

Lord Elgin.

Methuen's biographer, reviewing his performance thus far, considered that 'his aptitude in commanding 10,000 men cannot be questioned,' and that he could not be blamed for the inaccurate maps and scanty reconnaissance, or the inability to transmit information across the battlefield: 'Nevertheless, he did not manage to coordinate the movements of his division.'[30] A further charge, that he was reluctant 'to deviate from the lessons he had learned while serving in many successful colonial operations' seems a little unfair. What was certain, though, was that his greatest test was yet to come.

At a Boer council of war on 29 November, which de la Rey did not attend, the decision was taken to fall all the way back to Spytfontein, a distance of 10 miles, rather than to Magersfontein, some six miles back. De la Rey, when he heard of this, was outraged, telegraphing President Steyn over Cronje's head to protest. Steyn passed this on to Kruger, who in reply, asked him to go in person to put matters right, saying that it was 'the final moment of decision, whether we are to surrender the country.' He added: Brother, my age does not allow me and my eyes are too painful, or I would be there myself.'[31]

As he lay recovering from his wound, Methuen wrote to Buller to report. The battle of Modder River, he wrote, was 'one of the hardest and most trying fights in the annals of the British Army,' which was certainly something of an overstatement; it had been, though, an extremely difficult experience for troops facing a modern battle in conditions for which they were unprepared. As Pemberton wrote, 'it was farewell to the nineteenth century.'[32] He added that something more than a study of past campaigns was needed to keep Methuen and other generals, 'who had taken their profession equally seriously, abreast of the times, and that was a thorough appreciation of the extent to which advances in artillery – and rifle – fire, the quick firing gun, the magazine rifle, the use of smokeless powder, had revolutionised tactics.'[33]

In his despatch to Buller, Methuen set out the situation as he saw it and addressed the question of flanking operations:

> We are terribly handicapped. The maps are of little value, the information obtained still less, and the open country plus Mauser rifles render a reconnaissance impossible – add to all this a march before you come into action of eight miles, boiling sun, and sand mixed with salt, and I think I have described the situation on the day of the fight here. People talk of making a detour or sending a brigade round a flank; there is no use talking in that way with 8,000 horsemen in front of you, a river, and a position not to be turned. The job has got to be done, and we have taken an [important] position with less loss than I expected, for my casualties are light, no credit to me.[34]

Amery was sharply critical of this despatch to Buller:

> Lord Methuen hardly did himself justice in this rather incoherent document, penned while under the influence of a painful wound. His whole action at the opening of the battle shows clearly that the formation he adopted referred to an impression as to the course of the rivers,

30 Miller, *Methuen*, p. 112.
31 Pakenham, *Boer War*, p. 199.
32 Pemberton, *Battles*, p. 74.
33 Ibid., p. 76.
34 Miller, *Methuen*, p. 112n.

and as to the strength of the enemy, quite at variance with ascertainable, and, indeed partly ascertained facts. The frontal attack failed completely from the very outset, and the position was only carried by a successful turning movement on the left. But so completely had the whole force, including the artillery, been committed to the frontal attack, that the control of the battle almost immediately passed out of Methuen's hand.[35]

35 *Times History*, vol. II, p. 360.

10

Three Sieges

Despite Buller's initial pessimism, by the beginning of December it might be felt that Britain's military effort was beginning to take effective shape. The garrisons of Mafeking, Ladysmith and Kimberley, under siege, appeared to be able to resist the enemy without undue difficulty and operations for their relief were in hand. Methuen had fought three battles and was continuing to move north towards Kimberly while in Natal, preparations for a movement towards Ladysmith were well advanced.

At Mafeking, the garrison commander was Colonel Robert Baden-Powell. He had arrived in South Africa in July 1899 as one of a party of 10 special service officers intended to strengthen the British military presence there. Baden-Powell's orders were to organise a force in southern Rhodesia which it was hoped might detain part of the Boer army, poised as it was on the border of Northern Transvaal. He was also required to raise a force of mounted infantry, based on Mafeking, which might hold back the burghers in the west of the Transvaal.

However, as Brian Gardner has pointed out in his history of the siege of Mafeking, Baden-Powell was subsequently somewhat contradictory in his account of his orders. He told the Elgin Commission that in the event of war he was 'to raise two regiments of mounted rifles for the defence of the Rhodesian and Bechuanaland frontiers,' and that in the event of war, was to raise local armed forces, keep the natives in order and especially, 'to draw as large a force of Boers as possible from opposing the British on their southern borders.'[1] In later years, Baden-Powell further embroidered his recollection of his instructions, although as Gardner points out, while making his role more dramatic, it weakened his position because in fact, he did not detain a large enemy force; although initially 7,000 Boers under Cronje moved on Mafeking, the force besieging the town soon decreased rapidly by 75 percent.

However, the task of defending Mafeking was considerable. It was a post of no military value at all; but a huge quantity of stores had been accumulated there and Baden-Powell was faced with the task of putting it into a state of defence. He moved one of his two regiments into the town in the middle of September; the other, under Lieutenant Colonel Plumer, he ordered to Tuli, near the junction of the Bechuanaland, Rhodesian and Transvaal borders. He formally assumed command of the garrison of Mafeking on 4 October, at which time he had a force of 1,251 officers and men, including the local police, railway detachment and town guard. His

1 Brian Gardner, *Mafeking: A Victorian Legend* (London: Cassell 1966) p. 35.

artillery was pitiable, consisting of four antique 7-pdrs, a 1-pdr Hotchkiss, a 2 inch Nordenfelt and seven Maxim machine guns.[2]

Initially, the commander of the Transvaal forces in the west of the Republic was Piet Cronje. His intention was to sweep aside the small British force at Mafeking and then take the much more significant objective of Kimberley before heading south to the Orange River to threaten Cape Province. This was an entirely valid policy as far as it went, although in the event it was to lead the Boers into making a serious strategic error, when in addition to Ladysmith, they found themselves besieging both Mafeking and Kimberley. With the valuable but entirely temporary advantage that they possessed in the early stages of the war, it was important that the Boers should not be bogged down in passive operations in this way. They should rather have pressed on to deal a decisive blow in Natal before Buller and his army corps could take a hand. The capture of a seaport such as Durban would send a dramatic signal to those Boers in Cape Province ready to stage a rising. This was the threat which Milner particularly feared; it would have been a political disaster. Neither Mafeking nor Kimberley had any military value (though the latter had very considerable political and economic significance) and at neither location was the garrison formidable enough to offer any serious threat. Both could have been masked without difficulty. Although White's force in Ladysmith was substantial, it was soon to become evident that it, too, could be contained with a relatively small force.

There has always been uncertainty about the total strength of the Boer forces in the field at the commencement of hostilities. It has been suggested that some 32,000 Boers crossed the frontier in October, of which about a quarter were with Cronje. The Official History estimates his strength at 7,000; most accounts suggest that it was of the order of 6,000, though as time passed, Baden-Powell began to magnify this figure until long after the war, it had reached 12,000.[3]

Such as it was, the siege of Mafeking began on 13 October, with a number of minor actions happening before. On 29 October, a 94-pdr French Creusot arrived to support the very ineffectual siege operations thus far mounted by the Boers. The subsequent shelling of the town by this gun and the lighter Boer artillery was, though, still relatively ineffective. The Boers were, on the whole, equivocal about the best way to deal with Mafeking. Cronje believed that he could take the town without difficulty; Kruger, on the other hand, correctly judging that it was not worth fighting for, was firmly against attempting to do so, and finally decreed that any assault must suffer no more than 50 casualties. Cronje did not object to this limitation on his freedom of action, since above all, he too wished to limit his losses. Subsequent operations were conducted for a while with rather more vigour, but casualties on both sides remained relatively light.

On 18 November, Cronje, prompted by urging from Kruger, gave up his attempt to take Mafeking, concluding that he was wasting time and the valuable services of his troops in the effort. *The Times History* observed:

> It is very characteristic of Boer methods at that stage of the war that no attempt was made to rush the town before withdrawing so large a force. Cronje and his men entrained at Klerksdorp on the 21st and were at once sent round through Johannesburg and Bloemfontein to meet Methuen's advance … At last, after sitting in front of Mafeking for five weeks, the

2 Ibid., pp. 44-45.
3 *Official History*, vol. II, p. 49; Gardner, *Mafeking*, p. 53.

absurdity of wasting nearly a third of the two Republics' available forces on the capture of one small town became obvious.[4]

Cronje took with him some 4,000 men. This would leave between 2,000 and 3,000 to continue the siege of Mafeking, although Baden-Powell later estimated a higher figure. Left in command of the siege operations there was Assistant Commandant General J. P. Snyman. He was not disposed to launch any active assaults on the town, confining himself to maintaining a blockade.

To the south stood Kimberley, where the diamond mines had made it the second largest town in Cape Colony, with a population of about 45,000. It was remote from other centres of population. It lay between the rivers Vaal, 30 miles to the north, and the Modder, the same distance to the south. Still further south ran the Orange; the three rivers converged some 90 miles southwest of Kimberley. The town was just outside the border of the Orange Free State. Its situation gave it no military significance; but its size and its enormous wealth, naturally made it an attractive target for the Boers and on 10 October, that attraction increased when Cecil Rhodes arrived in the town. The next day, the Boer ultimatum expired; on 14 October the telephone line to Cape Town was cut. On the following day, Lieutenant-Colonel Robert Kekewich, the garrison commander, proclaimed a state of siege, although by then, only a small part of the Boer forces had actually crossed the frontier.

For Cecil Rhodes, Kimberley was the source of his enormous wealth and power. By 1899, his company De Beers was producing 90 percent of the world's production of diamonds worth £5 million every year. It was not surprising that, as war approached, he should make his way to Kimberley, although he gave out that he was really on his way to Rhodesia but had been persuaded to remain in the town. His larger than life presence in Kimberley would prove to be an almost intolerable burden to the unfortunate Kekewich.

Kekewich, the commander of the 1st Loyal North Lancashire Regiment, had been dispatched by Milner in August to make a secret report on the defence of Kimberley; he was in no doubt that it was extremely vulnerable, and Milner arranged for half of Kekewich's battalion to reinforce the place, with six semi-obsolete 2.5 inch guns.[5] By the time war broke out, Kekewich had made considerable progress in establishing a defensible perimeter. In addition to his own 596 regular troops, his garrison consisted of 352 Cape police and a town guard of local volunteers that was 3,658 strong. Kekewich had been considerably assisted by an American, George Labram, who was chief mechanical engineer of the De Beers company.

It was not long before relations between Kekewich and Rhodes began to sour. The latter had a poor opinion of the military in any case and was accustomed to getting his own way; he soon began to bypass Kekewich and to send out messages to Cape Town and London calling for the urgent relief of Kimberley, stimulating reports about this in the British Press. Rhodes, from the outset, was solely concerned about the safety of his mines – which the Boers had threatened to blow up when they took the town – and he did not intend to leave any stone unturned for their protection. In his efforts to stimulate the army command in Cape Town to embark on Kimberley's relief, he wrote on 31 October to Baden-Powell at Mafeking to urge him to join his requests for urgent action: 'The Cape military authorities could easily have relieved us here … Do not be foolhardy and pretend you could hold out for months. My theory is, if you make out

4 *Times History*, vol. II, p. 298: Gardner, *Mafeking*, p. 87.
5 Pakenham, *Boer War*, p. 182.

that you are all right they will not bother about Mafeking but turn their attention to marching on Bloemfontein.'[6] Throughout the siege, Rhodes was able to get messages out of the besieged town, and he made extensive use of this facility.

In the early days of the siege of Kimberley, there had been little military activity. The Boers brought up artillery of a much larger range than possessed by the garrison, but when the bombardment started, it was of little effect. Meanwhile the relationship between Rhodes and Kekewich steadily deteriorated. Major O'Meara, a regular officer who had been sent to join Kekewich and who was serving as his chief staff officer, wrote:

> Rhodes was now becoming more and more impatient at the delay, which was taking place in the relief of Kimberley, and particularly so as Kekewich could give him no information as to what was being done in this matter by the commander-in-chief. The fact is that Kekewich was himself completely in the dark as to the intentions of his military superiors.[7]

Kekewich was doing his best to respect Rhodes' position as the head of De Beers, as an individual with enormous influence and as a privy councillor but was finding it harder and harder to put up with the barely concealed contempt which he faced on a daily basis.

When Buller had arrived in South Africa, he was told at Cape Town that the civilians at Kimberley were representing the situation as serious, and he sent off a despatch to Kekewich reporting this and calling for an immediate appreciation. Kekewich was quite unaware of Rhodes' correspondence with Milner among others and was extremely angry. He sent an immediate reply: 'Situation in Kimberley not critical.'[8] The Boers meanwhile repositioned their artillery in order that their bombardment of the town might be more effective, but it made little difference and the siege continued uneventfully.

At Ladysmith, once White had chosen to allow himself to be besieged, and Joubert had chosen to besiege him, the British had taken up positions on an inner line which measured some 14 miles in circumference. White had decided that it was impracticable to include several of the heights such as Middle Hill, Bulwana, Gun Hill and Surprise Hill which overlooked the defensive positions. The Boers began to occupy their line of investment on 2 and 3 November, at this stage with a force some 17,000 strong. In the following days, this increased to a total of 23,000 and thereafter, a further 4,000 more troops had arrived.[9] As the siege began, the garrison consisted of a total of 13,745 men.

The Boers at once began to entrench their positions and prepared emplacements for their artillery. This opened with a general bombardment on 7 November in preparation for an assault on Wagon Hill; when this was launched, the defenders beat it off without difficulty. An attack two days later on the position at Caesar's Camp was also entirely unsuccessful. Thereafter, the Boers confined their activity to a daily bombardment of the town, which was largely ineffective.

White, meanwhile, organised a mobile column, which he kept in readiness to cooperate with the relieving force when it should draw near. Apart from this, he maintained a largely passive defence, launching the occasional sally directed at destroying Boer artillery, which enjoyed some success, particularly at Gun Hill on 7 December. Throughout this period,

6 Brian Gardner, *The Lion's Cage* (London: Arthur Barker Limited 1969) p. 43.
7 W.A.J. O'Meara, *Kekewich in Kimberley* (London: Medici Society 1926) p. 58.
8 Gardner, *Lion's Cage*, p. 58.
9 *Official History*, vol. II pp. 539-540.

White was in constant touch with Buller by heliograph about the operations which the latter was preparing to undertake for Ladysmith's relief. Buller indicated that when he began to move, it would be on the line of Potgieter's Drift on the Tugela. As the days passed and it began to seem that an advance from the south might be imminent, White strengthened his mobile column and located his artillery in positions which were most likely to be useful in support of Buller's operations.[10]

While overseeing the preparations for his advance, Buller was, in the meantime, also concerned with the steps being taken for the defence of Cape Colony against Boer invasion from across the Orange River. A Boer force had seized the crossing at Norval's Point on 1 November, but thereafter moved south extremely cautiously and it was not until 14 November that Colesberg was occupied. At this point, proclamations were issued to the effect that it and other districts south of the Orange River which had also been occupied, were now Free State territory.

In order to prevent Boer raids from disrupting the crucial line of railway upon which Methuen's advance depended, Buller charged French with the task of organising a combined force to reoccupy Naauwpoort. French, accompanied by Major Douglas Haig as his chief of staff, left Cape Town by train on 18 November. Buller's instructions to him read as follows:

> I shall reinforce you as rapidly as possible; meanwhile do your best to prepare for a flying column, strength say, nearly 3,000 men, with which as soon as I get more troops I mean you to attack the Boers about Colesberg. I think such an attack should be based on Hanover Road. Do all you can to reconnoitre the country, to obtain guides and information, and to be prepared to start; keep your men in condition, and exercise horses and mules.[11]

French decided to make Naauwpoort his base and on 21 November, his cavalry came to within eight miles of Colesberg. He planned to attack Arundel, as to which Buller told Forestier-Walker that he should do so as soon as he felt strong enough, but not before. Buller wrote again to Forestier-Walker on 30 November: 'Suggest to French that a policy of worry, without risking men, might have a good effect on the enemy at Colesberg and keep him occupied.'[12] The subsequent despatch of the 12th Lancers to join Methuen left French with insufficient mounted troops for the moment, but he was reinforced by the New Zealand Mounted Rifles on 2 December, which enabled him to resume worrying the Boers at Colesberg. On 8 December he advanced, his mounted infantry seizing a hill two miles north of Arundel and pushing onwards, he outflanked the Boers at Taaiboschlangte, who fell back on Rensburg to a position sufficiently strong for French to conclude that he could, for the moment, do no more than reconnoitre it. It would not be until 11 December that he would feel able to resume his advance.

Further to the east, on 25 November the Boers had occupied the key rail junction of Stormberg, from which the British garrison had fallen back to Queenstown. Subsequently, the Boers destroyed the railway and telegraph running to the east of the junction. It was a particularly desolate part of the country:

> Stormberg is the name given to the great Drakensberg range in this part of Cape Colony. Bleak and inhospitable, it long resisted the advances of civilisation. Bushmen retreated

10 Ibid., p. 550.
11 Ibid., p. 277.
12 Ibid., p. 279.

> here, and their splendid artistry can still be seen on the walls of the many caves and on the rock faces of the cliffs.[13]

The only town actually within range was Molteno. Stormberg Junction itself was described by the journalist G. W. Steevens as a 'little junction station. A platform with dining room and telegraph office, a few corrugated iron sheds.'[14] Nevertheless, it was of considerable strategic importance.

Responsibility for this sector fell on Lieutenant-General Sir William Gatacre, the commander of the 3rd Division, who had arrived at East London with his staff on 16 November; the two brigades which had constituted his division had been sent up to Natal, so for the moment, therefore, he had few troops to resist the Boer invasion of Cape Colony at this point.

13 Farwell, *Great Boer War*, p. 115.
14 G.W. Steevens, *From Cape Town to Ladysmith* (Edinburgh: William Blackwood, 1900), p. 10.

11

Buller's Plan

Having spent 10 days at Pietermaritzburg organising his army's transport, supply and medical services, Buller went up to Frere on 6 December to join his troops who were encamped some 11 miles south of the Tugela. His arrival immediately improved their morale. 'I have never seen troops re-tempered like this by one man since I saw the extraordinary change which came over the American army on the sudden arrival of General Miles before Santiago', wrote J. B. Atkins, the *Manchester Guardian* correspondent.[1] Buller cared a great deal about the welfare of his troops and they knew it. Julian Symons described the effect of his arrival:

> It was not, however, what Buller did but what he was that inspired his men. The very sight of this big red faced man on his great bay horse gave them confidence. He spoke with an utter authority that convinced them of his ability to lead them to victory, and they discerned in his merry, twinkling, pig-like eyes a sympathy with and understanding of them that made them feel that he was one of themselves. Even his bursts of rage, when the little eyes would change from merriness to ferocity, was something that they understood, and in any case it was well known that this rage was vented most often on the officers surrounding him.[2]

Before leaving Pietermaritzburg for Frere, Buller had written to Lansdowne on 4 December to express his concerns about the difficulties which he faced:

> I am in great doubt how to attack Ladysmith. The main road through Colenso goes through a ghastly country exactly the sort made for the Boer tactics and they have strongly fortified it. I can turn it by going across the Tugela at Potgieter's Drift some 15 miles up the river and should have better ground to advance over but I should not be in so good a tactical position to help White, as I should be if I came up the main road from Colenso. I must leave it till I get up to Frere. I don't know that I ever had a problem that has bothered me more.[3]

1 Symons, *Campaign*, p. 148.
2 Ibid., pp. 148-149.
3 Pakenham, *Boer War*, p. 211.

In this letter, Buller told Lansdowne that he was happier than he had been, but that he could not say that he felt out of the wood.

At Frere, as he pondered the options open to him, Buller turned over in his mind what seemed to be the best way to defeat the Boer republics. He was later to tell the Elgin Commission of the way in which he had approached this:

> The war could only be carried to a successful conclusion by the actual conquest of every armed man in the field; this task promised to be doubly difficult owing to the extreme mobility of the enemy. It seemed to me, therefore, that the best chance of success, until our troops could have been trained in a novel style of warfare, was to allow the Boers, if possible, to take up some tactical position, and strive to crush them by sheer weight of numbers. But in any case I was convinced that my true objective was the enemy's force in the field, wherever it might be, and that any strategical movement undertaken, except in obedience to this guiding principle, would be a mere flourish in the air.[4]

The enemy's force in the field immediately before him, which Buller would seek to crush by weight of numbers, was not going to make it easy for him to achieve his objective. The Boer position along the Tugela was immensely strong. It ran from Potgieter's Drift on the west to the junction of the Tugela with Sunday's River, about 30 miles to the east of Colenso. On the northern bank of the Tugela lies a more or less continuous ridge of hills, separated only by narrow kloofs and dongas. At its western end, the ridge is connected by the Brakfontein Nek with a spur of the Drakensberg known as the Tabanyama range, while the eastern flank is covered by the lower slopes of the Biggarsberg, running parallel to Sunday's River in the area between that and the Buffalo. Colenso, roughly in the centre of this position, lay on the south bank of the Tugela, which in the Kaffir language means 'the terrible one.' At this point, it is about 200 yards wide and some 20 feet deep in places, while its banks were from 18 to 25 feet in height.

To the west of Colenso, the river could be crossed in five places; the drifts, or fords at Robinson's, Mungers, Skiet's, Maritz and Potgieter's. The first four of these were difficult for loaded wagons. Eastward, the only practicable drift was at the point at which the Weenen road crossed the river.[5] In considering the deployment of his troops to defend the position against a British advance, Louis Botha could depend on their mobility quickly to reach any part of this long line that was threatened. In order to attack him, Buller's forces must traverse much greater distances than the Boers must, in moving to block the advance. The heights which Botha held gave him a perfect view for miles to the south of the river. An attacking force must negotiate the steep and rocky southern face of the position; for its defenders, however, the northern slopes provide gentle gradients. Although the Boer forces immediately holding the line of the Tugela were, according to the intelligence reports available to Buller, no more than 6,000 or 7,000 strong, they were defending what the Official History describes as 'an immense natural redoubt.' Buller in fact, had very little information about the points principally occupied by the Boers, although he might reasonably assume that the whole line of the river was kept under close observation. When he got to Frere, Buller had twice accompanied mounted patrols towards the

4 Elgin Commission, *Minutes of Evidence*, vol. II, p. 171.
5 *Official History*, vol. I, p. 336.

river to see what he could of the Boer position by telescope, but he had not learnt a great deal. All reconnaissance had to be conducted in the plain view of picked Boer rifleman, and it was therefore extremely hazardous, and the results gained were very limited.

Essentially, the British had three options; to attack in the centre, launching a direct assault on the Boer positions opposite Colenso or to conduct a flank march to either the east or the west. To the east, the country beyond the left of the main Boer position was extremely broken, and movement through the hilly and wooded terrain would be extremely slow, while the army would be encumbered by a lengthy wagon train carrying munitions and supplies. All told, it would involve a flank march of some 60 miles, for which Buller's infantry, after their long sea voyage, were scarcely fit enough. On the other hand, it would enable the army, once across the river, to head straight for the railway line at Elandslaagte. Amery suggested that this option 'offered by far the greatest rewards for success:'

> The main Boer army at that date was still immobile and dependent on the railway to an extent that subsequent Boer exploits have somewhat caused to be lost sight of, and there can be little doubt that if Buller could have got within striking distance of the railway he would not only have broken up and dispersed the Transvaal forces but would have secured most of the guns on Pepworth, Lombard's Kop, and Bulwana, and the supplies in the laager at Modder Spruit.[6]

It was also true that such a movement carried with it the advantage that the hilly and wooded country, and the distance of the line of march from the main Boer position, might afford some measure of secrecy. It was possible that Buller's mounted troops might be almost on the railway line before the Boers knew what was happening.

But speculation in hindsight about the possibility of such a move cannot obscure the real difficulties which it would have faced. The German Staff History pointed out that 'it would have necessitated a long circuit through a wooded and hilly region,' and noted that the loss of time involved, as well as the supply difficulties caused its rejection.[7] Furthermore, the terrain was unfavourable for any sortie from Ladysmith, and White had indicated to Buller that he would be best able to support the advance of the relieving army if it moved by a flank march to the west, or directly through Colenso. In fact, judging by his letter to Lansdowne of 4 December, Buller had abandoned the idea of an eastern flank march before he left Pietermaritzburg.

When he reviewed the option of a direct attack through Colenso on the heights beyond, Buller found it also unappealing. What he had been able to see through his telescope had done nothing to encourage him to undertake a frontal attack on the forbidding position before him. The approach would be across an open plain, affording little or no cover. He knew little or nothing of the country; the terrain south of Ladysmith had never been properly mapped at all. A map had been prepared by his intelligence department at Pietermaritzburg from farm surveys and other sources immediately before the war, but this was now in Ladysmith; all that Buller had was a map hurriedly compiled at one-inch to a mile:

6 *Times History*, vol. II p. 425.
7 *German Staff History*, vol. I, p. 51.

> But even without full information the formidable character of the Colenso position and of the positions between it and Ladysmith was evident to anyone who saw, even at a distance, the frowning barrier of hills, who studied the character of the country on the most general map. Sir R. Buller realised it after his reconnaissances and came to the conclusion that Colenso was impregnable to a frontal attack and it would be necessary to turn the position by a wide flanking march.[8]

That left the western flank march as the only option available, the objective being to cross the Tugela at Potgieter's Drift. It was not without serious difficulties. It meant marching away from the line of the railway. Buller would have to take a wagon train estimated at nine miles long. It would involve temporarily cutting himself off from the telegraph to the Cape and to Britain. However, it seemed to him to be much less daunting than the alternative and on 7 December, he told White that this was the route which he would take; he hoped, he said, to begin operations on 12 December. His estimate was that it would enable him to relieve Ladysmith within five days. White replied that he would sally out from Ladysmith during the night before Buller crossed the Tugela and would 'work towards you as far as I can.' He added: 'As time is an all-important factor in cooperation, you will, I am sure, inform me of any change.'[9]

Accordingly, Clery's staff began work on the plans for the operation, which involved considerable logistical problems. In addition to these, they also had to consider ways of concealing the movement from the Boers as long as possible; they were posted on inner lines, so could reach the heights opposite Potgieter's Drift within three or four hours. Buller did not have unlimited confidence in some of his generals, feeling for instance, that Clery had fallen back to Estcourt quite needlessly at the time of Louis Botha's raid. Nor was he impressed by what he heard of Major General Geoffrey Barton, the commander of the 6th Brigade, or Lieutenant-Colonel John Byrne-Murdoch, one of his cavalry commanders. Rather different was the potential problem offered by the overconfident Major General Fitzroy Hart, the commander of the 5th Brigade, 'a man of the Penn Symons school, a fiery Irishman, beautifully dressed, a master of field-day tactics, who believed in the traditional virtues of close order and dash.'[10] Another of Buller's officers of a rather similar character was Colonel Charles Long, the artillery commander, who believed in taking his guns as close to the enemy as he could. It was he who had sent up the armoured train from Frere, a move which Buller thought was 'inconceivably stupid.' Immediately, however, a serious difficulty for the commander-in-chief was working through Clery's staff, his own staff having been widely dispersed as a result of the breakup of the army corps.

The news from elsewhere that had been reaching Buller during this time of preparation had been generally encouraging. Methuen, pausing after the three battles he had fought during the course of his advance, had paused on the Modder River before taking what was hoped would be a decisive step towards the relief of Kimberley. In Cape Colony, French, at Naauwpoort Junction, was pushing forward patrols towards the border of the Orange Free State, and Gatacre was moving up his troops towards the key railway junction at Stormberg.

Buller continued to keep White informed. On 11 December he told him that he could not be certain of his dates until his transport was in place; it would be best, he thought, for White

8 *Times History*, II, p. 424.
9 *Official History*, vol. I, p. 338.
10 Pakenham, *Boer War*, p. 213.

not to move until the relieving force had reached Lancers Hill, about six or seven miles west of Ladysmith, 'unless you feel certain where I am.'[11] In Buller's view, White should not commit himself to a major action unless they could be sure that the two armies would be in supporting distance of each other.

During 11 December, the necessary orders were issued for the army to march via Springfield on the Little Tugela to Potgieter's Drift. The next day, preparations for the advance began in earnest, when Buller moved Barton's 6th Brigade, with two 4.7 inch and six 12-pdr naval guns to a camp 2 miles north of Chieveley, where it was five miles south of the Tugela; these were to cover the flank march to the west.

That same day, Buller confirmed to Lansdowne the action that he proposed to take. He reported that after conducting a personal reconnaissance by telescope, he had reached the conclusion that 'a direct assault upon the enemy's position at Colenso would be too costly,' and that he had decided on the flank march to 'force the passage of Potgieter's Drift.' His intention, he explained, was then to advance to Ladysmith by the Acton Homes-Ladysmith road:

> It is open country to Springfield, and open country again about two miles the other side of the Tugela to Ladysmith, but I shall have a train of about 400 ox wagons, and shall have four miles of difficult country about the drift. The operation therefore is not a very pleasant one, but has this great advantage, I am sure to get water; on the other hand, the nine miles of fighting from Colenso to Onderbrook would have been in waterless country.[12]

He could not have set out his reasoning more plainly; but within a few hours he was to change his mind completely.

11 *Official History*, vol. I, p. 338
12 Ibid., vol. I p. 339; Coetzer, *Infamy*, p. 77

12

Stormberg, Sunday 10 December

On 18 November, Gatacre and his divisional staff moved up to Queenstown with the 2nd Royal Irish Rifles, 898 strong, and there found the original Stormberg garrison and some locally raised units together with an armoured train. On 22 November, he deployed the Irish Rifles, with the Berkshire Mounted Infantry and some Cape police to Putterskraal, four miles south of Sterkstroom. Five days later, he occupied the passes at Bushman's Hoek and Penhoek, 12 miles to the east, essential if he was to advance on Stormberg. The destruction of the railway and telegraph, to the west of Stormberg, meant that French at Naauwpoort and Gatacre at Putterskraal were cut off from each other. As in the case of French's force, Buller had been anxious that Gatacre should be very careful, reminding him on 18 November that 'the great thing in this sort of warfare is to be perfectly certain that one position is safe before you advance to another, and that we are not yet strong enough in troops to play tricks.'[1] Gatacre, in response to a suggestion that he move on Stormberg, had told Buller on 21 November that he was not yet strong enough to do so, but that when he was, he would occupy the junction and clear the country round it.

On 30 November, Gatacre wrote Buller what he described as a grumbling letter, saying that he was 'in a miserable state of inefficiency,' with only two regiments. He had, he said, 'orders to raise mounted volunteers, but have no salary, no equipment, no clothing to supply them with; it would be laughable if it were not lamentable and serious.'[2] Two days later, he telegraphed Buller saying that the 'military situation here requires dealing with extreme carefulness. Boers have occupied Dordrecht, and enemy is advancing in a southerly direction, evidently pointing for Queenstown.' The latter, he considered, was an indefensible position. He went on to ask for orders. To this, Buller replied that they must make the best of the situation: 'You have a force which altogether is considerably stronger than the enemy can bring against you. Cannot you close with him, or else occupy a defensible position which will obstruct his advance? You have an absolutely free hand to do what you think best.'[3]

On the following day, Buller sent Gatacre a message through Forestier-Walker, suggesting a move on Hennings Station; he followed this up with a fresh injunction to take care until the arrival of the 5th Division, which was hardly consistent with a move on Hennings Station,

1 *Official History*, vol. I pp. 286-287.
2 Beatrice Gatacre, *General Gatacre* (London: John Murray 1910) p. 226.
3 *Official History*, vol. I, p. 268.

which would be a considerable undertaking. By 6 December, however, Gatacre was reinforced by the arrival of two batteries of his divisional artillery and some other supporting troops, although having only just arrived from England, they were not in the best condition. Gatacre now decided to take advantage of the force that had been bestowed on him by Buller and began to plan for a night march on Stormberg, setting out from Molteno, where he had previously posted a small force to hold the place.

Gatacre intended that his advance should be a surprise attack on Stormberg but unfortunately, it soon became widely known that he was to undertake this, as Conan Doyle noted:

> The fact that he was about to do so, and even the hour of the start, appear to have been the common property of the camp some days before the actual move. *The Times* correspondent under the date December 7 details all that he intended to do. It is to the credit of our generals as men, but to their detriment as soldiers, that they seem throughout the campaign to have shown extraordinary little power of dissimulation.[4]

It was not a promising augury for the coming offensive.

Gatacre was an ambitious man, with a dictatorial nature which led him to drive himself and his men hard. Earlier in his career, G. W. Steevens had portrayed these characteristics:

> General Gatacre came up with a great reputation, which he seized every occasion to increase. His one overmastering quality is tireless, abounding, almost superhuman energy. From the moment he is first out of his hut at reveille to the time he goes nodding from mess to bed at nine, he seems possessed by a demon that whips him ever into activity. Of middle height, and lightly built, his body is all steel wire. As a man he radiates a gentle serious courtesy. As a general, if he has a fault, it lies on the side of not leaving enough to his subordinates.[5]

Such a personality was always going to make as much as he could have of the free hand he had been given. It is perhaps this which led Buller so often to enjoin him to proceed with care.

The Official History described the area in which Gatacre planned to launch his offensive:

> The buildings and sheds which marked the railway junction lie at the foot of a steep razor-back hill, called Rooi Kop, and on the eastern edge of the valley or vlei, about two miles in length from north to south, and one in breadth. This vlei, in which the enemy's main body was known to be, is shut in on the east by the Rooi Kop, which dominates all of the surrounding country. To the south and south-west, it is enclosed by a lower hill, named the Kissieberg, and on the north by a flat topped kopje on which forts had been constructed by the British garrison when in occupation of the junction. Between this kopje and the northern point of the Kissieberg, there is a gap of a mile through which pass out the spruit, which drains the vlei, and the branch line to Naauwpoort. '[6]

4 Conan Doyle, *Great Boer War*, p. 168.
5 Johannes Meintjes, *Stormberg: A Lost Opportunity* (Cape Town: Nasionale Boekhandel, 1969) p. 69.
6 *Official History*, vol. I, pp. 289-290.

The main railway line to Bloemfontein and the main road from Molteno to Burghersdorp cross a nek between the Kissieberg and Rooi Kop, running close to the latter.

Gatacre's plan involved a night march from Molteno which would aim at seizing the nek and the Rooi Kop before dawn on the morning of 9 December. He hoped that by moving out from Molteno in this way, he would take the Boers by surprise; however, what chance there was of this – bearing in mind the widespread awareness of what was intended – was further diminished by his being obliged to postpone his movement due to difficulties in collecting sufficient rolling stock to carry his troops from Putterskraal to Molteno. It was early on the morning of 9 December that the camp was struck at Putterskraal, and the force was assembled during the afternoon at Molteno. It was not without some anxiety that Gatacre approached the coming operation; he wrote on the previous day that he was 'frightfully busy and worried. The whole of this country is seething with rebels, and as they are all mounted, and I have only a few mounted infantry on half fed ponies, it is very difficult to cope with them.'[7]

The forces available to Gatacre consisted of the 2nd Northumberland Fusiliers, the Royal Irish Rifles, the 74th and 77th Batteries of field artillery and three companies of mounted infantry. He also intended to employ the detachments of Brabant's Horse and Cape Mounted Rifles that had been occupying Penhoek, but the message ordering them to support the force at Molteno, handed into the telegraph office at Putterskraal at midnight on 8 December, was overlooked and never sent, and was not accompanied by a request for an acknowledgement. These troops had been intended to move around the north of the Rooi Kop to cut off the expected retreat of the Boers on Burghersdorp. The total strength of Gatacre's force was approximately 2,600.

On the afternoon of 9 December, Gatacre assembled his commanding officers to personally give them his orders for the advance. His plan was for the troops to set off at 7.00 p.m., aiming to reach Goosen's Farm, some two miles short of the nek, soon after midnight, and there, rest for 2–3 hours before attacking. Just before dawn, the Royal Irish Rifles were to rush the ridge to the left of the nek, where the Boer artillery was believed to be concentrated, while the Northumberland Fusiliers occupied the lower slopes of the Rooi Kop. However, at this meeting, Gatacre had to take account of a report which had just arrived, that the Boers had entrenched the south face of the Kissieberg and the nek and had constructed a wire entanglement in front of their position.[8] The report was incorrect, but in the light of this, Gatacre determined to modify his original plan and to move out from Molteno by the Steynsburg Road, leaving it by a cross track which led northwards towards Van Zyl's Farm, which stood immediately to the rear of the western face of the Kissieberg, thus turning the enemy position on the nek. This, Gatacre understood, would mean a night march of nine miles; it was actually 10.[9]

It was, in theory at least, a sensible move, but it added to the difficulties of what was already going to be a tricky operation: 'It involved a night march across unreconnoitred and very inadequately mapped ground, and left the general entirely at the mercy of guides who might indeed know the ground but might completely fail to understand his ideas or the limitations of his men.'[10] Added to this, the process of entraining the troops for Molteno had been much delayed, and many of them had spent several hours under the hot African sun. The last of them finally disembarked at about 8:30 p.m. The problems of a night march were compounded by the fact

7 Gatacre, *Gatacre*, p. 228.
8 *Times History*, vol. II, p. 367.
9 *Official History*, vol. I, p. 292.
10 *Times History*, vol. II, p. 367.

that Gatacre would be entirely dependent on his guides, who had been recruited from the Cape Mounted Police; his two intelligence officers, one of whom was familiar with the ground, were both engaged on the lines of communication and unable to accompany the column. Even worse, Colonel Waters, the officer in command of the garrison at Molteno, had not been informed of the change of plan, so that when the machine guns, ammunition reserve and field hospital, which represented the third echelon of the column, advanced along the main road as it had been originally intended that they should, they found no troops in front of them. Accordingly, they halted and sent back to Molteno to find out the situation only for Waters to reply that as far as he understood. it was indeed the main Stormberg Road that was the route being taken by the main column.

The first echelon of this comprised the divisional staff and the infantry and the second the artillery and mounted infantry. These finally moved off from Molteno at about 9:15 p.m. The Royal Irish Rifles were ordered to march with fixed bayonets as a precaution. This was completely unnecessary and meant that they must carry their rifles at a particular angle which they could not shift to ease the strain which eventually numbed their arms. The change of plan had not been explained to the troops and as they marched through the night under a bright moon, most of them were under the impression that they were taking the main road to Stormberg.

The march proceeded at a decent pace, with Gatacre up with the leading troops of the column. Soon after midnight it crossed a railway line running across the road. This was the single track colliery line which branched off from the main Stormberg-Rosmead line west of Stormberg Junction and crossed the Steynsbug Road nine miles from Molteno. Gatacre, naturally enough, sought reassurance from his guides that they were on the right track. In the despatch which he subsequently wrote reporting on the events of 11 December, he recorded the position as it now appeared: 'The force marched, with the usual halts, for about eight miles by moonlight, and halted near Roberts's Farm at 12.30. The chief guide now reported that we were within one and a half miles of the enemy's position, and, after a rest of about three quarters of an hour, we marched off again in the dark.'[11]

Roberts's Farm was in fact, well past the point at which the column was to turn right, but at this point, Gatacre felt that matters were proceeding satisfactorily. He was pleased to note that, as he had been told, the route which the column was taking was shielded from sight from Stormberg for a large part of the way, judging by the dark mass of kopjes and ridges to their right. It seemed to him he was going to be able to achieve the surprise which his plan intended, and he rode on with the guides at the head of the column. However, having reached the colliery line, it was evident that the point at which it was intended to branch off to the right had already been passed, and Gatacre's optimism began to wane.

He now asked the chief guide, Sergeant Morgan, who was from Molteno, where the column had reached. Morgan reassured him; it was not that the guides had gone wrong, but they had gone beyond the scheduled turning point to avoid a wire fence and a section of the track which would have impeded the guns; as it was, the column was now at a point more or less directly in line with the Boer positions.[12] This, Morgan explained to an increasingly uneasy Gatacre, was within a mile and a half of the position which it had been intended to reach. Gatacre accordingly ordered the halt referred to above, and it was 2.00 a.m. before the march was resumed. By 3.00

11 Gatacre, *Gatacre*, p. 231.
12 Meintjes, *Stormberg*, p. 89.

a.m. Colonel Eager, the commander of the Royal Irish Rifles, was in no doubt that the guides had lost their way, as he told Gatacre. The general continually questioned Morgan about the situation of the column but received constant reassurance. In fact, the guides had gone wrong, but refused to admit it. The Official History observes that whether they had got lost and missed the true road, or whether they had – on their own judgement – changed the route in the belief that although longer, it would make for easier marching, either way it had a serious effect on Gatacre's plan of attack.[13] As it was, the column was not a mile and a half from the enemy's position, but about three miles.

The Boer defenders of Stormberg were led by Commandant Olivier. At and near Stormberg he had some 1,700 men with two guns and a maximum. A detachment under Swanepoel held the nek between the Kissieberg and the Rooi Kop. A picket of about 50 men had been posted on the western ridge of the Kissieberg, while another was located at the northern end of the vlei. The rest of Olivier's force slept peacefully on the lower slopes of the two hills, entirely unaware of the night march being undertaken by Gatacre's column.

Olivier had accordingly felt able to detach a force some 500 strong, composed of colonial rebels, under Grobbelaar and Steenkamp, to Steynsburg in order to recruit more men. This had reached a point about seven or eight miles from Stormberg, where it outspanned for the night about a mile north-west of Roberts's Farm. Thus, the Boer forces, although expecting an attack to be imminent, were quite unprepared for the assault which Gatacre had planned, while he had reached a position close to that from which he intended to launch it:

> But either the chief guide did not fully comprehend the General's intentions, or he had lost his bearings, for he pointed to a kopje nearly two miles off and said that was the real place. The wearied men continued to trudge along the road, which, skirting the lower western slopes of the Kissieberg, leads to Stormberg Junction. Day was breaking, but no change was made in the formation of the troops. The infantry remained in fours, with no flankers out, and still only eight men were in front as an advanced guard. The Boer picket on the Kissieberg saw the grey thread as it wound its way slowly along the foot of the hill within effective range of the crest.[14]

It was a lone sentry on the Kissieberg who first made out the British column in the first light of dawn, sounding the alarm and calling out to his comrades that the enemy were coming. At once, a handful of Boers took up a position along the boulders by the side of the path, and opened fire. Although taken by surprise, the Boers had the distinct advantage of knowing where they were and what they should do. There was no panic; though surprised, the Boers seized their rifles and hastened, some to their horses, others to the positions on the crest immediately above them, and before the British recovered from the first shock of surprise, Olivier's men were spreading everywhere along the heights and firing away wildly into the valley.

A Boer officer, Pieter Kritzinger, described the scene in the Boer laager when the firing broke out:

> Some of us were still peacefully sleeping, while others were enjoying their first cup of coffee. With the rifle reports came wakefulness and bustle. It did not take us a moment

13 *Official History*, vol. I, p. 294.
14 Ibid., pp. 295-296.

> to realise that speed would be our only means of salvation. Should the enemy reach the summit first, disaster and defeat would be our lot. For some minutes it was a scene of confusion. The horses, saddles, bridles, rifles and bandoliers, where were they? Some knew and had their equipment ready in a moment; others, less careful, did not know, and sought almost frantically for theirs. We made for the mountain and scaled it as swiftly as our feet could carry us. Exhausted and breathless, we reached the summit before the enemy.[15]

The range at which the Boers opened fire was about 400 yards. The British were still marching in column of route, making it impossible to convey orders to the individual companies. Their commanders had to act – so far as they could – on their own initiative, inevitably causing extreme confusion. Gatacre, who had been leading his horse at the head of the column, ordered the Irish Rifles to deploy and to seize the detached hill beyond the nek. The three leading companies formed front, extending at right angles to the road and charged forward to seize the kopje. As they did so, they suffered heavily from enfilade fire. The rest of the Irish Rifles, together with the Northumberland Fusiliers, without waiting for orders, began to deploy and to scramble up the rocky slopes to their right.

Their first charge carried them some way up the initial slope, but the western face of the Kissieberg was extremely steep and progress thereafter was slow. About halfway up, and almost along the whole length of the ridge, they encountered a series of *krantz*, perpendicular walls of rock, barring their way. Between these there were gaps in which there were large boulders and bushes. In the face of this, the advance came to a standstill; the officers ordered their men to un-fix bayonets and to try to help each other up the rocks. The enemy fire for the moment ceased to trouble them, as they were now more or less under the cover of the *krantz*.[16]

As they struggled through the gaps, a process which took some considerable time, a halt was called to let the men catch their breath, before they again attempted to continue their climb in the direction of the shoulder of the hill, where the Boers had placed a gun. This advance, however, was only in groups of two or three, and the Boer rifle fire again became effective as the British infantry came into view. The Boers, firing from concealed positions, offered no target: 'Within a few minutes almost the whole of Gatacre's infantry had fretted itself away in an objectless attack on the steepest and most difficult part of the Boer position, and the general was left with nothing in hand.'[17]

When the firing broke out, the two batteries under the artillery commander Lieutenant Colonel Jeffreys, moved off the track to the left for about 1,000 yards, and then continued up the valley. The best position for them would have been the ridge 2,000 yards west of the Kissieberg, but the urgent need to support the infantry meant that there was no time to reach it. Gatacre therefore ordered the artillery to come at once into action, the 77th Battery from the kopje seized by the Irish Rifles and the 74th Battery on the open veld to the west. The mounted infantry had come up on the left of the artillery to cover them and were thus practically in the Stormberg valley. The artillery came into action at about 4:30 a.m. One gun of the 74th Battery became stuck in a donga and was the target for a hail of rifle fire which wounded three drivers and shot down the horses of the team; it had to be abandoned, although part of the breech

15 Meintjes, *Stormberg*, p. 93.
16 *Official History*, vol. I, pp. 296-297.
17 *Times History*, vol. II, p. 375.

mechanism was removed.[18] The artillery concentrated its fire on the crest towards which the Irish Rifles were advancing; the Boer riflemen, firing on the gunners at short range, inflicted heavy casualties, subsequently severely wounding Major Perceval, the commander of the 77th Battery.

Meanwhile, the attack having lasted about half an hour, the three foremost companies of the Northumberland Fusiliers, advancing on the right of the Irish Rifles, had made some progress towards the summit, when the battalion's commanding officer (tactfully un-named in the Official History) apparently without reference to Gatacre, decided that his battalion must leave the hill. He gave the order to retire, evidently concluding that they could not reach the crest. In this, he may have been influenced by the sight of men dribbling back to the foot of the hill. However, the order did not reach the three foremost companies, commanded by Captain Wilmott, and they clung on to the position which they had reached, alongside the three companies of Irish Rifles. The other five companies of the Northumberland Fusiliers fell back in accordance with their commander's order to the donga at the foot of the hill. This, though, provided little shelter, and not without considerable difficulty, the retreat was continued across the valley to the low kopjes on the far side.[19]

The Official History quotes an eyewitness who described the retirement:

> The donga was too deep to be used as a line of defence, being six feet deep at least, with both banks washed away underneath, and with nothing for the men to stand on to enable them to bring their rifles to bear. It was here that the trouble in the retirement commenced. The men retiring from the hill rushed to this donga for cover from the heavy rifle fire, and on getting into it, and thinking they were safe from immediate danger, laid down and many went to sleep, and the greatest difficulty was experienced to get them on the move again and to leave the donga. Many men were by this time thoroughly done up and did not appear to care what happened to them. Many men still remained on the hill, some because they had not heard the order to retire, and some because, utterly weary, they had sunk down in sleep in the dead angle at the foot of the height.[20]

The nature of the terrain made it almost impossible for the artillery to aim at specific targets; the whole of the side of the ridge was in shade. Concentrating their fire on the crest of the ridge, the gunners of the 74th Battery were quite unaware of the progress being made by Colonel Eager and his men, and a series of shells burst right over them, severely wounding Eager, Major Seton and several other officers, which effectively halted the advance at this point. Just before this, Eager had been with Captain Wilmott in discussion as to what could be done to protect their men from friendly fire. Eager suggested that since the gunners evidently were unaware of their position, they must fall back, but Wilmott objected, saying that if a withdrawal was ordered, it would be very difficult to get the men to resume their advance. Eager, though, insisted, and the withdrawal began to get under way.[21]

This was conducted in better order than that of the Northumberland Fusiliers, the three companies of Irish Rifles withdrawing first, then the batteries in succession and finally, the

18 *Official History*, vol. I, p. 297.
19 *Times History*, vol. II, p. 377.
20 *Official History*, vol. I, p. 299.
21 Ibid., p. 298.

mounted infantry which covered the withdrawal. The batteries then came into action again on a spur on the western side of the valley. Perceval, although wounded, remained in command of his battery throughout. The artillery held this position for over an hour, allowing the infantry to form up in their rear. During this time the Boers brought a long-range gun into action; although fired with accuracy, most of its shells only burst on impact, or not at all.[22]

Gatacre had been horrified at the spectacle of his infantry streaming back from the heights, and realised that it would be impossible to support the Irish Rifles on his left, which was where he had briefly hoped to press home his attack. The need to retire was abundantly clear, and he gave the necessary orders. One of his aides-de-camp later wrote a not altogether dispassionate account of Gatacre at this time:

> The general, as soon as he realised the state of things, arranged for the retirement, quite cool under the hottest fire, encouraging the men and moving over the position in every direction, not recklessly, but with a fine courage, which did us all good to watch. The retirement was carried out in wonderful order, and, weary though the men were, they hastened to join their units, and marched home in fair order ... Throughout the retirement he was the last man of the column, beating up tired stragglers, and bringing in abandoned transport.[23]

There was a strong wind blowing from the west and the forces under Grobbelaar and Steenkamp were for a long time, completely unaware of the struggle that was taking place on the Kissieberg less than three miles from their camp on the heights west of the valley, only learning of it when two riders burst on them with the news, which was confirmed by the sight of smoke rising from the scene of battle.[24]

Advancing from their laager, these Boers took up a position lining the crest of the hill west of Bamboosberg, opening fire at long-range on the retreating British troops. Responding to what could have been an extremely serious threat, five guns of the 77th Battery swung round to face west, opening fire at a range of 1,200 yards, while the remaining gun, facing east, continued to fire on the Kissieberg to check any Boer pursuit. The Boers under Grobbelaar and Steenkamp were driven back by the British artillery and appear to have made only a rather half-hearted attempt to join in the battle.

Gatacre had made up his mind to fall back on Molteno and directed the line of march in the first instance on Van Zyl's Farm; the mounted infantry and artillery were to cover the retirement. However, as he endeavoured to supervise this, Gatacre was entirely unaware of a circumstance which would turn an annoying reverse into a serious defeat. He had received no report that a large part of his infantry had failed to rejoin their units:

> He had remained with the mounted infantry throughout the action and having seen numbers of men of both regiments crossing the valley, was under the impression that the battalions were now in fact behind the western ridge. An extraordinary number of them were, in fact, still missing; the largest proportion of these had probably never left the Kissieberg.[25]

22 Ibid., p. 299.
23 Gatacre, *Gatacre*, p. 234.
24 Meintjes, *Stormberg*, p. 96.
25 *Official History*, vol. I, p. 300.

A number of men – equivalent to two companies of the Northumberland Fusiliers – were certainly taken prisoner on the Kissieberg; the Official History makes no comment on the responsibility of the battalion's commanding officer for seeing that all his company commanders had carried out his order to retire from the height, or that all those who had taken refuge in the donga had rejoined the main body.

One historian, Johannes Meintjes, is inclined to blame Gatacre for this fiasco, suggesting that as he had been mysterious about everything he was 'no less mysterious about the retreat, and that the men did not know that a full-scale retreat was taking place … Gatacre was clearly too preoccupied with the problem of giving an adequate explanation of what had happened to notice that a third of his infantry was missing.'[26] This comment, which is unsupported by any evidence, seems entirely unfair. *The Times History* offers a more balanced judgement:

> It is almost inconceivable that regimental officers can have failed to notice the absence of nearly a third of their battalions. The most reasonable explanation seems to be that officers reforming their men behind the ridge assumed that the absent companies were lining the ridge, while those on the ridge in their turn believed everybody else to be behind them. But even that is no adequate excuse.[27]

It is said that one company commander of the Northumberland Fusiliers did receive the order to retire but disobeyed it because he considered that he was well placed to assist the turning movement when it took place.

As it was, the retreating column made its way back along the track towards Molteno, the exhausted infantry suffering badly from thirst. As they marched, their formation gradually disintegrated and by the time they reached Molteno, they were in complete disarray. The artillery and the mounted infantry covered the retreat, which was not followed up very closely by the Boers. The need to keep moving, though, meant that a second gun had to be abandoned at Klipfontein when it got stuck in a watercourse. Gatacre's force finally struggled into Molteno between 11.00 a.m. and noon. He did not regard that as a defensible position and that evening, pulled back, sending the artillery and the divisional staff by train to Cypher Gat, where they were joined by the mounted infantry. The two infantry battalions went by train to Sterkstroom and the Royal Engineers and two companies of the Royal Scots, by train to Bushman's Hoek.

It had been a shambles. Total British casualties were 25 killed, 110 wounded and 561 missing. The Boers lost eight killed and 26 wounded. Among the injured was Colonel Eager, who later died of his wounds, as did Commandant Hans Swanepoel. Meintjes reckons that of all the Boer commanders present, he might have but for his wound, been capable of leading a much more energetic pursuit than actually materialised. Gatacre's widow and biographer naturally puts the best face she can on the battle, suggesting that 'the day was almost won,' and that if the infantry had been able to hold on for another quarter of an hour, they would have found the defences evacuated.'[28] This, sadly, was extremely improbable; the commander of the Northumberland Fusiliers may have been too precipitate in ordering a retreat, but the situation of the British infantry was almost impossible. Gatacre himself accepted that it had been 'a lamentable failure,' but added: 'The fault was mine, and I was responsible of course. I went rather against my better

26 Meintjes, *Stormberg*, p. 99.
27 *Times History*, vol. II, pp. 378-379.
28 Gatacre, *Gatacre*, p. 234.

judgement in not resting the night at Molteno, but I was tempted by the shortness of the distance and the certainty of success. It was so near being a brilliant success.'[29]

Gatacre may not have been a commander of outstanding ability, but he had been the victim of extreme ill luck. Nonetheless, he cannot escape some blame for the débacle. Nor can his staff; considering that the whole divisional staff was present and that it had to manage a force of no more than brigade strength, its performance was woeful. A series of errors contributed to the disaster. First, the delay on 9 December caused by a serious miscalculation of the time it would take to move the infantry from Putterskraal, left the troops sweltering in trucks for hours. The employment of Sergeant Morgan as principal guide while an intelligence officer familiar with the terrain was left on other duties, was another grave error. The failure to ensure that the Penhoek detachment took part was yet another avoidable mistake. For his part, Gatacre might have been quicker to realise that the column had lost its way, while choosing to continue to march in fours with inadequate advanced guards, made deployment extremely difficult. The commanding officer of the Northumberland Fusiliers exceeded his authority in ordering his battalion's retirement without consulting Gatacre. Finally, the oversight that left nearly 600 men to fall into the enemy's hands, was grossly incompetent. Taken altogether this was a grim litany of mismanagement. Buller, when he received the news, was unsurprisingly dismayed. However, Black Week had only just begun.

29 Ibid., p. 235.

13

Magersfontein, Monday 11 December

President Steyn, in response to Kruger's appeal, had not hesitated to go to the front to intervene personally in the discussions about what should be done. He arrived on 4 December and visited each of the Boer laagers to read the message Kruger had sent, which ended with the rallying cry that 'even though we must lose almost half of our men, we must still fight to the death, in the name of the Lord.'[1] Steyn's visit made a considerable impression; he was able to report to Kruger next day that the burghers were 'full of heart.' Next, he convened another council of war. This gave de la Rey the chance to put his case against facing the British northward advance in the Spytfontein position. He argued that if the British were allowed to occupy the heights of Magersfontein, they would have commanding artillery positions from which to fire on the defenders of Spytfontein. The better course, he submitted, would be to occupy the Magersfontein heights, obliging the British to advance on them across open country, devoid of cover.

De la Rey went on to apply the practical lessons to be learnt from the fighting at Modder River, arguing that the best way to defend the position was by locating entrenchments on the plain in front of the line of kopjes dominated by Magersfontein. There, securely dug in, the troops would be safer from artillery, and would be able to take advancing British infantry by surprise. Should it become necessary, there would still be the option of falling back to Spytfontein.

Cronje, who had incorrectly assumed that the British would follow up the battle on the Modder River almost at once, was not convinced by de la Rey's arguments. Steyn, however, was immediately persuaded and in the course of further discussions, the council of war endorsed the plan. The president's intervention had been of decisive importance. As *The Times History* remarked, 'it is impossible not to admire the activity and resolution President Steyn showed … Through all the long struggle that followed he was to be the heart and soul of the national defence, the very incarnation of uncompromising reckless resistance to the end.'[2] Having inspired his burghers in this way, and having ensured that the most effective tactics would be pursued, he departed for Bloemfontein, although not before dismissing Prinsloo, whose weak and ineffective performance had contributed substantially to the Free Staters' loss of morale. This followed another feeble performance on the part of Prinsloo, when with about 1,000 men,

1 Pakenham, *Boer War*, p. 199.
2 *Times History*, vol. II, p. 385.

he had launched an abortive attack on Enslin Station, which was held by two companies of the Northamptonshire Regiment. Mindful of how unsteady some of the Free Staters had been during the earlier fighting, many of whom were now unmounted, de la Rey proposed that they be located in the centre of the defensive position; they would fight better, he concluded, if they had no obvious means of escape.[3]

Work began at once to fortify the position at Magersfontein. It would be defended by about 8,200 men, following the arrival of further reinforcements from Mafeking. About 6,000 of them were mounted and de la Rey ensured the units on either flank were selected from these. The Boers were not, however, particularly strong in artillery. They had five field guns distributed along their line, with two pom-poms on Magersfontein Hill, and three more behind the low scrub covered ridge that ran down towards Moss Drift on the Modder River.[4]

The Boer position lay on the eastern side of the railway. It consisted of a line of four kopjes dominated at its south-eastern end by the height of Magersfontein itself. This, some two miles from the railway, rose steeply above the surrounding plain. On the western side of the railway the position was prolonged by a lower ridge running for about three miles north eastwards to Langeberg Farm. The road to Kimberley northward from the Modder River ran to the east of Magersfontein; between it and the river lay a low scrub covered ridge curving down to Moss Drift. From Langeberg Farm to Moss Drift the position was some nine miles in length.

Pemberton described the daunting nature of the position facing the British which the Boers were preparing to defend:

> Sweeping up from over the north-west horizon, it cut diagonally across the British front to end sharply to its north-east in a steep bluff. Towering 190 feet above the surrounding country, it resembled some dismasted Leviathan ploughing its way through a bare and featureless plain. Beyond the bluff came a gap or *pan*, two-thirds of a mile in width, and then once more the skyline was broken by what Methuen described as an 'underfeature' which curled round in a southerly direction. It was in effect two parallel folds of ground, thickly covered with scrub and about two and a half miles in length.[5]

As soon as the council of war had made its decision, de la Rey threw himself into the task of preparing the defences. In accordance with his strongly held conviction as to the advantage of entrenching the ground immediately in front of the heights, he called for the digging of deep and narrow trenches, particularly in front of Magersfontein, from three to five feet deep, vertically sided to give maximum protection against shellfire:

> Instead of being in one continuous line the shelter trenches were placed in groups to suit the conformation of the ground, and so as to be able mutually to flank one another. Their profile was such that their occupants were protected to the utmost possible extent against shrapnel fire. The nature of the soil permitted the interior and exterior slopes to be nearly perpendicular, and, by hollowing out the former, still better cover was obtained. The

3 Pakenham, *Boer War*, p. 200 *Times History*, vol. II, p. 387.
4 *Official History*, vol. I, p. 308.
5 Pemberton, *Battles*, p. 77.

> parapets were kept as low as possible and covered with brushwood and stones in places, so that the trenches were only visible a very short distance away.[6]

These trenches were located some 200 yards in advance of the heights.

Cronje, to his credit, soon overcame his initial reluctance to accept de la Rey's proposals, and energetically supported the work of entrenchment. *The Times History* was, justly, to describe the scheme as 'one of the boldest and most original conceptions in the history of war.' The work of digging the line of trenches was largely undertaken by the African labourers who had been commandeered to carry out such tasks. It was extremely demanding work; whereas at the Modder River the soil had been 'as soft and black as chocolate cake; here it was red and stony.'[7] While the work of digging the trenches on the plain went on, some defences were also prepared on the heights, the intention being that these would draw British artillery fire.

At first, the work of preparing the position concentrated on the section in front of Magersfontein Hill and on the western end of the line. The right wing was thrown well back, extending from the railway north of Merton Siding to Langeberg Farm. East of this there was a gap of about two miles, before the principal line of trenches around Magersfontein, which were about 4,000 yards in length. Thus it was that by 10 December, little had been done to fortify the eastern end of the position along the ridge curving to Moss Drift. It was only then that some work began there, since it was realised that an attempt might be made to flank the main position by an attack at that point. Since from one extremity to the other, the Boers were defending a line 12 miles long, it was inevitable that there were long sections that could not be strongly held and at the eastern end, the defenders of the ridge would be largely dependent for cover on the bushes and stony outcrops there.

Meantime, at Modder River, Methuen had been resting and reorganising his force. He had remained formally in overall command following the battle of 28 November, although in hospital recovering from his wound, until 2 December, when he handed over command to Colville. Even though still heavily bandaged, he resumed command on 6 December. He seems not to have felt a great deal of confidence in Colville, later in the war remarking that he was 'a most peculiar fellow.'[8]

The pause in the advance gave Methuen's exhausted troops time to rest and recuperate and enabled his engineers to complete the temporary bridge over the river alongside the original bridge which the Boers had blown up. This would be essential if Methuen was to carry out his orders to evacuate the civilian population of Kimberley. The delay also enabled him to accumulate supplies and ammunition which poured in daily up the railway from the south.

Any anxiety which Methuen may have felt for the immediate safety of Kimberley was dispelled by Kekewich's telegraph message that the town could hold out for 40 days, so there was no pressing need for him to resume his advance before he felt ready to do so.[9] Telling Kekewich that there would be a slight delay, he ordered him in the meantime to work on strengthening his defences. At Modder River, Methuen in addition to the construction of the temporary bridge, ordered the building of a number of redoubts on both sides of the river to defend the crossing when the column did resume its advance.

6 *German Staff History*, vol. I, p. 89.
7 Pakenham, *Boer War*, p. 200.
8 Miller, *Methuen*, p. 125.
9 *Official History*, vol. I, p. 304.

Meanwhile, the most important consequence of the delay was the arrival of significant reinforcements. By 10 December, the whole of the Highland Brigade had joined Methuen's force; this was regarded by many as the best fighting unit in the entire British Army. Commanded by Major General 'Andy' Wauchope, it consisted of the 2nd Black Watch, the 2nd Seaforth Highlanders, the 1st Highland Light Infantry and the 1st Argyll and Sutherland Highlanders. In addition the 12th Lancers, G Battery of horse artillery and the 65th (Howitzer) Battery had arrived, together with some mounted infantry; the Naval Brigade had also been reinforced, and was now 375 men strong, with one 4.7 inch gun and four 12-pdrs. Other units had come up to protect the lines of communication, while the most recent arrival, the 1st Battalion Gordon Highlanders, brought the total strength of the force at Methuen's disposal to about 15,000.[10]

With these forces now in hand, he turned to the question of how to proceed. He was mindful that it was not only his own force that had been able to benefit from the delay, writing in his subsequent report:

> The longer I remained inactive, the stronger the enemy would become. Therefore, on the day my last reinforcement arrived, I decided to continue my advance. It was out of the question to follow the railway, owing to the large kopjes on either side, which had been strongly entrenched. Besides, by that route there was not sufficient water.[11]

He had been sending out regular reconnaissance patrols, and he had recently received a balloon which it was hoped would be able to carry out a survey of the enemy's position. Unfortunately, the information gathered so far was not of much value, and after 4 December, when the Boers began to occupy Magersfontein, the patrols could not get within 1,000 yards of the enemy's position.

Methuen did, however, know of the full extent of the Boer line, although he was poorly informed about the defences on Magersfontein Hill and had no idea whatsoever of the trenches at its foot. He was also quite unable to form an accurate estimate of the size of the force which he would encounter. He and his staff guessed that it was probably between 12,000 and 15,000 strong, with six or eight guns.[12]

In considering how to undertake his further advance on Kimberley, there were several crucial considerations which Methuen had to bear in mind. Simply bypassing Magersfontein, and leaving it in the hands of the Boers, was not an option. From there, the Boer artillery could effectively interdict the use of the railway to and from Kimberley, not only threatening Methuen's line of communication, but also rendering the proposed evacuation of the civilian population altogether far too risky, while a wide flank march would be extremely hazardous. The Official History summarised the projects which were considered and rejected:

> A purely frontal attack upon the kopjes between Langeberg and Magersfontein Hill involved the crossing of a wide extent of open level ground, with the danger of a counter-attack by the enemy from the low ridge held by the left wing of Cronje's army. To the west of Langeberg Farm the country was so waterless as to preclude any attempt in that

10 Ibid., p. 308.
11 Captain A.T. Mahan, *The Story of the War in South Africa* (London: Sampson Low Marston and Co., 1900) p. 162.
12 *Official History*, vol. I, p. 309; Miller, *Methuen*, p. 129.

> direction. A flank march up the Modder River to Brown's Drift, and thence to Abon's Dam, about 16 miles north-east of Jacob, seemed feasible, for the British column would turn the works of Magersfontein and then fall upon the eastern flank of Spytfontein, the northern of the two lines of heights which lay athwart the railway between the Modder River and Kimberley.[13]

Leo Amery, looking back from the pages of *The Times History*, considered that the latter option was the best to select. He argued that the Boers would not have risked coming into the open to attack and that such a move would result in the abandonment of Magersfontein itself. According to him, it was at the suggestion of Colonel Charles Douglas, Methuen's new chief of staff, that this move was finally rejected.[14] It would have exposed the Modder River camp, with all its accumulated supplies – and the newly built bridge – to attack by a portion of the extremely mobile Boer army, and to protect this – and the long lines of communication on which Methuen depended – a substantial part of his force would be required. Prinsloo's abortive attack on Enslin had shown just what the enemy might be able to do if the attack was pressed with more vigour than had been the case on that occasion.

These considerations, coupled with the ever-present problem of the water supplies, turned Methuen's mind firmly against a wide-ranging flank march. He did consider the possibility of launching an attack on the left wing of the Boer position on the low ridge which ran from Magersfontein to Moss Drift, but rejected it on the ground that the bush covered ground would limit the effectiveness of the British artillery, and expose the infantry to heavy casualties:

> Therefore, it was finally decided to carry the heights of Magersfontein, and after their occupation and entrenchment to make a turning movement against the left flank of the Spytfontein range. The tactics of Belmont were to be repeated. After a vigorous bombardment of the hill of Magersfontein in the late afternoon of the 10th, the Highland Brigade was to march at night to its foot, and at dawn on the 11th attack this, the key of Cronje's position.[15]

On Saturday 9 December, Wauchope rode out from the camp of the Highland Brigade over to Methuen's headquarters, which were located in the Crown and Anchor Hotel, to discuss the plans for the forthcoming assault on the Boer positions. Wauchope was one of the most distinguished and popular men in the British Army. Now aged 53, he had taken part in three colonial wars, in each of which he had been badly wounded. He had also taken a considerable part in British public life, coming from an enormously wealthy Scottish mining family. On two separate occasions he had almost brought off an improbable victory against the odds at Parliamentary elections.

The plan which Methuen and Colonel Douglas now put before Wauchope was for the night march on Magersfontein to be preceded by heavy bombardment of the Boer position on the afternoon of 10 December. To carry this out, a column consisting of the 9th Lancers, some mounted infantry, five batteries, the Highland Brigade and the 2nd Battalion of the King's Own Yorkshire Light Infantry was to advance from Modder River towards the southern end

13 Ibid., pp. 309–310.
14 *Times History*, vol. II, pp. 392-393.
15 *Official History*, vol. I, p. 310.

of Magersfontein Hill. The Highland Brigade was to halt near Headquarters Hill, out of rifle range, while the KOYLI Battalion marched to Bridle Drift and entrenched there against attack from all sides. The cavalry would cover the advance on a line from the railway to the river. Pole-Carew's brigade was to take up a position to the west of the railway.[16] On the following day, the bombardment would be resumed, but not directed at Magersfontein Hill itself, since this would be the objective for the Highland Brigade, attacking at dawn after a night march to the foot of the hill.

Wauchope listened to Methuen's exposition of this plan with considerable unease. When he came out of the meeting, he said to Douglas: 'I do not like the idea of this night march.' Douglas urged him that in that case, he should go back to Methuen to tell him so, but Wauchope did not, returning thoughtfully to his brigade. He received his written orders at 7.00 a.m. on 10 December; they left him with a wide discretion as to how he was to carry out the actual assault on the Boer position. Methuen later wrote: 'No detailed orders as to the formation to be adopted were given by me.'[17]

It was later suggested, particularly by Amery in *The Times History*, that Wauchope had in fact, strongly protested to Methuen about the planned assault, and that he did not 'hesitate to express to his commander the doubts that rose up in his mind at the thought of the hazardous venture to which his brigade was being committed.'[18] Methuen's biographer carefully examined the claims that a serious disagreement had arisen between the two men, quoting a letter which Methuen wrote to his wife after the battle:

> There is a false rumour in a low paper that poor Wauchope asked me for guides, and that I refused saying I command all the division; that he then said: 'I will obey your orders.' He never said a word, for I remember saying to him, 'are my orders quite clear?' And he said: 'yes.' I looked at him wondering if we should meet again.[19]

Stephen Miller is firmly of the view that the accounts of Wauchope's alleged objections to the plan are incorrect. He quotes in addition, a contemporary biographer, George Douglas, who wrote that Wauchope was 'too staunch a soldier and too well-trained to allow his own feelings to interfere.'[20] Nevertheless, though he probably did not openly express his disagreement, it is entirely likely that Wauchope thought the plan to be extremely hazardous, which it certainly was.

On the morning of 9 December, Methuen had ordered the 4.7 inch naval gun to fire a few ranging shots with lyddite at Magersfontein Hill from a position three miles up the railway from Modder River. This was in preparation for the bombardment planned for the following day. Methuen was confident that this would have a crushing effect on the enemy, inflicting heavy casualties and seriously damaging morale. He had not previously had lyddite available for his bombardments during the previous battles and was in no doubt that its use now would greatly increase the effectiveness of his artillery. Accordingly, at 3.00 p.m. on 10 December, his troops moved to take up the positions assigned to them to cover the artillery during the bombardment.

16 Ibid., pp. 310–311.
17 Pemberton, *Battles*, p. 88.
18 *Times History*, vol. II, p. 397.
19 Miller, *Methuen*, p. 137.
20 Ibid.

The Highland Brigade accordingly marched forward to occupy its position near Headquarters Hill, while the batteries got into their positions, the howitzer battery close to Headquarters Hill and the field batteries further forward and to the east. At 4.00 p.m. the artillery opened fire, concentrating on the south-western face of Magersfontein Hill. The 4.7 inch naval gun, further back than the rest of the artillery, was firing at a range of 7,000 yards, the howitzers at 4,000 yards and the field batteries at 2,700 yards. The bombardment lasted for approximately three hours.[21] As a spectacle, it was all that could have been wanted. The watching war correspondents found it awe-inspiring, one writing that shells tore through the air with precisely the noise of an express train rushing at full speed. Pemberton depicted the scene:

> Above the bluff of Magersfontein looking to some like the Rock of Gibraltar, great mushrooms of acrid yellow smoke from the famous lyddite shells bellied up and jagged rocks were tossed in the air like so many pebbles. The Boers made no more reply to this than they had to the advance of the Black Watch; they were no more inclined to betray the whereabouts of their few guns than that of their secret trenches. As dusk fell the scene grew more dramatic and spectacular, the exploding shells and shrapnel resembled tiny sparks, but the bursting lyddite flung up sheets of lurid flame. Nothing, Methuen was convinced, could live through such an inferno.[22]

The truth, however, was completely different. Methuen had been entirely deceived about his bombardment's effect. It had inflicted total casualties amounting to three Boers wounded. The true consequence of the bombardment was that the Boers had been put on notice that a frontal attack was intended, as indeed they expected, and they were entirely prepared for the assault when it came. Methuen, in his later report of the battle, frankly admitted his mistake: 'I think now that the bombardment was a mistake, but we were all deceived by the reported terrific power of lyddite, which we believed would drive the enemy from the kopje.'[23] Pemberton, quoting this report, goes on to suggest that one observer at least was able to draw an important conclusion from watching the bombardment. A sergeant of the Black Watch noted that, when some shells fell short of the hill, dust of a peculiar colour was thrown up, and deduced from this that there must be trenches there. No account, however, was taken of this.

Amery was scornful about the pointlessness of the bombardment; the Boers, he reckoned, gained not only information about the pending attack but also greatly increased confidence:

> They now knew that the expected attack on Magersfontein was not far off. They also knew that to men securely entrenched, the appalling roar of bursting shells meant little more than the din of a thunderstorm. De la Rey could not have arranged a better demonstration of the soundness of his tactics, or found better means to exhort the burghers to stay in their trenches, than this ineffectual and purposeless cannonade.[24]

As the bombardment due to its close, Methuen held a final meeting with Wauchope and Colville. He sat with his injured leg resting on the box seat of a wagon and went over his plans for the

21 Miller, *Methuen*, p. 131.
22 Pemberton, *Battles*, pp. 84-85.
23 Ibid., p. 85.
24 *Times History*, vol. II, p. 394.

following day. The Guards Brigade, together with the 9th Brigade, would be held in reserve, the assault being conducted in the first instance solely by the Highland Brigade. Wauchope had nothing to say about this; when Colville remarked to him that it looked as if his brigade would not see much fighting, the Highlander replied: 'Things don't always go as they are expected. You may not be in reserve for long.'[25]

Methuen had found time that afternoon to write to his wife to tell her of the battle that was about to take place:

> My reinforcements were complete this morning, so I began firing this afternoon, and anticipate three days hard work and then the relief of Kimberley a gigantic job. I have said that any civilians who remain in Kimberley unless he [*sic*] has some valid reason will be turned out by me, and have to find food and transport, which means death. I have now 13,000 men and 30 guns, so the Boers must suffer. I fired a long navy gun with lyddite at their position *four miles off* at daybreak yesterday.[26]

He reckoned that he had to face 10,000 to 12,000 Boers but thought that he was in a stronger position than he had been so far.

Following the discussion with Methuen and Colville, Wauchope went back to his brigade. It had been raining most of the afternoon; now, as the evening drew on, the weather deteriorated further. It began to rain more heavily with thick clouds in the north-west; the wind was rising and there were intermittent rumbles of thunder. It was plainly going to be a very dirty night. Wauchope now met with his battalion commanders to explain his intentions for the assault, which were recorded by the commander of the Seaforths, Lieutenant-Colonel Hughes-Hallett:

> The plan was to march direct on the north-east spur of the hill held by the enemy. On arrival near the objective his intention was to move the Black Watch to the east of the hill where he believed the enemy to be posted under shelter, while the Seaforths were to march straight to the north-east point of the hill with the Argylls prolonging the line to the left and the HLI to be in reserve while the attack was developing[27]

Wauchope intended that the brigade should move in a compact mass of quarter columns, which meant a marching column of 30 companies, one behind the other. The ranks would be closed up as densely as possible, each man grasping the clothing of his neighbour, with NCOs on the left holding guide ropes which ran from front to rear. Wauchope, on foot, with part of his staff, would lead the column as it advanced. Methuen had assigned the task of guiding the column to its objective to Major George Benson, who had during the reconnaissance, taken the compass bearing of Magersfontein Hill. The ground over which the Highlanders would march was known to be obstructed by boulders, ant hills and patches of brush, so Benson's task in navigating the march of the brigade was not going to be straightforward.

After briefing his commanders, Wauchope lay down in his sleeping bag. His staff woke him at midnight. Not many of his men were able to get much sleep, passing a cold, wet and thoroughly miserable night. Methuen had ordered that officers were not to carry swords, but Wauchope

25 Pakenham, *Boer War*, p. 203.
26 Miller, *Methuen*, p. 130.
27 Pemberton, *Battles*, p. 86.

decided to take his old claymore. At 12:30 a.m. the march began, with the Black Watch leading, followed by the Argylls and Seaforths, with the Highland Light Infantry bringing up the rear. On the directing flank, the brigade major, Lieutenant-Colonel Ewart, passed up and down the files of marching men, having the names of the officers repeated to him so that he might identify each company and thus see that they did not lose close touch.[28] Wauchope led the column, with some of his staff and Major Benson. In its marching formation, the brigade was half a company's length (or 45 yards) wide, and 330 yards in depth.[29] The heavy rain drove into the troops from the north-west as they marched towards their objective; the Boers, of course, were perfectly aware that they were coming.

Benson's compasses had been severely affected, not only by the ironstone over which the column was now marching, but also perhaps by the lightning of the storm and the metal of 4,000 rifle barrels. As a result, the course pursued was far from straight; one of those who survived the battle wrote: 'We were tacking about in the most extraordinary way and making frequent stops to change direction.'[30] At 2.00 a.m. the column halted; Benson was convinced that it had tended away towards the left and Wauchope sent back for Ewart. After a hurried consultation, the column moved off again, changing its direction slightly to the right.

Sometime later, just as it was possible for the first time to see the top of Magersfontein Hill, in a flash of lightning, the head of the column encountered a patch of mimosa bushes which brought it to a halt. By now, Wauchope was aware that he must soon deploy. Benson, indeed, was strongly of the view that the time for this had already come, but Wauchope wanted to get a few hundred yards closer to his objective. First, however, in order to negotiate the obstruction, he led the Black Watch in single file through the bushes, while Ewart led the rest of the brigade around them. Once this was done, Wauchope issued instructions for the deployment of the Black Watch, but with the Seaforths to come up on the left and the Argylls on the right, with the HLI in reserve. The Official History concludes that Wauchope, having originally intended that both the Seaforth and the Argylls should come up on the left, changed his mind at the last moment to ensure that his right wing should completely overlap the eastern flank of the hill.[31]

Just as the battalions began to execute these orders, at 4.00 a.m., with streaks of dawn lightening the sky, all hell broke loose in the Highlanders' front, as a concentrated volley of rifle fire burst out from the Boer trenches. It came at the worst possible moment as the brigade was in the act of changing from the mass of quarter columns into its fighting formation. The surprise was complete. The column broke up; parties of men led by their officers charged towards the enemy, as the battalions became intermingled. 'Never were troops caught at a more terrible disadvantage than the hapless Highlanders … It was an awful moment, destined to haunt forever the memories of those who lived through that day.'[32]

It could have been even worse. Although the Boers were anticipating the assault, not all of them were aware just how close the enemy was,and only some were ready to join in the first volley. The Boers, too, had passed an uncomfortable night numb with cold and many had yet to stir, while it was, in the half-light, difficult to identify their targets, and much of the rifle fire passed over the heads of their attackers.

28 *Official History*, vol. I, p. 317.
29 Pemberton, *Battles*, p. 87.
30 Ibid., p. 89.
31 *Official History*, vol. I, p. 318.
32 *Times History*, vol. II, p. 400.

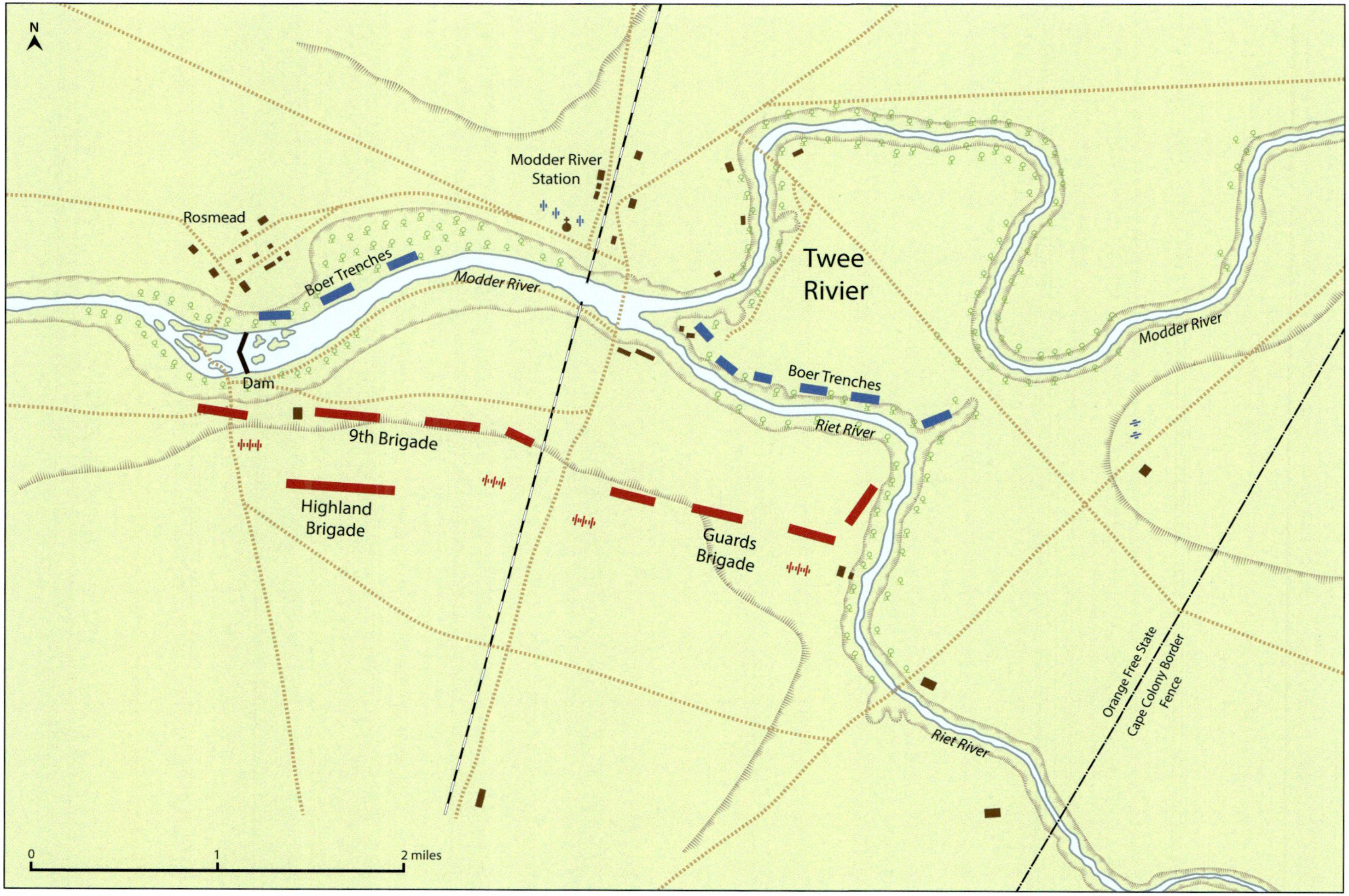

Modder River, 28 November 1899.

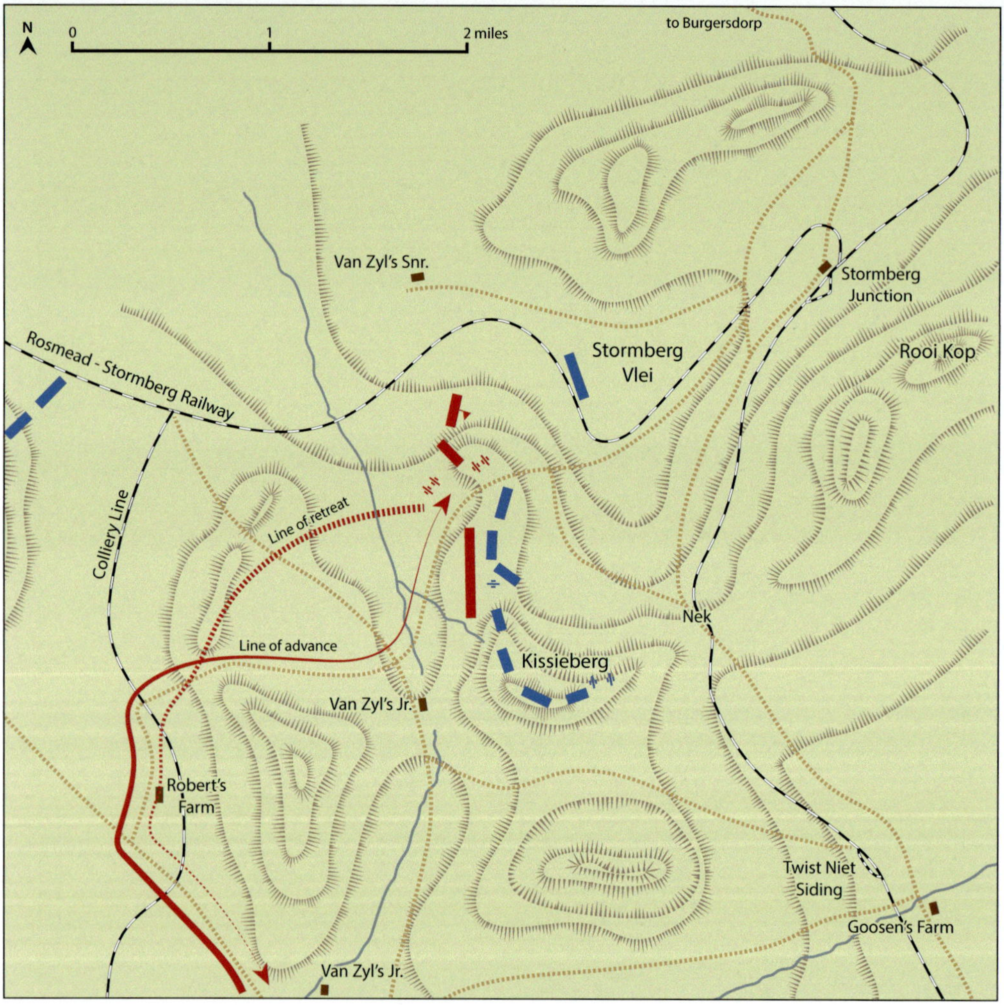

Stormberg, 10 December 1899.

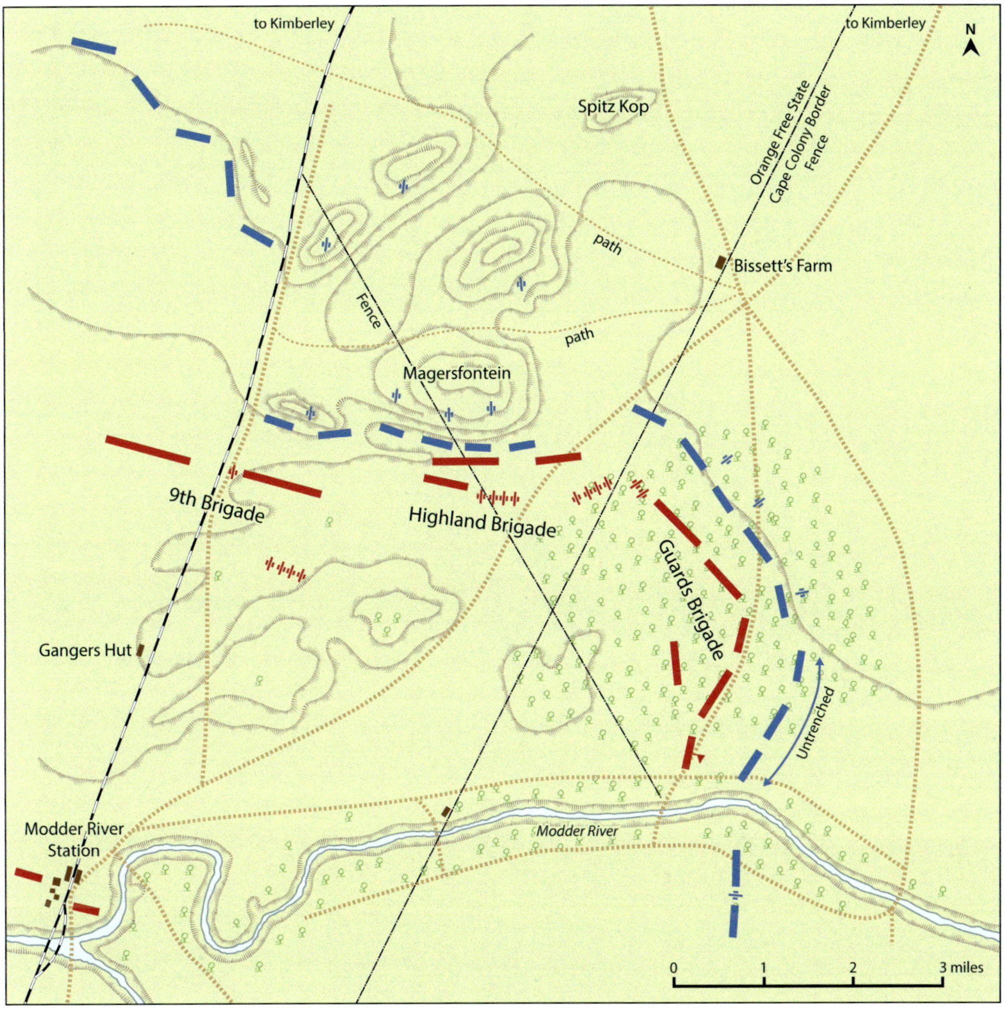

Magersfontein, 11 December 1899.

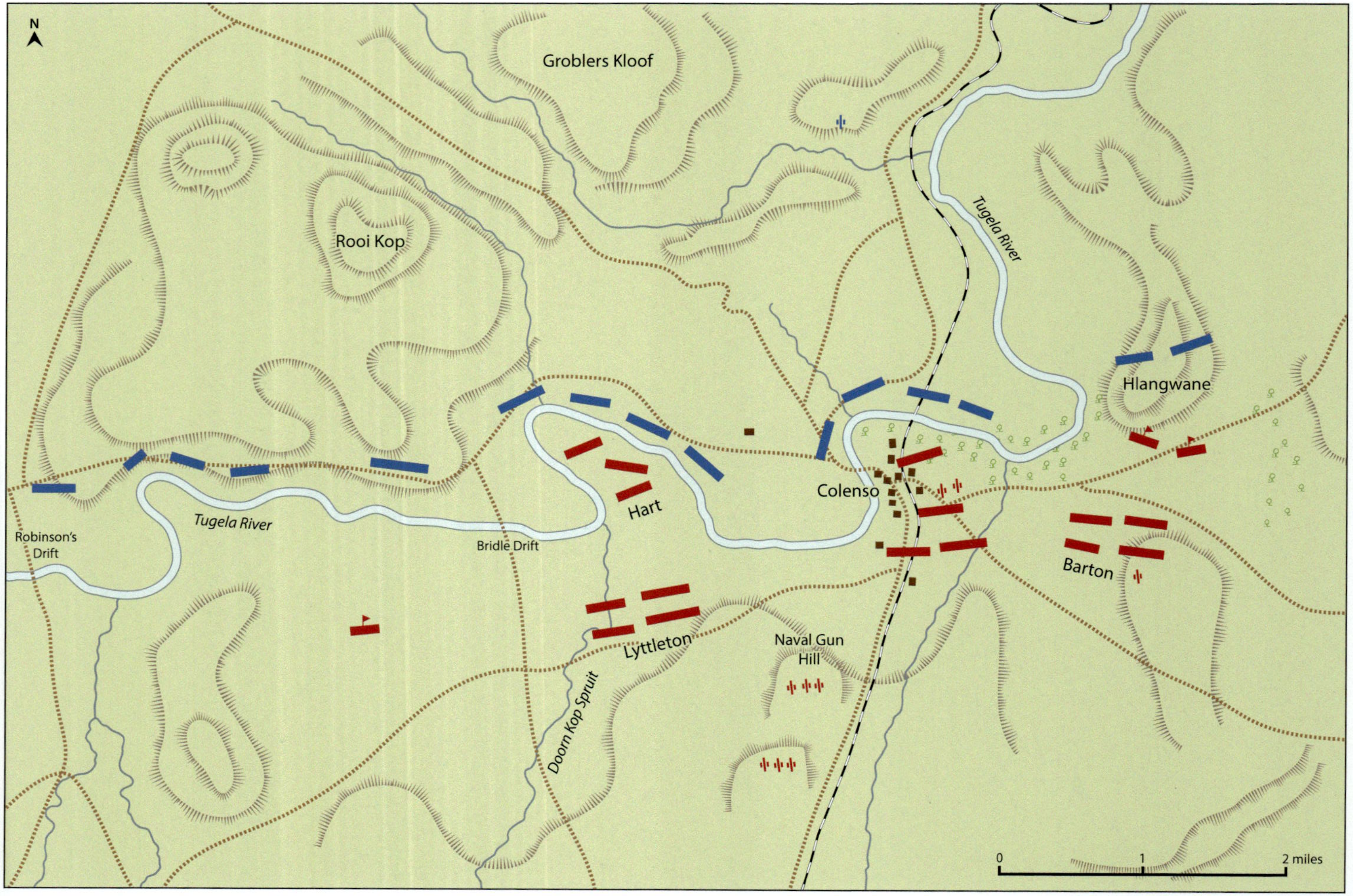

Colenso, 15 December 1899.

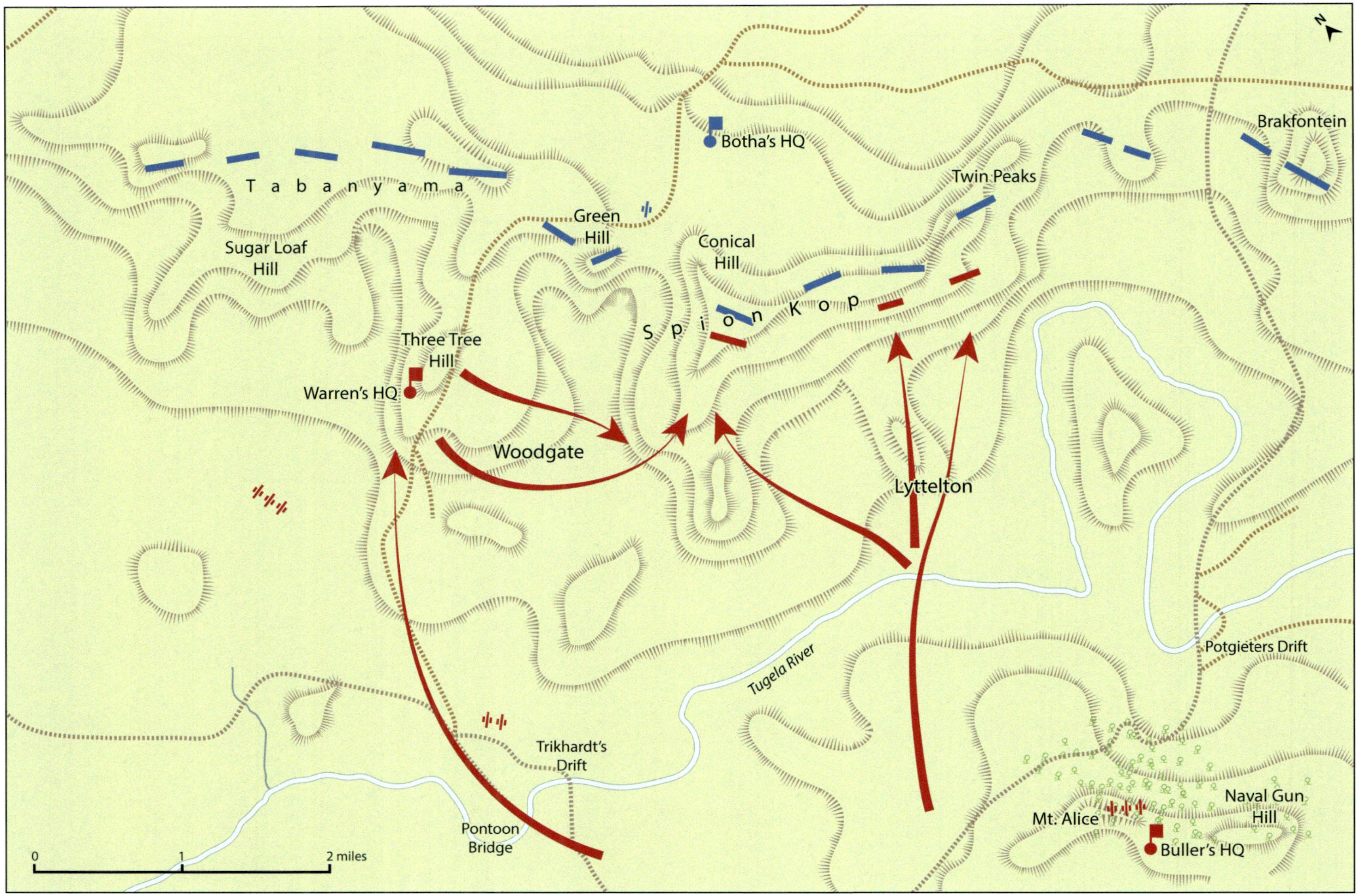

Spion Kop, 23-34 January 1900.

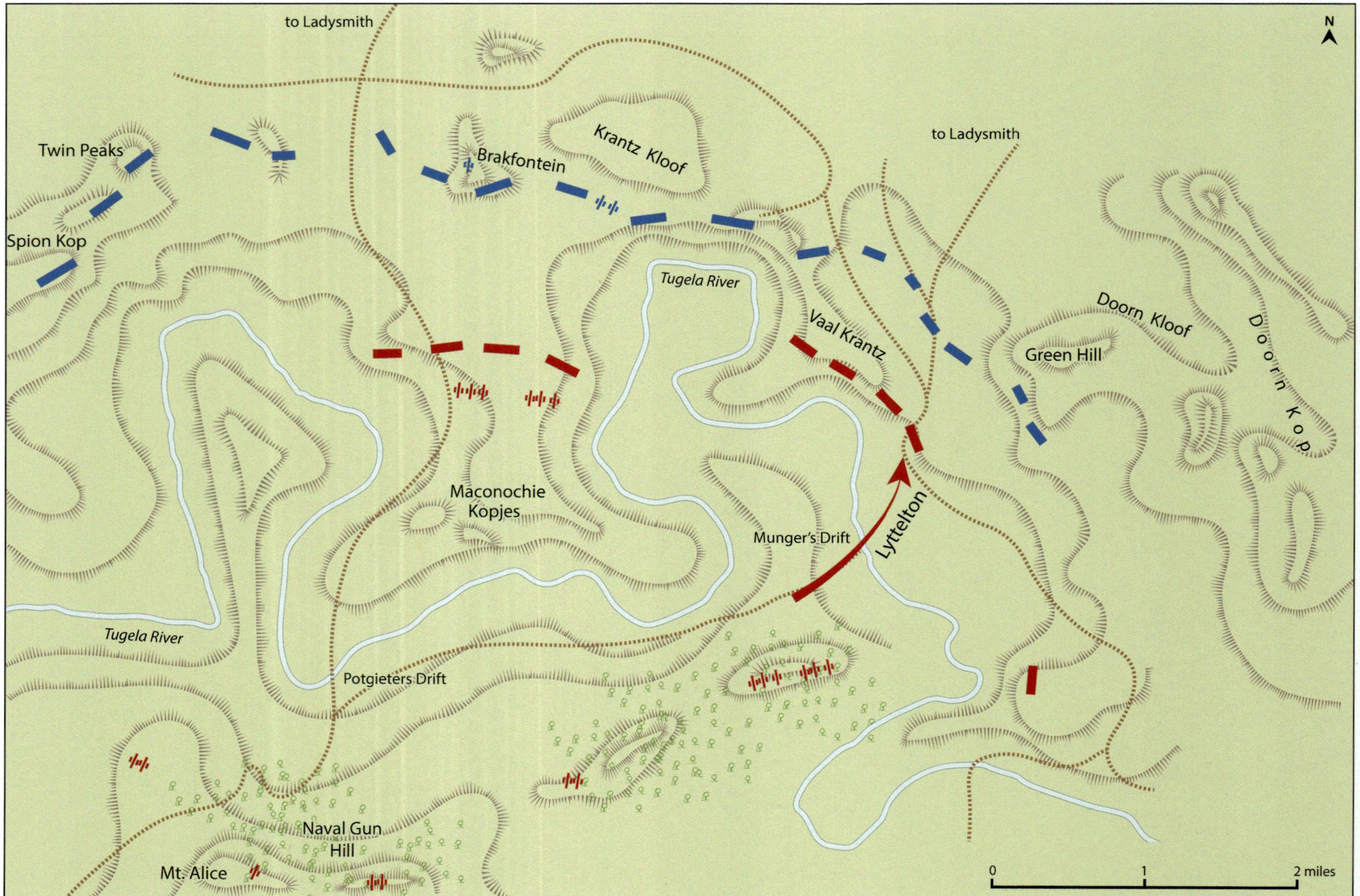

Vaal Kranz, 5-7 February 1900.

In the chaotic situation, Wauchope shouted the order to fix bayonets and charge. He, however, fell within minutes, two bullets striking his body and one his head. His body was later found just 200 yards from the Boer position. The men of the three leading battalions were completely intermixed and the confusion increased as the rear ranks pressed forward, through the tightly packed formations ahead of them. Some men, it is thought, may have panicked, and shouted 'Retire!' Certainly numbers of men did fall back, leaving perhaps half the brigade lying down and endeavouring to take cover from the hail of Boer fire. Before he fell, Wauchope had sent his cousin, Arthur Wauchope, who was one of his ADCs, to Colonel John Coode, the commander of the Black Watch, with orders to reinforce the right. Returning to where the general had fallen, Lieutenant Wauchope was also hit. Coode, endeavouring to carry out Wauchope's order, was killed, as was the commander of the Argylls, Lieutenant-Colonel Gerald Goff, leaving Hughes-Hallett as the ranking officer in the brigade, though he was unaware of it.[33]

It was close to impossible to establish any sort of order in the turmoil, even if there was anyone in a position to attempt it. The German Staff History noted: 'No one can cast a stone at the brave men, who, in clumsy formation, were helplessly sacrificed point blank range to magazine fire, and were then partly dashed back in disorder.'[34]

On the right of the Highland Brigade, the Boer line was held by the men of the small Scandinavian commando, posted at the point where the Boer left joined its centre. They had been able to enfilade the advancing Scottish infantry but now, as the latter came around the foot of the hill at close quarters, they were able to fall on the Scandinavian commando and effectively destroyed it, giving several groups of Highlanders the opportunity to try to storm Magersfontein Hill. About 90 to 100 men of the Black Watch under Captain MacFarlan, made some progress up the steep slopes, and another 100 of Seaforths and Black Watch under Lieutenant Wilson did the same. A third group of Seaforths under Lieutenant Cox, also made progress. At this point, however, the British artillery, aware that the Highland Brigade had been held, opened fire on the Boer position with shrapnel, effectively driving back the men under MacFarlan and Cox. Those with Wilson, however, were able to press on until they were suddenly taken in flank by heavy fire from the right. It was an unlucky chance:

> Cronje, who had been sleeping at a farm six miles from the centre of his line, was aroused by the sound of battle, and galloping to the hill, chanced to arrive at this moment. The rifles of his escort suddenly smiting Wilson's men from an unexpected direction at short range, checked them, and possibly changed the issue of the day.[35]

There now came up Boer reinforcements from the northern end of the low ridge on which was based the Boer left, and these opened fire on Wilson's men from the rear, and the attack withered away and fell back. Some of Wilson's men were captured; others retreated to the right of the brigade. Following this up, the Boers gradually drove back the most advanced units of the Highlanders' right wing, which retired at about 8.00.[36]

The forward movement of the Highland Light Infantry, as the brigade's reserve, could make no progress, and the Highlanders' front line, consisting of scattered groups of men, could do

33 Miller, *Methuen*, p. 142.
34 *German Staff History*, vol. I, p. 102.
35 *Official History*, vol. I, p. 320.
36 Ibid.

little but lie under the ceaseless rain of rifle fire from the hidden Boers no more than 400 or 500 yards away. Occasional attempts were made by parties of men to rush forward, but all were unsuccessful. For many hours, the stalemate continued. The exhausted British infantry lay, without food or water, under the blazing African sun, while the Boers, naturally, remained in their trenches.

As was so often the case, it was the artillery who provided such help as was possible to the hard-pressed infantry. The 4.7 inch naval gun opened fire from the same position as on the previous day. To its right was the howitzer battery, while the three field artillery batteries commenced firing at 4:50 a.m. from a point north-east of Headquarters Hill, at a range of 2,000 yards. Once it was realised that the Boers were mainly in trenches at the foot of the hill, the gunners adjusted their range accordingly, and later moved to a position closer to their target.[37]

Methuen, on Headquarters Hill, was able to do little to influence the fighting. The German Staff History observes that 'he watched the course of the battle without interfering in details, but when his Highland Brigade was overtaken by disaster, he appeared to have acted the part of a mere spectator.'[38] This is unfair. The Guards Brigade was moving up to support the Highland Brigade and at 11.00 a.m., after receiving information that Boer reinforcements were arriving from Spytfontein and Abou's Dam, Methuen ordered the Gordon Highlanders forward. In his report, he somewhat repented of his decision that the Guards Brigade should begin to move forward at midnight, rather than at 7.00 p.m. on the previous evening, which might have put it in a position to exploit the gap briefly created in the Boer line. It was, though, a remote possibility and Colville's only orders to his brigade were designed to prevent it becoming too closely engaged.[39] All that he had heard from Methuen was a hurried order reading: 'Highland attack has been checked. May fail. Keep your brigade in hand so as to protect Highland right and retirement if necessary. Perhaps retirement of whole force.'[40]

Thus it was that apart from the artillery support, very little help was afforded to the exhausted Highlanders, as they lay taking what cover they could from the constant Boer rifle fire. The German Staff History observes that 'the idea that an attack might turn the tide of battle seems to have vanished from the minds of the divisional staff, although more than half the force had not yet been in action.'[41] Certainly the role of Pole-Carew's 9th Brigade was ineffectual. Its two tasks were to make a feint towards the Boer right, advancing either side of the railway and to protect the camp. He, with his headquarters staff, the Northumberland Fusiliers and three companies of Northamptons, took up a position near the railway line; the rest of the Northamptons remained at the camp, to the north-west of which stood outposts of the lst Loyal North Lancashire Regiment[42]

The Times History is fiercely critical of the failure to employ Pole-Carew in a more offensive capacity:

> There can be little doubt that if he had received orders to push on, and had been reinforced by another battalion, he could have effected a lodgement on the lower ridge immediately to

37 *Official History*, vol. I, p. 321.
38 *German Staff History*, vol. I, p. 111.
39 Miller, *Methuen*, p. 143.
40 Pemberton, *Battles*, p. 98.
41 *German Staff History*, vol. I, p. 105.
42 *Official History*, vol. I, p. 326.

> the east of the railway. Once in command of that hill Pole-Carew could have enfiladed the whole of the centre trenches. But from the first Methuen never seems to have entertained the thought of taking any aggressive step to retrieve the failure of his first plan.[43]

This judgement is firmly rejected by Methuen's biographer, who points out that Pole-Carew's actions for the most part had little effect on the Boers since they had no need to reinforce their right flank during the battle: 'In addition, even Amery realised that this task would have required reinforcement, but failed to emphasise that none was forthcoming. Methuen knew that if the 9th Brigade had advanced, the camp would have been extremely vulnerable to an attack.'[44] If the camp had been broken up, Methuen would have had no option but to retreat, even if he had won the battle.

It was only on the extreme right of the British line that any real initiative was taken. Shortly before 4.00 a.m., Babington, with an escort of the 12th Lancers, most of the mounted infantry and the horse artillery, had advanced eastwards towards the low ridge on the Boer left. His aim was to turn the enemy flank here. When the sound of firing came to him from Magersfontein, he ordered the horse artillery to open fire on the ridge, which for the moment silenced the opposing rifle fire. He now sent the 9th Lancers along the north bank of the river with the aim of reaching Brown's Drift; they were, however halted at Moss Drift, and could make no further progress. In front of the ridge, it became clear to Babington that his horse artillery would be more useful supporting the Highland Brigade, and he ordered Major Bannatine-Allason, the battery commander, to move his guns north-east. As they approached what became known as Horse Artillery Hill, it became necessary to halt to cut a way through the wire fence and Allason decided to run his guns up by hand and locate them on the reverse slope. From here, he was able to shell the trenches at the foot of Magersfontein Hill at a range of 2,200 yards, and also the low ridge in his immediate front, which was a few feet higher than Horse Artillery Hill, at 1,400 yards. He continued in action at this point for some 24 hours.[45]

Meanwhile, along the bank of the Modder River, the KOYLI had been posted at Voetspads Drift. Its commander, Lieutenant Colonel Barter, became aware that a Boer force was moving downstream towards Moss Drift and on his own responsibility, advanced up river in that direction. He was himself held up before he could get to Moss Drift, but his move had checked any Boer advance at this point.[46]

At the foot of Magersfontein Hill the situation of the Highland Brigade was about to get worse, when at 1.00 p.m. the Boers began to outflank its right and right rear. The half battalion of the Gordon Highlanders had pressed forward in support of the Highland Brigade to a point less than 300 yards from the Boer trenches, where it remained. At 1:30 p.m. Hughes-Hallett, with the Seaforths, became aware of the Boer movement. He was still not aware that he was the senior surviving officer of the Highland Brigade. He sent messages to Colville appealing for help to cover his flank, but these failed to reach their destination. He later described the action he took to counter the threatening move:

> About 1.00 p.m. I found that a large party of the enemy were getting around my right flank and a very heavy fire was poured in on us from here and at the same time from the left. I

43 *Times History*, vol. II, p. 409.
44 Miller, *Methuen*, p. 144.
45 *Official History*, vol. I, p. 322.
46 Ibid., p. 325.

> then saw it was necessary to swing round a bit to my right to intercept this movement and I ordered the men near me to get round to the right, which we did under very heavy fire from the trenches in front. At this moment an order was passed down to retire.[47]

The immediate consequence was disastrous. In the confusion, the order to retire was taken to be of general effect:

> The officers strove hard to effect an orderly change of front; but their signals were misconstrued by many of the rank and file, who began to retire. First the right gave way; then at about 1:30 p.m. the movement became general and, covered by a very rapid and well-aimed hail of shells from the field artillery against the works at the foot of Magersfontein Hill, nearly all the Highlanders who were immediately in front of the Boers, gradually and with considerable loss ebbed away to the guns.[48]

The retirement quickly became a rout. Lieutenant Roger Poore, who was with a party escorting the guns, described the scene:

> Then I saw a sight that I hope I may never see again: men of the Highland Brigade running for all they were worth, others cowering under bushes, behind the guns, some lying under their blankets, officers running about with revolvers in their hands threatening to shoot them, urging on some, kicking on others; staff officers galloping about giving incoherent and impracticable orders. One came up to me and asked if I had any men? I said I was escorting the guns with a section of MI. He told me to 'Advance!' 'Where to? With what object and under whom?' 'God knows – only advance!'[49]

The correspondent of the *Morning Post* shared Poore's dismay at the scene: 'Back they came in a way that no officer could stop … One could see them swarming like bees over the veld till they were almost out of range and the guns left out in the open with no one to support them. It was, perhaps, the most unpleasant sight that a British soldier of today has ever beheld.'[50]

Unsurprisingly, the dramatic collapse of morale left bitter feelings; typical was the remark of one soldier of the Black Watch who declared that his regiment had been 'led into a butcher's shop and bloody well left there.'[51] There were many similar comments and much blame would be freely attached to Methuen for the disaster.

At about 4.00 p.m. the Boer artillery, which had been silent all day, suddenly opened fire from Magersfontein Hill. Their first shells burst over the demoralised Highland infantry, which had been collected behind the British field artillery. This fresh assault was more than they could take, and in spite of all their officers could do, the men retreated in small parties until they were safely out of range, and the brigade was not properly reformed until after dusk.[52]

47 Pemberton, *Battles*, p. 105.
48 *Official History*, vol. I, p. 327.
49 Pemberton, *Battles*, p. 108.
50 H.W. Wilson, *With the Flag to Pretoria* (London: Harmsworth Brothers, 1900), p. 193.
51 Farwell, *Great Boer War*, p. 112.
52 *Times History*, vol. II, pp. 412-413.

During the rest of the afternoon, fire gradually slackened. The Guards Brigade remained in position in front of the ridge, providing support when it was called for by Babington, whose dismounted lancers and mounted infantry had for a while become closely engaged. In places, the respective lines were only about 100 yards apart, but Colville had not sufficient strength to launch a major offensive in this sector, even if his instructions had not forbidden him from doing so. There was a moment at about 5.30 p.m. when it appeared that the Boers were about to launch an attack on the Guards Brigade, but nothing came of this. Meanwhile, the artillery continued in action throughout the day, although as the afternoon wore on, the rate of fire declined. During the battle, the 18th Battery fired 940 rounds, the 62nd about 1,000 rounds, the 75th 721 rounds, the horse artillery 1,179 rounds and the 4.7 inch naval gun 73 rounds.[53]

The German Staff History, noting that British writers had commented on what appeared to them to be the great amount of ammunition expended, was unimpressed: 'Careful consideration shows that this expenditure was not only in no degree large, but was, indeed, remarkably small, and the conclusion is either that the available supply was insufficient, or that there were difficulties in the way of bringing up ammunition.'[54] This conclusion was reached after comparison with the ammunition carried by a German battery.

By 7.15 p.m. all firing had ceased. It was Methuen's hope that the Boers, having checked the British advance, would do as they had done at Modder River and retreat from their positions overnight. This, however, as Methuen found from a personal reconnaissance at dawn next day, was not the case, and he was coming round to the view that he must now retreat. Colville, who joined him soon after, was optimistic, urging him to hold on in the hope that the Boers might still fall back, and Methuen was prepared to consider this, sending his chief engineer with Colville to look at sites for field works. However, at a council of war of his brigade commanders and headquarters staff an hour or so later, the general opinion was in favour of withdrawal, and Methuen ordered that this commence at noon. The Boers had no intention of abandoning their extremely powerful position and in the ensuing weeks, they worked hard to strengthen it further. Ironically, the architect of their victory, Koos de la Rey, was not present during the battle, having gone to Riverton near Kimberley to recuperate from his wound, which was continuing to trouble him.[55]

Although judged by the standards of later wars, the total of British casualties was not shatteringly high but they were considerable; 210 had been killed, 675 wounded and 63 were recorded as missing. It was, of course, the Highland Brigade that bore most of the loss, suffering 199 killed and 559 wounded and missing. Total Boer losses were believed to be 87 killed and 188 wounded.[56]

Historians have analysed the failure at Magersfontein in very considerable detail. It did, as Amery observed, provoke much embittered controversy. Most commentators have noted that Methuen himself was scrupulously careful not to publicly blame Wauchope; Amery, though, asserted that Methuen believed that the Highland Brigade had failed him and was the sole cause of his defeat, and that this appeared when addressing the brigade's officers on the following day, ' In a speech which, however kindly in its intentions and conciliatory in its language, still betrayed only too plainly the mistaken assumption underlying it.' If this was the case, the

53 *Official History*, I, p. 327.
54 *German Staff History*, vol. I, p. 118.
55 Trew, *Generals*, p. 219.
56 *Official History*, vol. I, p. 329.

resentment which was caused, and which led to so much blame being heaped on Methuen's head, was hardly surprising.[57]

Methuen's biographer looked at a number of possible reasons for his defeat at Magersfontein. First, there was the failure of reconnaissance, due to the lack of mounted troops and insufficient training for those carrying it out. Next, was the flawed decision to launch the preparatory bombardment, in which Methuen reposed undue confidence. His use of artillery was at fault, in that it was never used to support a specific infantry attack. The night march, conducted in adverse conditions, was, Stephen Miller considers, a sensible step to take; Methuen's error lay in not properly preparing the men for the advance. A serious tactical error was in the use of the reserves, placed as they were too far behind the Highland Brigade; when the Guards Brigade came up, 'it did not attempt to do anything but prop up the faltering line.' It should, instead, have been used directly in support of the initial assault. Methuen was mistaken, in Miller's view, in subscribing to an erroneous view of the need to hold back a reserve. Another factor in the defeat was the army's lack of preparation of the individual soldier for a modern battle.[58]

Miller identifies one final contribution to the defeat for which he considers Methuen may be fairly indicted; this being his failure – once his initial assault had been checked – to do much to direct the ensuing course of the battle. There was, it appears, no contingency plan in place. Miller quotes a writer in the *Sunday Chronicle* on the point: 'When his men had been brought within striking distance of the foe the general's business was done. The rest of the work and of the responsibility devolved upon his subordinates, the brigadiers.'[59] Methuen, though, never put this forward to cover up his error, and he accepted full responsibility for the battle, as indeed he should have.

Methuen's choice of a direct assault on Magersfontein Hill has been variously defended. Babington commented that 'you could have done the attack in no other way;' two high-ranking Boer officers are said to have told Methuen that 'you attacked at the right spot.'[60] The German Staff History was able to say that 'the idea of approaching the enemy under cover of darkness was, considering that the ground was devoid of cover, an excellent one, and an attack was bound to be all the more effective if it should partake of the nature of a surprise.'[61] Not all the circumstances which combined to lead to Methuen's defeat can be laid at his door, and it is understandable that he should have described it as 'the worst bit of luck I ever knew.' However, it brought the British advance up the railway line to a shuddering halt and was to have an immediate effect on operations in Natal.

The news of Magersfontein reached London in time for the Press to react on the following day. *The Times* commented:

> The failure of Lord Methuen's attack upon the position of the Boers at Magersfontein is the most serious event that the war has yet produced. The British arms have received a severe check at an exceedingly critical moment in the campaign, and the results cannot at present be fully estimated. The time has come for far greater efforts than have yet been made if the situation is to be retrieved and the war is to be carried to a successful conclusion. It is

57 *Times History*, vol. II, p. 417.
58 Miller, *Methuen*, pp. 147-151.
59 Ibid., p. 151.
60 Pemberton, *Battles*, p. 115.
61 *German Staff History*, vol. I, p. 111.

> necessary for the Government to act at once and to prove to the nation that it at length recognises the gravity of the military position.[62]

The Times had some practical suggestions to put forward:

> It is necessary to call up the whole of the available reserves in this country, and to turn the militia and volunteers to account. There are militia battalions which would certainly be willing to volunteer for service in South Africa, and from the large force of Volunteers a considerable body could quickly be raised for any duty. Efforts must be made to increase the local colonial forces, who have already proved extremely valuable in the field, and further offers of troops from Canada and other colonies must be sought and accepted. There is widespread patriotism throughout the Empire sufficient to enable us to meet a far greater emergency than the present. To organise and to turn that patriotism to account is the plain and urgent duty of the government.[63]

62 *The Times*, 14 December 1899.
63 Ibid.

14

Colenso, Friday 15 December

As his despatch to Lansdowne had made clear, Buller was in no doubt that of the three options he had been considering for an attack, the one for Potgieter's Drift was much the best, and the officers of Clery's staff continued to work on the orders. On 11 December, Buller received news of Gatacre's defeat at Stormberg but this had no effect on his determination to undertake the lengthy flank march. However, during the following day, news arrived of Methuen's defeat at Magersfontein and this at once caused him to reconsider his planned attack. After the war, in the course of his evidence to the Elgin Commission, he was naturally asked about his abrupt change of mind and whether it was simply on the ground of the encouragement which these events gave to the Boers. His reply was unequivocal: 'It was on the ground that my two other forces in the field had been brought to a standstill, both of them.'[1]

Buller's immediate reaction was to send an emphatic reply to Methuen's telegram that had brought news of Magersfontein:

> I at once telegraphed that he must either attack Cronje or fall back to Orange River, since it would be better to lose Kimberley then to hazard the isolation of his force. I also telegraphed to General Forestier-Walker that if Lord Methuen did retire, I regarded the first phase of the campaign is closed, and that both Methuen and Gatacre must take up tactical posts and prepare movable columns to operate around them. 'Through no fault of ours, 'I said, 'the enemy had the initiative and has used it well. We have staying power and must now use that.'[2]

In this changed situation, Buller now concluded that his own position had become quite different:

> With an enemy disheartened by failure, I thought myself warranted, in the peculiar circumstances, in making a flank march of fifty miles with an enormous wagon train, even though it might involve the uncovering of my communications. With an enemy elated by success, this was no longer justified. I therefore determined to try to force the direct road

1 Elgin Commission, *Minutes of Evidence*, vol. II, p. 196.
2 Ibid., vol. II, p. 174.

> to Ladysmith and reported as much by telegram to the Secretary of State on the 13th. In a letter to the Secretary of State on the same day, I added that whether I succeeded or failed, the time had come both in Natal and Cape Colony to stand on the defensive until the winter.[3]

He had, he said, changed his plans almost directly he received the news of Magersfontein.

Lord Elgin asked what Buller had in his mind at that point as to the consequences of the changed situation:

> But you had it distinctly before you, as your letter shows, at that time that if you failed you contemplated the loss of Ladysmith as the best way out of the situation? – I fully appreciated the enormous difficulties of the task in front of me … I did think that it was quite possible that if I failed I might not be able to get into Ladysmith in time to relieve it.[4]

Buller's letter to Lansdowne had emphasised that it was the risk to his communications which had led to his abandonment of the projected Potgieter's Drift operation; but he added a sentence that revealed a startling loss of morale: 'From my point of view it will be better to lose Ladysmith altogether than to throw open Natal to the enemy.'[5] In the following days, this suggestion was to cause the most profound anxiety in London.

Buller's abrupt change of plan reveals the almost total lack of confidence with which he confronted his situation. Amery was sharply critical:

> From the first Buller had been curiously slow to grasp the essence of the military situation, namely, that the Boers were more formidable in the field than had ever been suspected, and the last disasters taught him no more than White's failure and the confusion in Natal had taught him a month before. Nor did he possess the strength of purpose necessary to enable him to postpone all non-strategic consideration, to the one consideration of victory.[6]

It is not perhaps correct to suggest that Buller had not grasped how formidable the Boers were proving to be; indeed, in some respects he overreacted to this, and approached the task immediately in front of him in a decidedly pessimistic spirit. Later, after the war, he explained his state of mind at this moment of decision to Sir Arthur Bigge, who had been Queen Victoria's secretary. He regarded both of the projected operations, at Potgieter's Drift and at Colenso, as in the nature of forlorn hopes. The difference between them was, he said, that 'Colenso was in front of me. I could control the result. But Potgieter's Drift … I could not pretend that I could control that. I might easily have lost my whole force.'[7]

The decision made, Buller heliographed on 13 December a message to White to the effect that he had been forced to change his plans and would be coming through via Colenso and Onderbrook Spruit and later that day, told him that the actual date of his attack depended on the difficulties he met with, but would probably be 17 December. White accordingly prepared

3 Ibid.
4 Elgin Commission, *Minutes of Evidence*, vol. II, p. 197.
5 *Official History*, vol. I, p. 379.
6 *Times History*, vol. II, p. 247.
7 Pakenham, *Boer War*, p. 213.

his force for a sortie to be undertaken when he heard further. After these messages, Buller appears to have put White out of his mind and concentrated on the orders to be issued for the attack at Colenso.

A brief account has already been given of the position which Buller was about to attack. Commentators have been almost unanimous in considering it as virtually impregnable. The Official History described it as follows:

> The hills facing Colenso from the north form a great amphitheatre, the western horn of which reaches down to the river near E. Robinson's Farm about 4 miles due west of the village, the eastern horn being Hlangwane. Immediately after completing the loop in front of the village, in which lie the road and railway bridges, the Tugela turns sharply to the north for two miles, and then dashes north-eastward down a series of rapids through an abrupt gorge in the hills, ultimately resuming its course towards the east. Hlangwane, the eastern horn of that amphitheatre, which, with its included area, formed the Boer position, lies on the southern bank of the river.[8]

The fact that Hlangwane was on the right bank, and hence could be assaulted without the need for a river crossing, has led some commentators to conclude that this was potentially a serious weakness in the Boer position. However, experience was to show that if properly defended, it was an extremely tough nut to crack, requiring an advance through very broken country, which would soon involve entering bush country. In addition, as the Official History points out, even if it and the crossings close to Colenso had been captured, only the first stage of the task would have been accomplished: 'Further severe fighting would have been necessary before the defiles and the very difficult country to the north-west or north could have been forced.'[9]

In the centre of the Boer position, south of the Onderbrook Spruit which crossed the amphitheatre from west to east, stood the Colenso kopjes, which Buller described as 'four lozenge-shaped, steep-sided, hog-backed hills, each as it is further from the river, being higher and longer than the inner one.' The southernmost kopje, known as Fort Wylie, had been occupied by the British as a bridgehead over the Tugela before the retirement to Estcourt.

Even with the limited information which he had regarding the Boer position, it is no wonder that Buller had originally concluded that it would be too costly to assault. What is surprising, therefore, is that it took only a belief that the Boers would be greatly encouraged by the news of Magersfontein and Stormberg for him to abandon the notion of a flank march to Potgieter's Drift and undertake an assault on the Colenso position.

Botha had made effective use of the three weeks which he had been allowed to strengthen the whole of the mountain redoubt, and had made the most of the free hand he had been given:

> The trenches had been constructed with remarkable ingenuity, so as to be almost invisible from the south bank. They ran for the most part along the lower slopes of the great hills on the west and across the flats round which circled the amphitheatre. The only part of these defences which caught the eye from the far side of the river were the tiers of entrenchments covering the Colenso kopjes, and especially Fort Wylie. Emplacements had been

8 *Official History* vol. I, p. 340.
9 Ibid.

> constructed in many more places than there were guns available to fill them, and, in order to ensure that the exact positions from which shells would be actually thrown should be unknown to the British commander, the guns were shifted from gun-pit to gun-pit the night before the battle.[10]

Unknown to Buller, Botha had been having a problem with the defence of Hlangwane. From 30 November until 13 December, it had been occupied by a force of between 400 and 500 men under a commandant named Dirksen. When Barton's brigade moved out from Chieveley, this force lost its nerve and that night, in defiance of Dirksen's orders, the men withdrew completely from Hlangwane to the left bank of the river. At first, Botha appears to have acquiesced in this, but Dirksen, realising the threat to the Boer position, telegraphed Kruger to tell him, saying that 'if we give this kop over to the enemy, then will the battle expected at Colenso end in disaster.' Schalk Burger, who with Joubert's illness was Acting Commandant General, saw at once the force of this, and telegraphed Botha that the position must not be abandoned.

Kruger, when the matter was referred to him, instinctively saw at once the serious risk of leaving Hlangwane unoccupied, and sent Botha an emphatic instruction:

> Gentlemen, I have received report that you gave up position. Understand please, if you give up a position there, you give up the whole land to the enemy. Please stand fast, dead or alive, each man at his place, and fight in the name of the Lord. The kop on the other side of the river must not be given up because then is all hope gone with it … And fear not the enemy but fear God … If you give up position, and surrender country to England, where will you go then?[11]

Schalk Burger was strongly in support of the president's position and as a result, a hasty *krigsraad* was convened, which unanimously decided that Hlangwane must be reoccupied. A force of 800 men under Commandant Jozua Joubert was assembled, selected by lot from five commandos and this took up a position on Hlangwane during the night of 14/15 October.

Amery, in *The Times History*, doubted that the force sent to occupy Hlangwane was really adequate, given the importance of the position, reckoning that a smaller force would have sufficed to hold the main position. He considered that a larger force on Hlangwane would not only have ensured the security of the Boer position but would, if the chance arose, have been the ideal place from which to launch a counter-attack:

> The true explanation, unquestionably, is that Botha never for a moment doubted that the main British attack would be directed straight against the Colenso kopjes, and only feared that if Hlangwane were entirely unoccupied some detachments on the British flank might be tempted to seize it and might then realise its importance. Nothing indeed, at this stage of the war, is more astonishing than the contempt the Boer generals showed for their opponents, except the fact that that contempt was almost invariably justified by the event.[12]

10 *Official History*, vol. I., p. 342.
11 Pakenham, *Boer War*, p. 221.
12 *Times History*, vol. II, p. 432.

The Boers had shown remarkable confidence in entrusting the command to the youthful Botha and in accepting his prescription for the conduct of the defence. As a result, the principal defences of the position were to be found in the low kopjes close to the river, rather than in the higher range of hills behind. Botha was determined to ensure that the British, when they came to launch their attack, would be taken by surprise. From his bed, the ailing Piet Joubert sent Botha a lengthy telegram of advice about the need for fire control:

> I cannot neglect to reiterate pointing out to you and begging you to insist sternly with the officers and men against wild firing at long and almost impossible distances … Our burghers with their rapid-fire rifles begin to shoot at so great a distance, and it is much to be feared that in a fierce fight lasting a whole day, they fire away all their ammunition to no purpose without hurting the enemy, and the enemy is then able to make use of lance and sword after exhausting their ammunition.[13]

Joubert also urged Botha to be on his guard against any move by British cavalry to pass around his rear, and to place supports so that new forces could advance to prevent this. He ended his message: 'It is bitter to lie here on my back and think and advise from such a distance, but God's will be done, just in heaven as on earth. Best wishes.'

Buller had advanced Barton's brigade on 12 December, accompanied by two 4.7 inch and six 12-pdr naval guns, to a camp some two miles north of Chieveley, in order to be in a position to cover the proposed flank march to Potgieter's Drift. Now, on the following day, having changed his plans, he ordered the guns to be located on an eminence known subsequently as Naval Gun Hill, to commence a bombardment of the Boer positions. This lasted for some three hours, and continued on the following day. To this, Botha made no reply; but the movement of the rest of the British Army to a position north-west of Chieveley left him in no doubt that Buller was about to launch a frontal attack. Should they do so, he was confident in his ability to repulse it, and he planned to launch a counter-attack from the force on Red Hill, on the right of his position, under Commandant Fourie.

To resist the imminent assault on his position, Botha had a total of approximately 4,500 men available. He possessed only five guns, including a 120mm howitzer and a pom-pom, which he intended to move from point to point as the occasion demanded. He faced an opponent who was 19,378 strong, with two 4.7 inch and 12, 12-pdr naval guns and five field batteries with 30 guns, together with 18 machine guns. This force was made up of four infantry brigades, totalling 13,937 men; a naval brigade of 310 men; 2,867 mounted troops; 1,113 artillerymen; 453 engineers; 230 Army Service Corps personnel; medical units of 494 men; and a staff of 171.[14] Thus, Buller certainly had the kind of overwhelming force that he had prescribed as necessary to crush the enemy; it remained to be seen, however whether even with this army, he was strong enough to force the position facing him. He may previously have spoken jauntily of crushing the enemy; now he approached the task in a gravely pessimistic frame of mind.

During the morning of 14 December, Buller rode forward to examine again by telescope, so far as he was able, the position that he was about to attack. He may have been struck by the failure of the Boers to make any response to the lengthy bombardment of their position,

13 *Official History*, vol. I, p. 344.
14 Ibid., p. 470.

and perhaps concluded after all that his estimate of the probable heavy cost of an assault had been overly pessimistic. At all events, that afternoon he assembled his subordinate commanders and their staffs to tell them of his plans and to give instructions for an assault to be launched the following day. His written orders were not issued until 10.00 p.m., reaching the brigade commanders at about midnight.

In drafting these orders, neither Buller nor the staff can have failed to have in mind that in launching a contested river crossing, they were undertaking one of the most difficult of military operations. What is surprising is that it was to be undertaken with only a very limited understanding of the Tugela and its crossings. If the British had been approaching from the south into totally unknown territory, their ignorance of the topography around Colenso might be understandable; but this was not the case. Before the withdrawal to Estcourt at the beginning of November, the British had held Fort Wylie and the adjacent Fort Molyneux as a bridgehead and many of those involved must have had some familiarity with the surrounding terrain. In addition, there must have been a number of local inhabitants from whom an accurate picture could have been obtained.

Yet, as the Official History observes, the information available was far from complete:

> In this section of the Tugela, the only crossings which seem to have been known to Sir Redvers Buller's staff, before the battle, were the two bridges, the drifts immediately above and below that over which the road passes, and the 'Bridle Drift' four miles upstream to the south-east of E. Robinson's farm ... The river, in consequence of the difficulty of approaching it, had not been systematically reconnoitred, nor had the known drifts been tested, although, as elsewhere in South Africa, they are subject to sudden variations, here dependent on the rainfall in the Drakensberg. The Tugela is, as a rule, fordable at this season of the year at the regular passages and has an average breadth of some 120 to 150 yards.[15]

The orders suggested that the Boers were only occupying the kopjes immediately north of the river and it was there that would be the focus of the attack. This would be led by Hildyard's 2nd Brigade, which was to move off at 4.00 a.m. in the direction of 'the iron bridge,' a reference to the road bridge, crossing the river at that point to seize the kopjes. Hart's 5th Brigade, starting half an hour later, was to march to the Bridle Drift, crossing the Tugela here before moving along the left bank towards the kopjes. Lyttelton's 4th Brigade would advance to a point between the Bridle Drift and the railway, from where it could support either the 2nd or 5th Brigades. Barton's 6th Brigade was to move at 4.00 a.m. to a point east of the railway towards Hlangwane, covering the right flank of the 2nd Brigade. It would also support Dundonald's mounted brigade, which was to advance on Hlangwane with 1,000 men and one battery, from where it could enfilade the kopjes. The two regular cavalry regiments under Burn-Murdoch, would cover the left flank. The six naval guns, two 4.7 inch and four 12-pdrs, presently north of the 4th Brigade, would advance on the right of the field artillery. The 14th and 16th Field Artillery Batteries were to move at 3:30 a.m. east of the railway and, covered by the 6th Brigade, take up a position to prepare the crossing for the 2nd Brigade, accompanied by the remaining six naval guns under Lieutenant Ogilvy.[16]

15 Ibid., p. 341.
16 Ibid., pp. 347-350.

One aspect of these orders later gave rise to a major dispute between Buller and Long, the artillery commander. Buller, in his subsequent despatch, suggested that he had personally explained to Long that he was to come into action with the naval guns only, 'as the position was not within effective range for his field guns.' Long, in the following March, flatly denied this in a letter which in due course, would come before the Elgin Commission, writing bluntly, 'Sir Redvers Buller never gave me that order.'[17]

In considering this dispute, the subsequent accounts given by Buller and Long are neither altogether trustworthy. Buller's suggestion that he indicated that the field guns were not to come into action is plainly inconsistent with the written orders that they were to proceed to a point from where they could prepare the crossing for the 6th Brigade. On the other hand, Long's use of the term 'medium-range,' which does not appear in the orders, as Buller's indication of what he was to do, is suspiciously imprecise. *The Times History* (which says that Buller gave Long a note) offers an explanation of Long's proceedings:

> Long was a convinced believer in a theory which had for some time been growing up among some artillerists in favour of pushing guns right forward and securing an overwhelming short-range fire … Possibly, too, a certain ambiguity in Buller's note may, instead of deterring, have piqued Long into attempting to put his theory in practice against the Boers.[18]

On the face of it, the orders issued for the attack appeared reasonably clear; but Pemberton points out that their meaning was in some respects anomalous. First, the instructions to Hart were that he was 'to cross the Bridle Drift immediately to the west of the junction of the Doornkop Spruit and the Tugela:'

> But reference to the map … will show that there are two spruits running into the Tugela, each with a drift to its west. The nearer was a pont drift impassable on foot, the farther a bridle drift, fordable except during spates. Between the two the river made a great loop to the north-west, difficult to detect from a distance and for that reason possibly unknown to Buller. In the map issued to Hart, based presumably on Buller's master map, the farther of the two spruits (actually a mere watercourse, dry for half the year) was incorrectly named the Doornkop; and there is reason to believe that the loop was not marked.[19]

Secondly, it is unclear to which bridge Buller was referring when giving orders to cross 'the iron bridge.' There were two bridges, the broken railway bridge being directly opposite Fort Wylie: 'There is, however, nothing in Buller's published correspondence to show that he knew it to be damaged. For that reason it would seem that he meant Hildyard to cross that bridge and no other.'[20] Pemberton goes on to cite Buller's biographer Colonel C. H. Melville who says that Buller had in mind the railway bridge. The Official History, on the other hand, assumes that he meant the road bridge, while *The Times History* thinks that it is clear that he meant the railway bridge.[21]

17 Elgin Commission, *Appendices*, pp. 341-342.
18 *Times History*, vol. II, pp. 440-441.
19 Pemberton, *Battles*, pp. 125–126.
20 Ibid. p. 126.
21 Colonel C.H. Melville, *Life of Sir Redvers Buller*, vol. II (London: E. Arnold, 1923), p. 101; *Official History*, vol. I, p 346; *Times History*, vol. II, p. 436.

The point is not unimportant; the road bridge, or Bulwer bridge, would take Hildyard in a westerly direction, and he would then have to move to his right to seize the kopjes, while the railway bridge would take him due north to Fort Wylie. It was to become a point of academic interest as the battle developed, but if the railway bridge had been intended, it is extraordinary that no mention in the orders was made of the road bridge, past which Hildyard would have to march with it on his left. At the least, it should have been seized, since it would have been invaluable in getting troops over the river to support Hart if his crossing had been successful and he was moving eastwards.

Whether the attack about to be launched was really practicable became later the subject of divided opinions. Ian Hamilton, when he visited the battlefield some months later, wrote emphatically to Spenser Wilkinson: 'I only wish you could see the place. I trust I am right in saying that there are but a few subalterns in the British Army who would not recognise that an attack on Buller's lines must fail.' Roberts, much later, would describe it as 'sheer murder.'[22] On the other hand, Julian Symons quotes Lyttelton, whom he considered one of the two or three most intelligent commanders on the British side, as thinking that 'either operation (a flank march or the direct attack) was feasible, provided it was carried out in the proper way, Colenso probably the easier.' Lyttelton apparently said afterwards that there had been 'no proper reconnoitring of the ground, no certain information as to any ford by which to cross the river, no proper artillery preparation, no satisfactory targets for the artillery, no realisation of the importance of Hlangwane.'[23]

Amery, in *The Times History*, is in no doubt at all that the plan was almost inconceivably bad:

> Whether, undeterred by the fate of others, Buller still believed at heart that a force of British infantry such as his could 'do anything and go anywhere,' or whether, on the contrary, he was so bewildered by the terrible responsibility of his position and by the paralysing intangibility of the enemy as to be unable to think out any better plan, it is impossible to say. Whatever the true psychological explanation of the plan for the attack on Colenso, the fact remains that a worse plan could not have been devised. Only by a miracle of good fortune could it hope to succeed.[24]

All these opinions were of course expressed after the event, liberally applying hindsight and perhaps do not give sufficient weight to the pressure on Buller to do something quickly if he was to relieve Ladysmith. Lyttelton's comments on the way in which the assault was launched do however seem entirely just.

Pakenham, reviewing the Tugela position, reckons that it was not an impregnable position, pointing out the great length of the line that must be defended, the fact that the southern part of the plain where Buller would attack was barely within rifle range of the Colenso kopjes, and the need to extend the eastern end of the line across the river to defend Hlangwane. The debate in the Boer high command on where to locate the line of defence echoed the discussions before Modder River and Magersfontein, and Botha dealt with the issue, as de la Rey had done, by recommending a sophisticated entrenching of the position. It was this that turned a strong position into one which was indeed, not far short of impregnable.

22 Symons, *Campaign*, p. 155.
23 Ibid.
24 *Times History*, vol. II, p. 439.

It was still dark when the British troops began their advance. This, for the men of Hart's 5th Brigade, was preceded by half an hour's drill, an exercise which tells us something about their commander's rigid thought processes. Buller, meantime, made his way to Naval Gun Hill, taking up a position close to the 4.7 inch guns from which to watch the battle. Across the river, the moving lights in the British camps told the Boers that the anticipated assault was about to commence. Botha had been woken at about 1.00 a.m. As dawn lightened the sky, he stood beside the 5 inch Krupp howitzer, watching the long columns of British infantry moving towards the river. Pakenham was struck by the contrast between the stately formality of a British commander-in-chief isolated even from his brigadiers and the modesty of Botha's manner of leadership. He noted how sparsely furnished was the latter's tent and how he would give up the only chair and sit on the ground when an elderly burgher entered. 'There he sat, as a procession of visitors tramped through the tent. He ate, drank, slept and wrote his official despatches under their gaze. It won everybody's heart.'[25] As he watched the British troop movements, Botha was in no doubt at all that with all their wagons and guns they must head for the wagon bridge.

At 5:20 a.m. the six naval guns on the height beside which Buller had taken his position, began to shell the kopjes on the far side of the river. For more than half an hour the Boers made no reply. Meanwhile, the rest of Buller's artillery were getting into position. The 14th and 16th Batteries and Ogilvy's naval 12-pdrs had crossed the railway line at 3:30 a.m., where they joined the 6th Brigade and moved northward. Long, in accordance with Buller's express instructions, accompanied them. The 2nd Brigade marched off at 4.00 a.m. followed half an hour later by the 4th Brigade, heading towards Colenso. Dundonald's brigade, accompanied by the 7th Battery, had also begun to move at 4.00 a.m., as had Barton's 2nd Brigade.

The orders had provided for the 64th and 73rd Field Batteries under Lieutenant Colonel Parsons to follow Lyttelton's 4th Brigade, but since Buller had ordered him to pass at least one of his batteries across the river with Hart, Parsons marched with his guns to the rear of the 5th Brigade.[26] At the head of that brigade rode Major General Hart, with a Kaffir guide and a local colonist as interpreter to help him find the Bridle Drift. He had a copy of the one-inch map, such as it was, that the staff had prepared; this, regrettably, was inaccurate on three points; it showed the Doornkop Spruit as running into the Tugela at the western end of the loop; it showed the Bridle Drift as close to the junction with the spruit; and placed to the west of the drift, another loop of the river. Only a short deep donga entered the river at the western end of the loop; the Doornkop Spruit in fact entered the river at the eastern end, and the Bridle Drift lies a mile from the western end, not close by. There is no second loop.[27] Hart had been told that his guide lived nearby and was entirely familiar with the crossing. What neither he nor Buller knew was that there was another drift at the head of the loop which might have been fordable, breast high, and another immediately below the junction of the Doornkop Spruit with the Tugela.

The patrols sent forward by Colonel Burn-Murdoch, from the Royal Dragoons riding to protect the flank of the 5th Brigade's advance, had soon reached the river bank, where they could see the Boers across the river moving to positions to meet Hart's column. Three gallopers in succession were sent to Hart to warn him that the Boers were in strength all along his front and to his left. Hart's response was to say that he would take no notice of the Boers unless they

25 Pakenham, *Boer War*, p. 219.
26 *Official History*, vol. I, p. 352.
27 Ibid., 352-353.

attacked him in force. He would march on, in close order, to the Bridle Drift in accordance with his orders, displaying what Pakenham described as one of the great traditions of the British Army: 'Courage matched only by stupidity.'[28]

After breaking camp, Hart had marched north westwards to the first drift over the Doornkop Spruit and then northwards towards the Tugela. The column was led by the 2nd Royal Dublin Fusiliers, followed by the 1st Connaught Rangers, then the 1st Border Regiment and finally the 1st Royal Inniskilling Fusiliers. At about 6:15 a.m., as the head of the column reached a newly ploughed mealie field and from where Hart could see the river, it seemed to him that the map was misleading. He asked his Kaffir guide where the drift was; through the interpreter the reply was that it was up the loop, the guide pointing in that direction. He appears to have thought that it was the so-called pont drift for which the 5th Brigade was aiming, which lay at the head of the loop, rather than the Bridle Drift.[29]

It was at this moment that, contrary to Botha's orders, the Boer gun located below Grobbelaar Mountain opened fire, the first shell passing over the rear of the column, the second in front of the Connaught Rangers and the third bursting among the men of that battalion. The Dublin Fusiliers immediately formed front and extended to the right, the following battalions deploying to the left in single rank with intervals opening from two to three paces. The brigade now moved forward by a series of rushes; as it advanced, it came under heavy fire from the long Boer trench to the north. The battalions quickly became intermingled; those on the left were cramped for space by the riverbank. The Kaffir guide, meanwhile, had bolted, and the location of the drift to which the brigade was supposed to be advancing was unknown. Hart's brigade major had ridden upriver to look for it; he found what appeared to be a ford, but when he entered the river he was soon out of his depth.[30]

Meanwhile, the men of the brigade continued to work their way up the loop by short rushes, suffering heavy losses as they did so from sustained rifle far from the Boer trenches. Hart had by now, virtually lost all control of his brigade:

> Nobody knew where the drift was or had any clear idea what was happening. The eagerness to get across the river somehow and come to grips with the Boers carried the men forward 'like waves of the sea without any special guiding from anyone.' A fold in the ground gave limited protection, and detachments of the Dublins and Connaught Rangers, thus sheltered, penetrated as far as some African kraals at the apex of the loop. The majority peeled off to the left to face the flanking fire from across the river and devised such cover as they could out of ant hills and tufts of grass.[31]

Hart, who lacked nothing in courage, walked calmly about urging his men forward, but he had no more idea than they did of where they were going other than to continue to follow the Kaffir guide's indication. Captain Romer of the 1st Dublins, succinctly described their situation: 'Nobody knew where the drift was. Nobody had a clear idea of what was happening. All pushed forward blindly, animated by the sole idea of reaching the river bank.'[32]

28 Pakenham, *Boer War*, p. 230.
29 *Official History*, vol. I, p. 354.
30 Ibid., p 356.
31 Pemberton, *Battles*, p. 130.
32 Pakenham, *Boer War*, p. 228.

The commander of the rearmost battalion, the Inniskillings, had led his men to form a single line parallel to the river instead of remaining in two ranks as Hart had intended, and they had worked their way towards the left of the loop in the direction of the Bridle Drift. Hart was annoyed at this deployment and ordered the Inniskillings back into the loop, a decision which merely confirmed the extent of his defeat.

On Naval Gun Hill, Buller had watched as Hart's brigade at first headed for the Bridle Drift and then veered off to its right. Up to this point there had been no artillery preparation; Parsons now unlimbered the guns of his two batteries and opened fire, although he had no specific targets at which to aim and in fact, some of his shells fell among the men of the Irish Brigade. Buller, seeing that things were going seriously wrong, had before the firing began, sent off a galloper to order Hart to stay out of the loop. Unfortunately, this officer's horse got stuck in marshy ground near the river and he never arrived. As the situation continued to deteriorate, Buller sent off his ADC, Captain Algy Trotter, this time with orders for the brigade to retire, but by now the situation was so confused that even an orderly retirement was going to be almost impossible. Under continuous and heavy fire, the Irish Brigade was completely pinned down: 'There was no enemy to see and nothing to fire at … All we had to do was to lie as close to the ground as we could, watch the bullets pitting the earth around us and wonder whose turn it would be to be hit next.'[33]

It was at 7.15 that Buller had concluded that he had seen enough and sent off the order to retire; he then rode down to Lyttelton, whose 4th Brigade had in accordance with its orders moved to a position from where it could support either the 5th Brigade or the 2nd Brigade. To Lyttelton, Buller said: 'Hart has got into a devil of a mess down there. Get him out of it as best you can.'[34] There was not, though, a great deal that Lyttelton could do. He advanced four companies of the Rifle Brigade to a point where they could give supporting fire. By now the order to retire had begun to spread through the 5th Brigade and parties of men had begun to retreat out of the loop when Lyttelton arrived on the scene. Among them was Hart himself, who told Lyttelton: 'The men have all fallen back. We'll form up in the rear.'[35] Hart was in fact quite mistaken, as Lyttelton could see for himself; the ground ahead was covered with figures, wounded and unwounded, lying flat. As he watched, Lyttelton saw one group rise up suddenly to make their way back, only for many of them to be shot down. Parsons' batteries, still endeavouring to engage the enemy, inadvertently opened fire on the men of the 4th Brigade; at the time, Lyttelton was sheltering from the Boer rifle fire behind the wall of a sheepfold and was startled to find himself under fire from both directions.

Things had not been going well in other sectors of the battlefield. Barton's 6th Brigade had moved off on the eastern side of the railway line in a roughly north-easterly direction. At first, Long, with the artillery, had accompanied the 6th Brigade, the field artillery leading and Ogilvy's six naval guns in the rear; but after a while, the artillery began to diverge and Barton ordered two companies of Royal Scots Fusiliers to act as escort. The rest of the 6th Brigade halted at 5.30, about two miles short of the river.[36]

Long, however, had continued to advance with his two batteries. Hearing heavy firing from the left, he was anxious to get into position as quickly as he could. He understood that Buller

33 Pemberton, *Battles*, p. 131.
34 Symons, *Campaign*, p. 159.
35 Pakenham, *Boer War*, p. 232.
36 *Official History*, vol. I, p. 358.

wished him to come into action at medium-range against the three kopjes immediately behind Fort Wylie, so he pushed on. In the account which he gave in the letter previously quoted, he wrote: 'The light was deceptive and I got a bit closer than I intended,' adding that the position which he took up was 'a better and less dangerous one than I could have got further back.'[37] Long's advance so close to the enemy may, however, not have been as accidental as he claimed; Powell quotes a conversation recorded by Atkinson, the *Manchester Guardian* correspondent, on the ship to South Africa, in the course of which Long spoke of the importance of getting guns close to the enemy 'because the only way to smash these beggars is to rush in on them.'[38]

Long had by now reached a point some 1,000 yards from the river and 1,250 yards from Fort Wylie (which, he said, he did not know was held by the Boers). Ogilvy had protested to him at the continued advance of the guns but as it turned out, his six naval guns had lagged behind the field artillery.

Long ordered his batteries to come into action at a point about 80 yards north of a broad and shallow donga running at right angles to the railway just in front of the position taken up by his guns. Up to this point, both Boer artillery and riflemen, who had been astounded to see the British guns advancing in this manner in the open, had remained silent, but Botha now gave the order to open fire. Despite indifferent marksmanship, the volume of Boer rifle fire was so intense that Long's gunners at once began to suffer casualties. Among the first of these was Long himself. The Boers knew the exact range, having left whitewash marks on the railway fence and the nearby stones. Two of Ogilvy's naval guns came into action some 400 yards back; the native drivers of the oxen trains of the other four bolted and it was some time before they could be cut free and be manhandled into position to open fire.

Hunt, Long's second-in-command, was also down, as were a number of other officers, but the 12 field guns continued firing methodically until about a third of their crews had been killed or wounded, at which point the rest took shelter in the donga. Command had passed to Major Bailward. The second line ammunition wagons were, like the guns, left standing in the open plain. By now, the two field batteries had used up practically all their ammunition, having fired about 1,000 rounds within an hour. Two officers, Captains Fitzgerald and Herbert, now rode back to get help.[39]

Buller, on Naval Gun Hill, had been astounded when Long's guns had opened fire. He sent a staff officer to see what they were doing. The latter returned to say that although a little under fire 'they seemed quite comfortable.' Soon after this, Colonel Stopford, Buller's military secretary, rode up to say that Long's guns were badly out of position; Buller replied grimly that he knew that already. He mounted his horse and rode off to see the position for himself, meeting Fitzgerald and Herbert, who gave him an alarmist and exaggerated account of the situation of the batteries, suggesting that all the guns were out of action and most of the men killed or wounded.

Buller rode on to Hildyard, who of his own motion had halted the advance of his 2nd Brigade. According to the Official History, his reason for doing so was because he was awaiting the completion of the artillery preparation before advancing to Colenso.[40] To Hildyard, Buller said that Long's guns had got into a terrible mess and that he doubted whether they could attack

37 Elgin Commission, *Appendices*, pp. 341–342.
38 Powell, *Buller*, p. 150.
39 Pakenham, *Boer War*, p. 231.
40 *Official History*, vol. I, p. 363.

Colenso that day. It was now about 8.00 a.m., and Buller made up his mind at once to call off the attack. Pakenham, considering his reasons for doing so, concluded that 'the emotion evoked by the news of Long's guns and of Hart's fiasco on the left, was suppressed rage, not despair.'[41] Buller, having decided to abandon the attack, was now concerned to save the guns and he ordered Hildyard to push forward two battalions to cover the process of recovery.

These now advanced, the 2nd Queens on Colenso and the 2nd Devons towards Long's guns, in open order; Hildyard's other two battalions formed a second and a third line. As the brigade advanced it came under heavy fire but suffered few casualties. By 9.35. a.m. companies of the Queens had occupied Colenso, while two companies of the Devons had reached the donga in which Long's men were sheltering.

Having given his orders to Hildyard, Buller rode forward with his staff, coming under heavy fire in which his medical officer, Captain Hughes, was killed and he himself hit by a shrapnel bullet. When he reached the point from which Ogilvy's naval guns were firing, he ordered their retirement, which they managed with the help of artillery horses. Buller saw no hope of bringing Long's guns back into action:

> Since the batteries ceased fire, Fort Wylie had been reoccupied by the enemy, and the fire therefrom, and from the neighbouring trenches, was so heavy that Buller considered that it was impossible that troops could live in the open by the guns. He sanctioned a series of gallant attempts being made by volunteers to withdraw them. Limber teams were collected for this purpose, in the rear donga.[42]

The Times History assigns some blame to Buller and Clery for the plight of the guns:

> Clery or Buller, by the naval guns, must have known the moment fire broke out that Long's batteries were engaged at close range with the Boer trenches, and ought either at once to have sent a galloper to order Long to withdraw his guns or to have accepted the situation and ordered Hildyard's and Barton's brigades to advance to the attack without delay. Buller's attention was, it would seem, at that moment absorbed by the infantry attack on the left which was just developing.[43]

By the time Buller had reached the donga from which Ogilvy's guns were firing and from where he could see Long's guns, he was angry, demoralised and in not inconsiderable pain; Pemberton considers that he 'was no longer capable of appraising the situation with coolness and reason. The site of the dozen forlorn guns without sign of their detachment seemed to have further stunned his faculties.'[44] Among the volunteers who came forward were Captain Walter Congreve, the press censor, his friend Lieutenant Freddie Roberts, the son of Lord Roberts and one of Clery's ADCs, Captain Schofield. They hooked two teams into the limbers and cantered towards the guns, Congreve watching as Roberts laughed 'and slapped his leg with his stick as though we were on the Mall at Peshawar again.'[45] As they neared the guns, both men were hit

41 Pakenham, *Boer War*, p. 231.
42 *Official History*, vol. I, p. 365.
43 *Times History*, vol. II, p. 443.
44 Pemberton, *Battles*, p. 137.
45 Pakenham, *Boer War*, p. 235.

but Schofield and a Corporal Nurse managed to hook onto two guns and bring them back to safety. Other attempts were made fruitlessly, until Buller, who had meanwhile remained in the donga, finally refused to allow any more.

Congreve had been wounded in the leg. He later described it as the most beastly day he had ever spent: 'no water, not a breath of air, and not a particle of shade and a sun which I have never felt hotter even in India.'[46] He found Freddie Roberts, unconscious, fatally wounded in the stomach and dragged him into a shelter. Subsequently, parties of Boers appeared and surrounded the donga in which they and a large number of wounded lay, including Long, Congreve and Roberts, as well as a group of men from the 2nd Devons. Among them was Colonel Bullock, their commanding officer and these, together with the unwounded gunners, were taken prisoner. The Boers allowed the injured to be brought back by the ambulance men. The courage of those that had engaged in the attempts to retrieve the guns was later recognised by the award of six Victoria Crosses.

Buller's distress at these events, coupled with his own wound and the exhaustion of long hours spent in the saddle, had combined to break his spirit:

> Utterly losing heart, indifferent to all consequences, and intent only on making an end of a miserable business, he decided to abandon the guns to the enemy and get back to camp. At 11.00 he sent word to Hildyard to tell the Queens and Devons to retire at once without waiting for the removal of the guns. Then, after ordering Ogilvy's naval guns to be withdrawn from the big donga, he rode off to the east to recall Dundonald.[47]

There had not been much success in the eastern sector either. Dundonald, with a mounted brigade that was not much more than 1,000 strong, with one battery, had been ordered to try to take up a position on Hlangwane, from where he would be able to enfilade the kopjes north of the iron bridge. Captain Birdwood, one of Dundonald's staff officers, reckoned that to carry out such an operation, 5,000 men supported by sufficient artillery would have been required.[48]

The 7th Battery which accompanied Dundonald's force had come into action as early as 6.00 a.m., firing on Fort Wylie and the other kopjes. At about 7.00 a.m. when Dundonald's main body reached a point some two miles from Hlangwane, scouts reported that the hill was occupied and the battery switched its fire to its south-western slopes at a range of between 2,000 and 2,600 yards. Dundonald pushed forward the South African Light Horse against the southern slope, while sending Thorneycroft's Regiment and the Composite Regiment to work round by the Gomba Spruit to the east. Thorneycroft advanced about a mile to the north-east, and then northwards through the bush, coming into contact with Boers dug in about 300 yards from the base of the hill. An attempt to advance further was prevented by another party of Boers which outflanked Thorneycroft from the ridge to the east, and he reported to Dundonald that he could make no further progress.[49]

Realising that he could get no further without infantry support, Dundonald rode back to Barton to ask for a battalion to assist him in carrying the hill. The orders which Barton had received for the 6th Brigade had been to move to a position where it could support the flank

46 Ibid., p. 237.
47 *Times History*, vol. II, p. 453.
48 Pemberton, *Battles*, p. 139.
49 *Official History*, vol. I, p. 368.

of the 2nd Brigade and if necessary, the mounted troops moving towards Hlangwane Hill. However, Barton had by now, received further orders not to commit his brigade and refused to support Dundonald with as much as a company; without support Dundonald could do no more than hang onto the lower slopes which his men had occupied. Pemberton is severely critical of Barton's lack of initiative: 'Strictly, Barton was in the right; but a general of a different calibre would not have hesitated to use such discretion which should be implicit in carrying out orders of that nature. By Barton's refusal the last chance of redeeming the day was lost.'[50]

Buller now arrived to see for himself the situation in this sector; he heard from Dundonald the latter's opinion that he could carry the hill with one or two battalions but from Barton, the view that the whole of his brigade would be needed to achieve this. Buller concluded that taking Hlangwane 'would be useless unless he had first forced the passage of the Tugela at Colenso, and of this he had already relinquished all hope.'[51] Accordingly, Buller ordered Dundonald to retire; when the latter protested, asking that his men should stay there until dusk, when they could fall back more safely, Buller refused, insisting that they must retire at once. He had no wish to prolong an unfortunate day longer than absolutely necessary.

In the centre, the retirement of Hildyard's brigade had gone relatively smoothly. Beginning at about 11.00 a.m., it was more or less complete by 2.00 pm. Some of the Devons had begged to be allowed to remain in Colenso village in the hope of recovering the guns after dark, but Buller's orders had been absolutely clear. However, either the order to retire had not reached Bullock and the party of 2nd Devons which accompanied him, or he declined to obey it, and as a result, he was taken prisoner with the abandoned gunners in the donga.

The retreat of Barton's 6th Brigade was largely uneventful, save for a group of Royal Scots Fusiliers which had at around noon, taken up a position in the donga behind Long's guns. The order to retire failed to reach them and they were also taken prisoner when the Boers surrounded the donga. This only occurred after the four 4.7 inch naval guns on Naval Gun Hill were withdrawn and the Boers felt able to cross the river. Thereafter, the Boers were able to limber up the guns and their ammunition wagons and take them back over the river. There was a moment when Dundonald, falling back with the 7th Battery, saw the Boers swarming round the guns, and was about to open fire on them, when it was seen that men in khaki from the British ambulances were among them, and it was impossible to fire, to the rage and frustration of Dundonald's officers.

In the western sector, the extrication of Hart's 5th Brigade had proved rather more complex. Lieutenant-Colonel Parsons had brought the 64th and 73rd Field Batteries over the Doornkop Spruit, closing up to the rear of the left of the brigade to a position from which he could fire over them. Here, he was only some 1,200 yards from the river, and came under enemy rifle fire, though suffering few casualties. His batteries, supported by the 4.7 inch naval guns, silenced the Boer artillery at this point. However, the difficulty of transmitting orders meant that the most advanced units of the 5th Brigade did not receive the order to retire until 10:30, and some men, fighting along the river bank, were cut off and unable to retire at all and were taken prisoner.[52] Gradually, however, the rest of the brigade retreated through the positions taken up by the men of Lyttelton's brigade, and were reformed and marched back to camp.

50 Pemberton, *Battles*, p. 141.
51 *Official History*, vol. I, p. 369.
52 Ibid., p. 374.

Across the river, Botha was frustrated. It had been his intention that the commandos who had been posted to the west of the loop should cross the river higher up and attack the flank of the 5th Brigade as it fell back. However, these commandos were Free Staters and declined to obey his order: 'But as, irrespective of the Irish Brigade, a cavalry regiment, two batteries, and two fresh battalions were available to repel any counter-attack, it was perhaps fortunate for the Boer Commandant General that his orders were disregarded.'[53]

Botha, although satisfied to have won a considerable victory, had another reason for disappointment, as he testified after the war. He had hoped to lure the British over the river without firing a shot,and having got them there in the open, destroy them. As it was, the rash advance of Long and his guns had the effect of obliging him to open fire, removing the opportunity of the comprehensive ambush he had in mind. Long had, ironically, saved Buller from a much more catastrophic defeat.

A large number of British war correspondents accompanied Buller's army, which ensured that British newspaper readers had a full and almost immediate, account of the battle, frequently written in highly coloured prose. Typical of these was Bennett Burleigh, the correspondent of the *Daily Telegraph*, who wrote of Colenso:

> Backwards and forwards wove the shuttle of death from the trenches covering the low ground and foot-hills and the walled crests across the Tugela. The enemy's lines were crowded with riflemen, and the flash and puff of musketry ran ever up and down their front. Our naval guns in the centre, helped now in a desultory way by others, hammered away at the Boer trenches. Five minutes after they opened with their rifles, the enemy's gunners followed suit with half a score of cannon. Our infantry and batteries were ploughed with 6 inch Creusot shells, lesser Krupps, and the aggravating rat-a-tat-tat of the one pounder Maxims and Hotchkiss machine-cannon. Ah! I should have added that, for it was part of the hurricane of iron and lead our infantry and gunners dauntlessly faced and advanced against. What wonder that all who saw the soldiers' heroism were enthusiastic in the admiration of Tommy![54]

British casualties during the battle amounted to a total of 1,139 officers and men, of whom 143 had been killed and 756 wounded, with 240 missing. Boer losses were six killed, one drowned and 22 wounded. The Official History mournfully remarked:

> The British commander's plan for the passage of the Tugela was undoubtedly so hazardous that only the most exact sequence of the phases of its execution, as conceived by Sir R. Buller, could have brought it to a successful issue. Imperfect knowledge of the topographical conditions of the problem, and of the dispositions of the enemy, combined with misapprehension of orders, sufficed to wreck it at the outset.[55]

As always, the Official History is extremely sparing of criticism. It has been left to other historians to examine more critically the failings which produced such an unfortunate outcome. Pemberton observes that of the many commentaries on Colenso, the briefest are the best; he

53 Ibid., pp. 370–371.
54 Rupert Furneaux, *News of War* (London: Max Parrish, 1964), p. 198.
55 *Official History*, vol. I, pp. 374–375.

cited the German Staff History, which recorded that 'the general and not his gallant force was defeated;' the comment by Leslie Renton: 'We all hammered our heads against a stone wall of which nobody knew anything;' and a Dublin Fusilier: 'Fight? Och, it was no fight at all, at all.'[56]

Buller, exhausted and depressed, had returned to camp at Chievely by 5.00 p.m. That evening he asked Stopford, rather than his servant, to assist him to undress: 'The shrapnel blow had left him black and blue from shoulder to loins, and he wanted no one else to know. Sixty-one years old, he had been on the go for thirty-six hours without a break, fourteen of them in the saddle.'[57] It was in this condition that he sat down to compose a report of the day's events.

56 Pemberton, *Battles*, p. 144.
57 Powell, *Buller*, p. 152.

15

Britain's Response

Weary and dispirited though he was, Buller wasted little time before sending his report to Lansdowne of the outcome of the battle. Overall it was a sober and reasonably measured account of what had occurred. He regretted, he said, to report a serious reverse. He described the plan of attack and its failure. Of the 5th Brigade's misadventures he wrote: 'Early in the day I saw that General Hart would not be able to force a passage and directed him to withdraw. He had, however, attacked with great gallantry.' He went on to describe the loss of the guns and the heroic efforts to rescue them. In a passage that the War Office censored he observed that it appeared that Long 'in his desire to be within effective range, advanced without any scouts or effective infantry supports close to the river.' He paid tribute to his men: 'The day was immensely hot and most trying to the troops whose conduct was excellent.'[1]

As the evening wore on, however, Buller's mood darkened. It was not only the grief and sadness over the events of the day which preyed on his mind. He was also nursing a considerable sense of grievance against Lansdowne over the latter's response to the news of Stormberg and Magersfontein, which had been to tell Buller that he should dismiss both Gatacre and Methuen. The latter was to be replaced by Lieutenant-General Charles Warren, the commander of the 5th Division, which was due to arrive at Cape Town in a few days. Buller had been expecting this as a reinforcement in Natal; he now assumed (incorrectly) that Lansdowne meant the division should go with Warren to the Modder River to take part in the relief of Kimberley. Buller was outraged at what appeared to be the deliberate overriding of his own advice. Without the 5th Division he did not think that the relief of Ladysmith was practicable.[2]

Considering his situation, Buller let his feelings of despair get the better of him, and at 11.15 p.m. he sent another telegram to Lansdowne that was to have immediate and far-reaching consequences:

> My failure today raises a serious question. I do not think I am now strong enough to relieve White. Colenso is a fortress, which I think, if not taken on a rush, could only be taken by a siege. There is no water within eight miles of the point of attack, and in this weather that exhausts infantry. The place is fully entrenched. I do not think either a Boer or a gun

1 Pakenham, *Boer War*, p. 238.
2 *Official History*, vol. I, p. 377.

> was seen by us all day, yet the fire brought to bear was very heavy. Our infantry were quite willing to fight, but were absolutely exhausted by the intense heat. My view is that I ought to let Ladysmith go, and occupy good positions for the defence of South Natal, and let time help. us. But that is a step. on which I ought to consult you. I consider we were in face of 20,000 men today. They had the advantage both in arms and in position. They admit they suffered severely, but my men have not seen a dead Boer, and that dispirits them. My losses have not been very heavy. I could have made them much heavier, but the result would have been the same. The moment I failed to get in with a rush, I was beat. I now feel that I cannot say I can relieve Ladysmith with my available force, and the best thing I can suggest is that I should occupy defensive positions and fight it out in a country better suited to our tactics.[3]

By the time that this reached London there had already been rapid developments. Buller's first telegram had reached the War Office in the early evening of Friday 15 December. At that time, Salisbury, still only slowly recovering from the grief of his wife's death, was at Hatfield and his nephew Arthur Balfour, as Deputy Prime Minister, was minding the store. He was dining with the editor of *The Spectator* when he was called to the War Office to receive the news of Buller's telegram. The shocking outcome of Colenso led Balfour and Lansdowne to an immediate conclusion; Buller must be replaced and this must be done without consulting either Wolseley, as commander-in-chief, or the Queen. They were in no doubt as to where they should look for a new supreme commander in South Africa.

Lord Roberts had been attentively watching the course of events in South Africa. He was certain that he should be sent to South Africa as commander-in-chief but for the moment bided his time. On 22 October he wrote to Lansdowne to express his satisfaction at the news of the battles of Talana Hill and Elandslaagte, while noting that 'White will have plenty to do during the next three weeks or so.' He ended his letter with the hope that all would go well with Buller and White, 'but if either should be incapacitated, I hope you will send me to South Africa.'[4]

As the situation developed, Roberts began to increase the pressure, writing to Lansdowne a week before Colenso, to review Butler's performance to date

> I am concerned at the very gloomy view Buller takes of the situation … As, I think, I have often remarked to you, it is impossible to gauge a general's qualities until he has been tried, and it is a remarkable fact that not a single commander in South Africa has ever held an independent command in the field. It is the feeling of responsibility which weighs down most men, and it seems clear, unless I am very much mistaken, it is having too frequent an effect on Buller. He seems to be overwhelmed by the magnitude of the task imposed upon him, and I confess that the tone of some of his telegrams causes me considerable alarm. From the day he landed in South Africa he seemed to take a pessimistic view of our position, and when a commander-in-chief allows himself to entertain evil forebodings, the effect is inevitably felt within the army. I feel the greatest hesitation and dislike in expressing my opinion thus plainly, and nothing but the gravity of the situation and the

3 Ibid.
4 Andre Wessels, *Lord Roberts and the War in South Africa* (Stroud: Army Records Society, 2000), pp. 13-14.

> strongest sense of duty would induce me to do so, or to offer – as I do now – to place my services at the disposal of the government.[5]

Four days later, he wrote to Brackenbury, with whom on the previous day, he had had a conversation about the wretched state of the army in respect of its stores and munitions. It was fortunate, he wrote, that Brackenbury had been able to gauge the depths of the shortcomings. He was sure that Lansdowne would support his recommendations but said that he was ready to help in any way.[6]

Lansdowne could not fail to have been impressed by Roberts' letter, which he was told to show to no one save Salisbury. As an analysis of Buller's state of mind, it was pretty accurate, though Roberts was quite wrong in suggesting that Buller's gloom was having a bad effect on his men; remarkably, in the immediate aftermath of Colenso, his troops' morale, and their belief in Buller as a commander, were entirely unshaken. John Atkins wrote of the withdrawal from Colenso that Buller had 'gained laurels from his defeat that are not always won by victorious generals … A weaker man, a less correct soldier, would have carried the position with an appalling loss of life. Buller's decision to retire was a proof of his bravery and good generalship.'[7]

Roberts' campaign designed to achieve his appointment as commander-in-chief in South Africa, now culminated in an outspoken telegram which he sent to Lansdowne on the morning of 15 December, following the news of Stormberg and Magersfontein. He clearly felt that now was the moment to strike. Pakenham describes its terms as being even more despondent than Buller's second telegram, but it appears that the Cabinet never even saw it. It read:

> Methuen cannot apparently force his way to Kimberley. He should therefore be ordered to withdraw to the Orange River without delay. Otherwise his line of communications will be cut and as he cannot have any large amount of supplies and ammunition he would have to surrender. Kimberley and Mafeking ought not to have been held after the Orange Free State declared against us, and though their being left to their fate now would be deeply regretted it seems unavoidable. Ladysmith also ought not to have been retained but as White's force especially the Artillery and Cavalry portion would not easily be replaced it should be relieved and to do this effectually Warren should be sent round with every available man. Meanwhile Buller should be ordered to act strictly on the defensive.[8]

The appointment of Roberts to the command seemed so obviously the correct response to the news of Buller's defeat that no alternative seems to have been considered. The decision was taken to send him without consulting Wolseley or the Queen because it was feared that objections might be raised by either of them. Early on the morning of 16 December, a telegram went to Roberts to tell him to prepare to go to South Africa. A meeting of the Cabinet's Defence Committee was arranged for later that afternoon. As the day wore on, Buller's second telegram arrived, the terms of which came as an even greater shock to Balfour and Lansdowne, and must have strongly reinforced their conviction that the decision that the Defence Committee would be asked to approve, was indeed correct.

5 Powell, *Buller*, pp. 156-157.
6 Wessels, *Lord Roberts*, pp. 16-17.
7 Pakenham, *Boer* War, p. 240.
8 Ibid. pp. 244-245.

It was at this point that a young unknown captain on the staff of the Intelligence Department found himself at the centre of the British government's decision-making process. After reading Buller's second telegram, Balfour put it in his pocket and made his way to Queen Anne's Gate, on the opposite side of St James's Park from the War Office, in order to discuss the position with Sir John Ardagh, the Director of Military Intelligence, in advance of the meeting of the Defence Committee. The latter was ill in bed, so it was to the 39-year-old Captain William Robertson that Balfour addressed himself, and from whom he sought advice.[9]

To Robertson, Balfour explained that he did not understand Buller's telegram:

> What puzzled the minister was that there should be any such great obstacle to the relief of Ladysmith as that implied by Buller's proposal to abandon the attempt. In his view the advantages of position seemed to be with us, seeing that Buller's force outside and White's force inside were together numerically superior to the Boer force in the middle; we were the nutcrackers and the Boers were the nut, and he could not understand why they should not be promptly and completely crushed.[10]

Robertson did his best to explain that while all very well in theory, such an operation was not as straightforward as it seemed:

> Its successful application demands not only considerable superiority, either in numbers or morale, but also perfect timing, good intercommunication, and great determination on the part of the exterior forces and their commanders, and these are the very essentials which, in the given circumstances, are the most difficult to ensure.[11]

Balfour was not wholly convinced, but when Robertson pointed out that Ladysmith had had only 60 days' supplies when first besieged some six weeks earlier and could not hold out long after the end of the year unless rations had been reduced, he observed 'that the prospect of the country having a happy New Year was not very bright.' Robertson told Balfour that Britain had, in Wolseley's words, 'committed one of the greatest blunders in war, namely, we have given the enemy the initiative.' However, Robertson went on to offer some more encouraging comments. There was, as yet no reason to accept Buller's suggestion to 'let Ladysmith go;' the town could probably hold out much longer than had been suggested and its surrender would be extremely serious. There was, Robertson said, a pressing need for a change in the high command, since Buller could not properly conduct operations over a front of 600 miles; he should either give up. the command in Natal so that he could effectively command the whole of the campaign, or be limited to Natal, someone else being appointed to the supreme command. By the time he left, Balfour had been more than sufficiently reassured that his first reaction had been correct.[12]

With Buller's second telegram before them, the members of the Defence Committee had no difficulty in endorsing the decision of Balfour and Lansdowne to appoint Roberts to the overall command. There was also the ticklish question of implementing that decision without first

9 Field Marshal Sir William Robertson, *From Private to Field Marshal* (London: Constable and Co., 1921), pp. 101-103.
10 Ibid., p. 101.
11 Ibid.
12 Ibid., p. 108.

consulting Wolseley and the Queen. The first had a long history of hostility towards Roberts and he would certainly object to his appointment. Isolating the Commander-in-Chief of the Army from such a decision was a grave step indeed. Nor could the decision to bypass the Queen be taken lightly; she was strongly pro-Buller, as was the general's good friend Sir Arthur Bigge, her Private Secretary. Nevertheless, the need to ensure the speedy appointment of Roberts so that he might set off for South Africa with the minimum of delay, satisfied the Defence Committee that it must sanction the immediate implementation of the appointment, even if it had been made after no more than a discussion with a junior staff captain. The events of Black Week had been bad enough; but the wording of Buller's second telegram was decisive.

Its tone demonstrated, all too clearly, that Buller had more or less completely lost his nerve; and the suggestion of letting Ladysmith go was shocking in the extreme. The use of this phrase was to haunt Buller in the years to come and he was, naturally, called upon to explain himself. By the time he came to testify before the Elgin Commission, he was able to contend, with every appearance of conviction, that it did *not* mean allowing Ladysmith to fall. It was, he said, 'a well understood expression.' He added: 'I think every soldier really understands it. I am sure that Sir Henry Norman would say the same thing – that 'let go' does not at all mean let fall.' To this, Sir Henry Norman, the military member of the Commission, felt able to say 'certainly.'[13]

Buller went on to explain his overall thinking at the time when he sent his second telegram: 'I had to consider what I had better do, should I attack Ladysmith again, or should I do what I thought would be a rather easy way of getting a certain amount of advantage against the Boers – should I attack Kimberley?' He added that he did not like himself to leave Natal because he thought it would have encouraged the Boers to attack Ladysmith.

In this, as in most of his evidence to the Commission, Buller found it hard to offer any consistent explanation for the messages that he sent. He made, in fact, an extremely poor witness, confused and at times, contradictory as he struggled to avoid the obvious inference that in the immediate aftermath of Colenso, he had lost his nerve completely. That this was clearly the case became even more apparent when the text of his heliographed message to White on the morning of 16 December is considered:

> I tried Colenso yesterday but failed. The enemy is too strong for my force except with siege operations which will take one full month to prepare. Can you last so long? Stop. If not, how many days can you give me to take up. defensive position, after which I suggest your firing away as much ammunition as you can, and making the best terms you can. Stop. I can remain here if you have alternative suggestions, but I unaided I cannot break in … Whatever happens, recollect to burn your cipher and decipher and codebooks and any deciphered messages.

There have been various versions of this telegram; Pakenham quotes most of it, while Amery offers a slightly different version, while saying that it represents the purport though not necessarily the exact wording.[14]

Buller was also understandably pressed by the Elgin Commission as to the meaning of this remarkable document and he had a good deal to say about it. It was not published, he said, as

13 Elgin Commission, *Minutes of Evidence*, vol. II, p. 202.
14 Pakenham, *Boer War*, p. 239; *Times History*, vol. II, p. 460.

he had sent it 'but published as it was said to have been deciphered.' It was followed by another heliographed message to White:

> I find I cannot take Colenso and I cannot stay in force there as there is no water, but I am leaving there as large a force as I can to help. you; but recollect that in this weather my infantry cannot be depended on to march more than ten miles a day. Can you suggest anything for me to do? I think I could take Colenso but I can never get to Onderbrook,[15]

Long after the war, Buller would put forward a number of explanations for a telegram that he was obliged to admit to the Elgin Commission was 'stupid.' However, all that lay in the future. Now, in December 1899, his hasty and intemperate reaction to the defeat at Colenso had led to immediate consequences. When Salisbury learnt of the decision by the Defence Committee that Roberts should be appointed as commander-in-chief, he considered him too old for the post and insisted that Kitchener be appointed as his chief of staff.

The decision of the Defence Committee that the appointment be implemented without reference to either Wolseley or the Queen was described by Julian Symons as unthinkable:

> 'Nothing shows the government's distrust of the War Office and their fear of Wolseley better than the fact that they not only thought of the unthinkable, but actually did it, feeling no doubt that if they consulted Wolseley and then rejected his advice, they would be flying too obviously in the face of accepted military authority.'[16]

Wolseley's feelings were much aroused at this time. On that Sunday morning, still unaware of what had taken place at the meeting of the Defence Committee, he had had a serious row with Lansdowne, asserting that he had started a system at the War Office that was impossible for war, and would break down. When later Sir Arthur Bigge came to him from the Queen (who, having heard of it, did not at all approve of the appointment of Roberts) and asked Wolseley if he had been at the Defence Committee meeting; he said that he had not been asked to attend. Bigge did not at that time, tell him what had been decided and when he did hear from Lansdowne on Sunday afternoon of the decisions taken, Wolseley was taken utterly aback:

> He sent for me to say that the Cabinet yesterday decided to send out Lord Roberts as C-in-C to South Africa, with Kitchener as his Chief of Staff. He had previously given me no inkling of this, although I had seen him yesterday after the Cabinet, and this morning ... I was nearly struck dumb and said I thought it was a very unwise decision and that in my mind and according to my opinion Buller was much the abler soldier of the two and that of course he would resign ... What a set of people to serve.[17]

The government's response to Buller's telegrams came in a series of messages. The first, on 16 December read: 'Her Majesty's Government regard the abandonment of White's force and its consequent surrender as a national disaster of the greatest magnitude. We would urge you to devise another attempt to carry out its relief, not necessarily via Colenso, making use of the

15 Elgin Commission, *Minutes of Evidence*, vol. II, p. 206.
16 Symons, *Campaign*, p. 174.
17 Ibid., pp, 174-175.

additional men now arriving, if you think fit.'[18] To this, Buller replied briefly that this was what he wanted and that he had been in some doubt as to what weight he should attach to financial considerations at Kimberley. The next message he received, on 18 December, however, was less welcome:

> In Natal and Cape Colony distinct operations of very great importance are now in progress. The prosecution of the campaign in Natal is being carried on under quite unexpected difficulties, and in the opinion of Her Majesty's Government it will require your presence and whole attention. It has been decided by Her Majesty's Government under these circumstances to appoint Field Marshal Lord Roberts as Commanding in Chief, South Africa, his Chief of Staff being Lord Kitchener.[19]

Wolseley's prediction that Buller would resign proved incorrect. Instead, he expressed his feelings on the appointment of Roberts in a letter to his wife that same day:

> Just as I was writing to you an unpleasant surprise has supervened. A telegram has come to say that Lord Roberts is appointed C-in-C, and I am relegated to the command in Natal. I have expected this. Two days after I arrived here they ordered me to supersede Sir George White, and I would not, they then later ordered me to supersede Gatacre and I would not, and then Methuen and I would not, so now they have superseded me. I honestly confess I am not sorry, though I fear you will be disappointed. Personally I think they are right, this show is too big for one man, it is impossible for me to run this place and look after the Cape, which is a thousand miles away. [20]

Kitchener readily accepted the post of chief of staff, leaving Khartoum on 18 December, reaching Gibraltar eight days later where he was able to board the *Dunottar Castle* carrying Roberts to South Africa. While he was in transit, Lord Cromer, the British Consul General and de facto ruler of Egypt, telegraphed London that Kitchener wished to be given 'local rank senior to the other generals of whom I gathered he had a somewhat low opinion ... He seemed to attach so much importance to the point that I thought I had better let you know.' Jealousy of Kitchener was, however, still too strong to permit this; but Roberts agreed that he would not act as a chief of staff but would effectively serve as second-in-command.[21]

The decision to appoint Roberts without consulting the Queen naturally had not gone down well at Windsor, as Bigge made clear. Balfour went down to see the Queen and was able to smooth things over without undue difficulty. He found her in a determined frame of mind: 'We are not interested in the possibilities of defeat,' she said. Speaking to Bigge of the failure to consult Wolseley, Balfour was entirely candid: 'It was impossible to consult the commander-in-chief upon such an appointment, as his well-known jealousy of Roberts made his advice on such a subject perfectly worthless.'[22]

18 *Official History*, vol. I, p. 379.
19 Elgin Commission, *Appendices*, p. 342.
20 Powell, *Buller*, p. 155.
21 Sir Philip. Magnus, Kitchener: *Portrait of an Imperialist* (London: John Murray 1958), p. 158.
22 Halik Kochanski, *Sir Garnet Wolseley: Victorian Hero* (London: The Hambledon Press 1999), pp. 245-246.

Meanwhile Roberts, who had been put on notice on 17 December, made his way to London. Arriving there on the following morning, he went to meet with Lansdowne. News had since come in of the death of Freddy Roberts and Lansdowne had the painful duty of breaking the news to his father. He later described Roberts' response: 'The blow was almost more than he could bear, and for a moment I thought he would break down, but he pulled himself together. I shall never forget the courage which he showed.'[23]

Prior to departing for South Africa, Roberts went down to Windsor for an audience with the Queen. When she spoke of his son, he said: 'I cannot speak of that, but I can of anything else.' He spent the next few days recruiting those officers he particularly wanted to serve on his staff. They included Colonel William Nicholson, serving in India, who would act first as his military secretary and then as Director of Transport; and Roberts' personal friend Colonel George Henderson, the distinguished military historian who was a professor of strategy and tactics at the Staff College, who would be Director of Intelligence.

Roberts naturally also went to see Wolseley; it was a meeting that could not fail to be uncomfortable for each of them, but they were both on their best behaviour, and it passed off reasonably well, as Wolseley wrote to his wife:

> I was as 'gushing' as possible to him, so much so that he told Lansdowne afterwards I had been most cordial. He said, 'the one unpleasant thought he had in going was that it must naturally have been a great disappointment as his senior not to have been sent.' My ready answer was, 'I never expected to be asked,' which was quite true. But, added I, the man I was sorry for was Buller. However, we parted the best of friends, and I said everything that was nice to him, both officially, and on account of his sad loss in our last battle.[24]

The response of the British Press to Black Week generally was one of determination to overcome the military setbacks and to see the war through to a successful conclusion. *The Times* wrote on 18 December:

> The serious repulse of Sir Redvers Buller on the Tugela closely following the terrible reverse experienced by the Highland Brigade at Magersfontein and the disaster to a portion of General Gatacre's command, has gravely compromised the military situation. This is not the time for disseminating criticism, or for imputing blame to individuals. We have only to deal with the facts in so far as they appear in the official despatch.
>
> It is idle now to analyse the causes which have led, through a series of humiliating circumstances, to the present most unfortunate position. It is more satisfactory to turn, with a sense of relief, to the measures which the government, now awakened to the emergency, is determined to take, and which will be found embodied in an official announcement printed this morning. These measures are comprehensive, and their adoption will be hailed with satisfaction, more especially by the auxiliary colonial forces concerned.
>
> If these measures are taken swiftly and in a practical manner, as they doubtless will be, there is reason to hope that they will meet the requirements of an emergency which it is scarcely possible to take too seriously. Neither the Crimean War nor the Indian Mutiny

23 Pakenham, *Boer War*, p. 246.
24 Symons, *Campaign*, p. 176.

> gave rise to greater danger to the Empire than that with which we are now menaced … We stand united in firm determination to uphold our Empire at all costs. The responsibility of giving practical and effective expression to the will of the nation rests with the government.[25]

Three days later, the paper reiterated its confidence in the ultimate outcome:

> The nation is rising to meet the emergency, and the unity of the Empire is assuming the most practical form. The after-effects of this great movement will be far-reaching. Adversity has its uses, and even our bitterest foreign critics will not fail to recognise that we remain, as we have always been, essentially a fighting people, that prosperity has not enfeebled our manhood, and that we can show a strong and united front to misfortune.[26]

When on 23 December Roberts left London to board the *Dunottar Castle* at Southampton, *The Times* saw him off as a 'little, vigorous, resolute, sorrowful man in deep. mourning.'[27]

There is a glimpse of the view of the situation taken by members of the government in a letter which Selborne wrote to Curzon on that day:

> The present position is humiliating and unpleasant to the last degree, but I treat it philosophically. If there have to be two laughs, one at the beginning and one at the end of the war, well I prefer that my enemies should enjoy the former. There is much to be remembered for our future benefit and use. The first cause I have already hinted at to you. Want of a concentrated foreseeing grip. of the situation at home. Each department went its own way and the Cabinet as a whole neglected Milner's warnings about the military danger. If we had had a C-in-C at home in full vigour and authority he could have grasped the military position from the beginning and guided the Cabinet in insisting on proper military dispositions. But I need not tell you that the Wolseley of today did nothing of the kind. How different had he been the Wolseley of ten years ago![28]

This judgement on Wolseley was hardly fair, since he had come up. against real resistance from Lansdowne in the months before the war, but it reflected a widely held view. Wolseley was a convenient scapegoat for the troubles which the government had brought on itself.

Selborne ended his letter on an upbeat note: 'That the resolution of the nation is unshaken and unshakeable, that we shall win in the long run, by the mercy of God, I do not for a moment doubt.' He believed, he said, that the nation 'would emerge from this ordeal, chastened indeed, but stronger and more united.'

In this opinion, Selborne was entirely correct. The popular response to Black Week was entirely positive:

> There was no hysterical outcry, no witch-hunt. No one stridently proclaimed that some at least of the blame might be laid at the doors of ministries and politicians who wanted an

25 *The Times*, 18 December 1899.
26 Ibid., 21 December 1899.
27 Symons, *Campaign*, p. 176.
28 Boyce, *Crisis*, p. 98.

> Empire on the cheap, who loved to see red splashed on a world map. but strenuously opposed any increase in the estimates, designed to raise military efficiency and preparedness.[29]

The events of Black Week, and the appointment of Roberts and Kitchener 'were the signals for a great spontaneous effort on the part of the nation, spontaneous in the sense that it received acquiescence rather than encouragement from the Government.'[30] These sentiments were echoed by Amery, in *The Times History*, when he wrote: 'If the nation had been indifferent to the need for military efficiency it was not indifferent to the demands of patriotism. Its reverses, instead of proving it soft and without spirit, as its enemies confidently hoped, only brought out its highest qualities, its sober judgement and its unwavering resolution.'[31]

Important in fostering this national unity and confidence in the war's outcome was the attitude of the Liberal Opposition, whose leaders responded to Black Week with speeches that were in general, supportive of the government. The Leader of the Opposition, Sir Henry Campbell-Bannerman, had been hostile to Chamberlain and to the part he and Milner had played in bringing about the war. Now, on 20 December, he spoke in Aberdeen in terms which were comforting to the government: 'The end cannot be doubted. We have in the field the largest army that ever left these shores. It can readily be reinforced. We have a united people in the country and in every part of the Empire, and with these forces on our side – moral and material – success is certain.'[32] The reference to the Empire reflected the remarkable response from the British white dominions, in each of which a strong feeling of colonial patriotism had rapidly developed and from whose governments came immediate and generous offers of military support. This contrasted with the reaction on the Continent of Europe to Britain's war against the Boers, where the Press of all the major powers was almost unanimously anti-British.

It was at this point that there came before the government a document that revealed vividly, just how grave were the deficiencies in Britain's war machine. In February 1899, General Sir Henry Brackenbury had been appointed as Director General of the Ordnance. He had been the choice of Wolseley and had been a prominent member of the 'Ashanti Ring,' but was widely regarded as a man of outstanding ability, not least by Lansdowne who readily supported his appointment. Although Brackenbury had not held any senior command in the field, he enjoyed a high reputation and had held a number of important administrative posts. He had been appointed with a brief to review the processes of the Ordnance Department. This was responsible for equipment, stores, weapons, munitions and production facilities, and it had become apparent that all was not well in the way the Department was operating. Now, his report exposed shortcomings of the utmost gravity, many of which were due to a sustained policy of false economy on the part of successive governments. These shortcomings had undoubtedly, contributed to the poor start that the army had made in the South African War. Brackenbury found that the Department was totally unprepared for war and in particular, had virtually non-existent reserves of equipment.[33]

The reforms for which Brackenbury now called for were likely to be extremely expensive; they were strongly opposed by Hicks Beach, the Chancellor of the Exchequer. Brackenbury made

29 Pemberton, *Battles*, p. 146.
30 Symons, *Campaign*, p. 175.
31 *Times History*, vol. II, p. 466.
32 Pakenham, *Boer War*, p. 248.
33 Christopher Brice, *Brackenbury: The Thinking Man's Soldier* (Solihull: Helion and Co., 2012) pp. 242-243.

clear that if they were not implemented, his resignation would be on Lansdowne's desk. At this particular juncture, in the sensitive state of public opinion, a crisis of this kind was something that the government could do without. Hicks Beach arranged for the issue to be referred to a committee under Sir Francis Mowatt. This, perhaps unexpectedly, came down foursquare in support of Brackenbury's proposals, which were costed at a total of over £11.6 million.[34]

Wolseley had been prompted by events to demand of Lansdowne on 14 December that substantial reinforcements be sent to South Africa, telling him: 'We are face to face with a serious national crisis, and unless we meet it boldly ... [It will] lead to dangerous complications with Foreign Powers.'[35] He called for the immediate mobilisation of the 7th and 8th Divisions and for the acceptance of civilian volunteers; these proposals would produce a reinforcement of some 45,000 men.

Another reaction to the events of Black Week was the government's response to a telegram which Buller sent on the day after Colenso: 'Would it be possible for you to raise 8,000 irregulars in England. They should be equipped as mounted infantry, be able to shoot as well as possible and ride decently. I would amalgamate them with colonials.'[36] George Wyndham, the junior minister at the War Office, took up. the idea, which was immediately carried forward by the establishment of the Imperial Yeomanry, which caught the imagination of the Press and the public. Large numbers of volunteers came forward to join the new force. Wolseley, however, did not respond favourably, writing on 28 December:

> I am very anxious to supply the GOC in South Africa with 8,000 trained men accustomed to some sort of discipline; but to go to the highways and byways and pick up. any civilians who will volunteer to go to South Africa quite regardless of whether they have ever learnt even the rudiments of discipline, and to form them into companies or battalions is, according to my knowledge of war, a dangerous experiment.[37]

By now, however, Wolseley's influence was in steady decline, and the scheme went ahead despite his objections.

34 Ibid., p. 251.
35 Pakenham, *Boer War*, p. 252.
36 Ibid.
37 Kochanski, *Wolseley*, p. 251.

16

Warren

In the immediate aftermath of Colenso, Botha sent a message reporting the outcome of the battle to Kruger:

> The Lord of our fathers has today given us a brilliant victory. We have repulsed the enemy on all sides, at three different points. We allowed them, under violent bombardment from their side to advance 12 guns up to a point very near to the river. As soon as these were unlimbered we opened fire with our Mausers, killing the gunners and disorganising them to such an extent that they only succeeded in recovering two of their guns ... With a thankful heart I can congratulate you and the Afrikaner people on this brilliant victory.[1]

It had been, indeed, a brilliant victory; but it raised the question of how to make the best use of it. Black Week may have lifted Boer morale enormously but one result of it was unquestionable; Britain's government and its people were even more resolved than before to see the war through to ultimate victory. This meant that Boer victories, however dazzling, would, in the end, be 'Dead Sea fruit'. However, the only alternative strategy to an immediate offensive was one of attrition. Against an enemy with overwhelming resources, this ultimately, must fail unless that enemy's determination crumbled and in December 1899, there was no prospect that it would.

Additionally, Kruger's attempts to follow up the successes of Black Week met with realistic resistance from his generals. Cronje firmly rejected Kruger's suggestions, both for a raid on Methuen's communications and for a direct attack on the British at Modder River. Botha, though always offensively minded like most of the younger Boer leaders, responded on 17 December in a similar manner to Kruger's suggestion of smiting the enemy 'while the terror is so great in their hearts.' He pointed out that 'there are no hills [around Buller's camp at Frere] nor the least cover between us and the enemy and I am afraid to undertake something which, if it goes wrong, will hearten the enemy.'[2] The truth was that the Boers, at the end of 1899, had no exit strategy, other than to hang on, win battles when necessary and hope that British exhaustion would bring her to the conference table. That, in the existing situation, was never going to happen.

1 S.B. Bourquin and Gilbert Torlage, *The Battle of Colenso* (Randburg: Ravan Press 1999) p. 33.
2 Pakenham, *Boer War*, p. 257.

For the moment, therefore, the policy would be to stand on the defensive, as Joubert – temporarily returned to duty – made clear in a circular letter dated 29 December. In this, he predicted that Buller would attempt to win a successful battle before his successor could arrive, as Colley had done two decades earlier. For this reason, they must be on their guard against such an action. In particular, attention should be paid to organising outpost duty properly. He concluded his letter:

> Therefore, let the words of our Lord be impressed on the mind of everyone: 'Watch and pray, lest ye enter into temptation.' Our enemy is not only powerful, but also artful, and treason is continually taking place, for it appears from the newspapers that the enemy is even cognisant of our most secret plans, and we cannot advance, but remain stationary, while the enemy is continually strengthening himself.[3]

Notwithstanding this, at Kruger's urging, a *krigsraad* decided against Joubert's advice that an attempt should be made to storm the defences of Ladysmith. Due to the crucial importance of maintaining a strong force in the Tugela position, only 4,000 men were available for the attack, which was directed at the Platrand, an eminence to the south of the town, running from Wagon Hill to Caesar's Camp. The assault was launched in the early hours of 6 January; it fell on a position commanded by Colonel Ian Hamilton who had, regrettably, failed to prepare it adequately for defence. His force suffered heavy casualties during a battle which lasted until late afternoon, in the course of which the Boers came very close to success; had they been able to take the Platrand, they would have had the key to Ladysmith in their hands:

> The peril, the anxiety, and the magnitude of the issues at stake are not to be measured by the mere numbers engaged, or the length of the casualty list. Had the plateau remained in the enemy's possession the fall of Ladysmith would have been possible at any moment. The enemy, greatly encouraged, would not have guarded feebly their acquisition.[4]

British casualties amounted to 168 killed and 249 wounded; the Boers recorded losses of 64 killed and 119 wounded, although the actual total may have been somewhat higher. The British loss in killed was in fact, higher than at Colenso and in proportion to wounded, was more than three times as high due to the difference between the effect of long-range firing in the open and short range firing among rocks.[5] The failure of the assault seemed to support those Boer leaders who argued against an offensive policy. At any rate, thereafter, on neither side at Ladysmith was there much appetite for a great deal in the way of action.

On the Tugela, Botha would remain on the defensive and it would be Buller who made the next move there. Since Colenso and his receipt of the government's immediate and explicit instruction that he should make another attempt to relieve Ladysmith, he had been reviewing the alternatives open to him. He had soon recovered from the black despair which had led to his sending his unfortunate messages. His rapidly improving morale was buoyed up by the unbroken confidence in his abilities felt by his men. He reported to Lansdowne that when his reinforcements arrived, he would attempt to relieve Ladysmith by short stages.

3 *Official History*. vol. I, pp. 425-427.
4 Ibid., pp. 569-570.
5 *Times History*, vol. III, p. 202.

Mindful of the fact that Roberts was on his way, Buller prepared a memorandum for him on 28 December to await his arrival, summarising his views of the situation:

> The whole Tugela River is a strong position; there is no question of turning it; the only open question is whether one part of it is easier to get through than another. I tried Colenso, because, though unaided I could not have forced the defile north of Colenso, it was the only place in the whole line in which Sir George White's force could aid me in my advance from the Tugela. I am now waiting for reinforcements, and I am going to try and force a passage at Potgieter's Drift. If I can find water to use in the subsequent advance, I think I ought to just pull through; but the difficulties are very great. If I succeed, it should be about 12 January, and if then I join hands with Sir G. White, I think together we shall be able to force the enemy to retire and so free Sir G. White's force.[6]

Thereafter, Buller wrote, he would relieve Kimberley and then advance on Bloemfontein. He reckoned that time was in their favour and that in Cape Colony, when the 7th Division arrived from England, the disaffected Dutch would go back to their homes.

On his way to South Africa. Roberts had made clear to Buller that he considered it best for the moment to stand on the defensive: 'Although I should be delighted to hear of your joining hands with White, still the status quo until the 6th Division has landed does not seem to me to be altogether undesirable.'[7]

On 10 January, unmoved by Roberts's suggestions, Buller reported that he was leaving Chieveley on the following day, with the intention of operating towards Ladysmith via either Potgieter's Drift or Trickhardt's Drift, some five miles further up river. Reading this, Roberts still felt – as he later told the Elgin Commission – that it would have been better to delay the move a little longer.[8] However, he felt he was not in a position to judge how far Buller was committed or whether an immediate move was necessary, so he left Buller with a free hand and turned his attention to the operations to relieve Kimberley, which he decided had become immediately necessary.

Now that he was to have the bulk of the 5th Division to reinforce his advance, Buller had begun planning the westward move of his army. His intention was that this division would play a key role in the operation which he had in mind, led by its commander, Lieutenant-General Sir Charles Warren. The latter had had a somewhat unusual career. Born in 1840, he was commissioned as a second lieutenant in the Royal Engineers at the age of 17. During the 1860s, he was engaged for years in surveying Gibraltar; then, in 1867, he joined a team undertaking archaeological research in the Holy Land, later publishing a number of books on the subject. After his return to military duties, he went on to command a mounted force in the Transkei war of 1877–1878 and later, led a military expedition to Bechuanaland. In 1886, he was appointed as Commissioner of the Metropolitan Police. His term of office was extremely controversial and he resigned in1888 following extensive public criticism. Returning to the army, he served for five years in Singapore, during which he had a very quarrelsome relationship with the governor.

6 *Official History*. vol. I, p. 410.
7 Symons, *Campaign*, p. 192.
8 Elgin Commission, *Minutes of Evidence*, vol. I, p. 461.

Then, back in the United Kingdom, he was appointed to the command of the Thames District, serving there until he went on the reserve list with the rank of lieutenant general.[9]

On the outbreak of war, Warren wrote to Wolseley to ask if he could help in any capacity, which led to his appointment to command the 5th Division when it was mobilised. This was generally regarded as a surprise, since he was noted for tactlessness, intolerance of criticism and for an extremely short temper. Julian Symons wrote that it was 'easier to understand than excuse the appointment,' noting that Warren was a man whom Wolseley knew, and who was one of his own generation: 'It was one of Wolseley's most unfortunate weaknesses in old age that he could never wholeheartedly accept the worth of the younger generals like Kitchener, but clung to those who had made their reputations in his own shadow.'[10]

Another reason why Warren's appointment was unwise was that he was distrusted and disliked by Buller, feelings which were enhanced when Buller learned that Warren had been entrusted with a Dormant Commission to succeed him in the event that he was killed or wounded. This was a decision taken by Lansdowne and Wolseley while Warren was on his way to South Africa; he learnt of it in a letter from Wolseley in which the latter wrote: 'I look to Sir Redvers Buller and you to put an end to this folly. Our men and Regimental Officers have done splendidly. Our generals have been our weak point.'[11]

During his voyage round from Cape Town to Durban, Warren and his staff had devoted themselves to a study of the situation along the Tugela, playing a series of war games to decide what would be the best approach. Warren noted in his diary that 'there was a general conclusion that the route by Hlangwane was the most passable, but it was not taken in the exercises because General Buller had given it up, and it was therefore assumed that there must be some unknown difficulty that way.'[12] When Warren reached Frere on 26 December and met with Buller, he found the commander-in-chief 'rather reserved.' In his diary, he suggested that the series of reverses suffered by Buller and the loss of the guns, 'might well alter a man for a while.' He felt that he could not say what he wanted that night, so it was arranged to continue their discussion next day.[13]

When he heard of the plan to move westward to attack the line of the Tugela, Warren suggested that an assault on Hlangwane might be better; Buller's response was to ask him curtly what he knew about it, clearly resenting 'the coming of this smug, self-assured second-in-command, ready and no doubt anxious to step into his shoes.'[14] Warren mournfully recorded that there was a fundamental difference between them which had existed for years: 'He prefers to work in open country, where the Boers can pick you off at 2,000 yards … I prefer situations where our moderate ranged vision can be of more service, such as those of mountain warfare and bush fighting. It is just these two kinds of fighting that General Buller detests. I know it of old.'[15]

Buller issued his detailed orders for the westward move of his army on 8 January. With the reinforcements which he had received, he now had of the order of 30,000 men under command and he proposed to move west with some 23,000, shifting his centre of operations from Colenso

9 Symons, *Campaign*, pp. 178-171.
10 Ibid., p. 182.
11 Symons, *Campaign*, p. 183.
12 Ibid., p. 185.
13 Coetzer, *Infamy*, p. 114.
14 Pemberton, *Battles*, p. 149.
15 Coetzer, *Infamy*, pp. 114-115.

to Springfield, from where he planned to launch his attack on the Boer position on the Tugela. In *The Times History*, Amery had this to say about the proposed operation:

> But the fact is that what Buller had in view was not a flank march at all, but that entirely different thing, a march to a flank preparatory to a subsequent frontal attack. For it is not the direction on the map that constitutes a flank march, but the surprising of the enemy's flank before he can take up a new front. In Buller's plan this essential element of surprise was entirely lacking. There was no attempt to conceal the movement, none to delude the enemy by skilful feinting, none to outwit him by rapidity of movement. How little Buller troubled about mobility was shown by the enormous transport, which included tents and other disposable luxuries, and by the fact that 600 mounted men, nearly a quarter of the whole mounted force, were left with the garrisons at Chieveley and Frere.[16]

The Official History, on the other hand, as usual offers no criticism of Buller's plan or of his ponderous moves to get into position to execute it; but it is difficult not to concur in Amery's view. Although Botha only gradually began to build up his strength at the western end of his line, he had every opportunity to monitor Buller's movements and to prepare to meet the anticipated attack.

The plan for the move was that Clery, with the 2nd Division, would move out during the early hours of 10 January, while Warren with the 5th Division, would follow on the evening of that day. The order specified in great detail the ammunition, equipment and supplies to be taken and the medical arrangements. The columns, when they set off, were immensely long, and of course, entirely visible to the Boers on the other side of the Tugela. The conditions for the march were extremely unpleasant, as one of the war correspondents with Warren's division described:

> The rain came through the still air in a steady, teeming, straight downpour that threshed in one's ears. I wore an oilskin coat, but it was useless; the rain found available chinks or else beat its way through. The hills seem to melt down like tallow under heat; the rain beat the earth into liquid, and the thick, dark earthy liquid ran down in terraced cascades. From Estcourt to Frere the division waded, sliding, sucking, pumping, gurgling through the mud; the horses floundered or tobogganed, with all four feet together; the wagons lurched axle deep into heavy sloughs and had to be dragged out with trebled teams of oxen.[17]

Dundonald, with his mounted brigade, had ridden on ahead, entering Springfield early in the afternoon of 10 December, finding the place unoccupied. His scouts reported no contact with the enemy and he took the opportunity to seize Mount Alice and Spearman's Hill, which dominated Potgieter's Drift from the southern side of the Tugela. Early on the following morning, pursuant to orders which Buller had issued on 9 January, Hildyard advanced to the Tugela in an effort 'to induce the enemy to believe that our intention is to cross the River Tugela at Porrit's Drift.'[18] This move failed to draw any reaction from the Boers and by noon, Hildyard had returned to the camp established at Pretorius Farm. Dundonald, meanwhile, had succeeded in

16 *Times History*, vol. III, pp. 209-210.
17 Symons, *Campaign*, p. 194.
18 *Official History*, vol. II, p. 619.

capturing the ferry at Potgieter's Drift, when a party of swimmers crossed the river and brought it to the south bank in face of heavy enemy rifle fire.

By the afternoon of 12 January, the 4th Brigade had moved into a position close to Spearman's Hill and on the following day, two 4.7 inch naval guns were established there, ensuring that the drift was safe. Buller took the opportunity to ride up to Mount Alice to see what he could of the Boer defences. There, he found Winston Churchill, to whom he had given a temporary commission but who continued also to serve as a war correspondent. They could see that the projected operation was not going to be straightforward:

> The ground fell almost sheer six hundred feet to the flat bottom of the valley. Beneath, the Tugela curled along like a brown and very sinuous serpent. Never have I seen such violent twists and bends in a river. At times the waters seemed to loop back on themselves. One great loop bent towards us, and there the arch of this the little ferry of Potgieter's floated, moored to ropes which looked through the field glasses like a spider's web. The ford, approached by roads cut down through the steep bank, was beside it, but closed for the time being by the flood. The loop of river enclosed a great tongue of land which jutted from the hills on the enemy side almost to our feet. A thousand yards from the tip of this tongue rose a line of low kopjes crowned with reddish stones.[19]

Returning to Springfield, Buller issued a Special Order to his troops; the army was now advancing to the relief of Ladysmith and must be successful. The enemy, he told them, was clever and unscrupulous and would try to deceive them. Above all, if surprised by a sudden volley, there must be no hesitation: 'Do not turn from it, but rush at it. That is the road to victory and safety.' He concluded with a stirring call to his men: 'Let us bear ourselves as our cause deserves.'[20]

19 Winston S. Churchill, *The Boer War* (London: Octopus Publishing Group Plc, 1990), p. 117.
20 *Official History*, vol. II, pp. 623-624.

17

Spion Kop

The process of completing the army's movement went on under the watchful eyes of the Boers, who began to build up their own strength on the northern heights, particularly opposite Potgieter's Drift. It was a slow process and gave the Boers plenty of opportunity to prepare for the assault which was obviously imminent. For his part, Buller's observation of the position led him to conclude that the enemy's position at Potgieter's Drift was too strong to be taken by direct assault and next day, he telegraphed his revised intentions to Lansdowne. After describing the topography of the position, he wrote that 'the enemy's flanks are unassailable; their defences are in two and three lines, the second line being out of sight of the plain with eight guns. This position I do not think we can force.' He went on:

> I propose that Warren – taking 36 guns, field artillery, three brigades, and 1,500 mounted men – shall cross five miles to the west at Trickhardt's Drift; the mountain which forms right flank of enemy's defence will be turned by his advance, while we do the best we can here with one brigade and three battalions, howitzer battery and Naval guns. He agrees to this, but as he can only take supplies for three days, and I will have to march not less than 15 miles from the river, and as he will have difficulty in obtaining water, the operation is undoubtedly risky. But this is the only possible chance for Ladysmith, where supplies are running short, and the sick list is already over 2,000.[1]

Buller sent a message to White to tell him of his new plan. He was confident that Warren would encounter little resistance as he moved against the right of the enemy's position, which he took to end at Bastion Hill, above Venter's Spruit. This, Buller believed, was only weakly held; he estimated that there were no more than 400 men between Bastion Hill and Brakfontein. The Intelligence Department did receive a report of 16 January that a 'general move westward' was in progress, which can hardly have come as a surprise, but that 'there seemed to be nothing to show that the strength of the enemy so far to the west of Trickhardt's Drift was being much increased.'[2] The problem for the British was the impossibility of carrying out any effective reconnaissance of the Boer positions, other than what could be seen with the

1 *Official History*, vol. II, pp. 623-624.
2 Ibid., p. 347.

telescope. On 15 January, Buller rode to a point where on the previous day Captain Hubert Gough, Dundonald's intelligence officer, had seen parties of the enemy apparently engaged in building gun emplacements between Bastion Hill and Spion Kop. Buller, who was accompanied by Gough on his ride, saw nothing to prompt any change in his plan.

Later that day, he issued his secret orders to Warren. Since the enemy position at Potgieter's Drift was too strong to take by direct attack, he proposed to turn it by sending a force across the river at Trickhardt's Drift and up to the west of Spion Kop. Warren would have under his command, Dundonald's mounted brigade, six batteries of field artillery, Clery's 2nd Division, comprising the 2nd Brigade (Hildyard) and 5th Brigade (Hart) and Woodgate's 11th Brigade. All told, Warren would be in command of a force of 15,382 men, with 36 guns and 14 machine guns.[3] Buller explained that his idea was that Warren should, throughout his advance, refuse his right but throw his left forward until he should gain the open plain north of Spion Kop. From there, Buller reckoned Warren would command the rear of the Boer position at Potgieter's Drift, rendering it untenable. He reiterated his belief that Warren would encounter no more than 400 men on his left. Perhaps remembering the problems with guides at Colenso, he sent as a guide, a Devonshire man who had been employed on one of his own farms: 'He is English to the backbone and can be thoroughly trusted.'[4]

With the evident lack of a common understanding between him and Warren, it is astonishing that, in his plans for the coming offensive, Buller would put the conduct of the operation effectively in Warren's hands. Pakenham put the question bluntly: 'Why give Warren – a general who was quite untried in the conditions of the new warfare, and a man with whom Buller found personal relations so painful – why give him the bigger army and the bulk of the work?' Buller never gave an answer publicly to a question that has baffled historians, and Pakenham quotes a remark he made several years later: 'Warren had an easy task, merely to shoulder the Boers off his left; but I reserved to myself the difficult task, viz that of thrusting in my best [Lyttelton's] brigade when Warren's operations had caused a gap in the enemy's line.'[5] This explanation was adopted by Geoffrey Powell, Buller's generally sympathetic biographer:

> More acceptable is the explanation that, having divided his force to mount with poor communications and in rugged country an inevitably complicated operation, his place was near Lyttelton. By not having to exercise detailed control of the operations on his flank, he would be best placed to decide the right moment to commit Lyttelton's units, and so trap and perhaps destroy the Boers. Only recently at Colenso had he experienced the danger of becoming too involved in the immediate battle.[6]

That may have been how Buller later chose to look at his intentions, but it still leaves unexplained his decision to entrust Warren with so great a responsibility. Later, Buller was to suggest that Lansdowne had required that Warren should hold a position to which his rank entitled him; Lansdowne denied that this was the case when giving evidence to the Elgin Commission. It does seem entirely possible, though, that Warren's seniority influenced Buller.[7]

3 Ibid., pp. 624-626.
4 Ibid., p. 625.
5 Pakenham, *Boer War*, pp. 282-283.
6 Powell, *Buller*, p. 165.
7 Ibid.; Elgin Commission, *Minutes of Evidence*, p. 178.

The Official History, reviewing these orders, regards them as embodying 'a broad and bold conception:'

> Though Warren, taking with him the larger portion of the army was to force his way by Trickhardt's Drift up to the westward of Spion Kop, it was still the Boer position behind Potgieter's Drift at which the blow was really aimed. All Warren's manoeuvres were to be directed to passing to the rear of the enemy in that stronghold (paragraph 4, secret orders), and opposite it Sir R. Buller himself would remain with the rest of the force. With these troops he intended to create diversions in Warren's favour, to threaten Spion Kop and Brakfontein, and even to attempt a crossing at Skiet's Drift (paragraph 5, secret orders) under the shadow of Doorn Kop.[8]

In this somewhat contradictory analysis of Buller's plan, the authors of the Official History, appear to have accepted the explanation of the command structure as later described by Powell.

The balance between the two parts of Buller's army, giving Warren much the larger part, does however seem at odds with Buller's belief that only 400 Boers were likely to be in front of Warren. On the other hand, the latter, after he had himself reconnoitred Trickhardt's Drift on 15 January, had formed the view that hard fighting was likely to follow his crossing, a belief based 'more upon the immense visible strength of the ground north of the river than upon the numbers of the enemy who actually allowed themselves to be seen.'[9]

At 1.00 pm on 16 January, Warren issued his orders for the force under his command, which set off from Springfield at 5.00 p.m. and by 12:30 a.m. next morning, was within a mile of Trickhardt's Drift. No attempt was made at first to cross the river; instead, at 8.00 a.m., Warren began the task of building a pontoon bridge. Churchill commented on the timing of this:

> We all made quite sure that the bridges would be built during the night, so that with the dawn the infantry could begin to cross and make an immediate onfall. But when morning broke the whole force was revealed spread about the hills overlooking the drift and no sound of artillery proclaimed the beginning of an action … we all wondered what was the cause of the delay.[10]

Meanwhile, Warren ordered his artillery to shell the approaches to Wright's Farm. While this was going on, two battalions of Woodgate's brigade were ferried across. The bridge was completed by 11.00 a.m., and the rest of Woodgate's brigade and that of Hart crossed, and the mounted troops forwarded the river at the drift. A second bridge was completed by 7.00 p.m.

To the east, Lyttelton had moved out during the afternoon of 16 January, heading for Potgieter's Drift, with 8,000 men, one battery of field artillery, one of howitzers, eight 12-pdr naval guns and Bethune's mounted infantry. The work of restoring the ferry at the drift to working order was completed by 5:15 p.m., and six hours later, the 1st Rifle Brigade, Scottish Rifles and the 61st Howitzer Battery had crossed the northern bank of the Tugela. The kopjes close to the river, known as 'Maconochie's Kopjes' after the name of the manufacturer of the preserved meat rations issued to the troops at this point, were immediately occupied. At this

8 *Official History*, vol. II, pp. 347–348.
9 Ibid., p. 348.
10 Churchill, *Boer War*, p. 125.

time, the principal objective of Lyttelton's force was to focus Boer attention on Potgieter's Drift while Warren was crossing at Trickhardt's Drift.

During the morning of 17 January, Buller rode over from Mount Alice to join Warren at a point on the south bank where he was watching Woodgate's advance. The two men presumably discussed the way the operation was going, but in the course of their meeting, there is no sign that Buller was discontented with the progress being made. However, later that day, after he had returned to his headquarters, Buller sent a message to Warren:

> I am carrying coals to Newcastle probably, but on the chance I write to say I wish you would, if you had not already done so, point out to Woodgate that his advance from Smith's Farm today was all wrong. The one thing if we mean to succeed is to keep our left clear. He was at Smith's Farm; the Yorkshires had occupied a kopje to the east, and he had advanced north-east. This was wrong … If your direct road is blocked, we must go forward by moving off to the left, and this will have the further advantage that it will keep you near the water at Venter's Spruit … Until you have so far encircled the enemy that you can wheel to the east, pray always try to overlap their right with your left.[11]

There was nothing in this to emphasise the importance of moving quickly, which was something Roberts, in a message from Cape Town on 16 January, had stressed: 'It is, I am sure, needless for me to urge the importance of there being no delay on the road. Rapidity of movement is everything against an enemy so skilful in strengthening defensive positions.'[12]

Major (later Field Marshal Lord) William Birdwood, on Dundonald's staff, was painfully conscious of the delay in pressing forward:

> We all expected and hoped we should at once cross and attack before the Boers were ready for us; but no – several hours were passed putting up a pontoon bridge which should I think have been ready by dawn … Warren, instead of attacking or even crossing right away and reconnoitring the enemy's position, proceeded to occupy himself in superintending the passage of carts over the river, instead of leaving this to a staff officer, and until the whole of the supplies were over he would make no advance. It is the exact opposite of the Crimea where they starved. Here troops are if anything overfed and the generals are bound hand and foot by their supply columns.[13]

Warren did little more on 18 January than complete the crossing of his transport and reconnoitre in the direction of Fairview Farm. Dundonald, however, had been on the move. Setting off at 7.00 a.m., he reported to Warren four hours later that he was advancing on the Acton Homes road, and that it would be practicable for Warren's advance and less exposed than the road which ran close to the Tabanyama range. When he received this message, Warren was already unhappy with Dundonald, having discovered that there were no cavalry stationed to protect the camp, and nothing to prevent the oxen from being 'swept away.' He sent an order requiring that 500 mounted troops should be sent back for this purpose, an order which he repeated at 11.45 a.m.[14]

11 *Official History*, vol. II, p. 631.
12 *Times History*, vol. III, p. 221.
13 Pemberton, *Battles*, pp. 154-155.
14 *Official History*, vol. II, p. 631.

At 2.00 p.m., Dundonald responded, saying that he would assign the task of protecting the camp to the Royals. He went on to suggest that Warren should come up to where he was and see for himself. As the day wore on, Dundonald pushed on, and his advanced guard ambushed a party of Boers who had trotted forward to seize some low kopjes without realising the presence of the British troopers. Dundonald, believing that a considerable opportunity had now arisen, reported this in the evening, asking if the Royals could be returned to him. This elicited from Warren the reply: 'I did not intend you should force on an action until I had arranged to proceed from here and take the initiative; unless you are sure of success you should retire upon the camp. I am sending you three squadrons of the Royals to support you.' Dundonald sent two more reports with details of his action and his present position; Warren replied that it seemed to him that Dundonald was too far to the north-west, but that he was expecting his advanced guard to arrive at Venter's Spruit next day at 7.00 a.m. He followed this up in the morning to make clear his annoyance at Dundonald's activities:

> Our objective is not Ladysmith. Our objective is to effect a junction with Sir Redvers Buller's force and then to receive orders from him. By detaching your cavalry from me you are hampering all my movements and forcing me to alter my plans. I am moving up towards you and desire that you will not move forward unless you are actually forced to do so. I require your mounted men to act as part of my force.[15]

Dundonald, who might perhaps have given a more comprehensive account of what he saw as an opportunity to establish a significant force on the slopes around Acton Homes, was now sent for by Warren, with whom he had an extremely uncomfortable meeting, in the course of which he had to listen to a lecture on what the general considered was the proper use of cavalry. Birdwood recorded that Dundonald stood up to Warren and asked what he wanted him to do: 'When Warren told him that he thought our place was to ride up the hillside in front of the infantry Lord D. said he would only do so on his receiving a distinct written order as he regarded it as murder for cavalry to think of doing such a thing.' This enraged Warren still further; he told Dundonald that he must have 500 of his men close to him and the infantry, and he did not care what happened to the rest.[16]

It has generally been regarded as one of the great missed opportunities of the campaign. Symons thought that if Warren had reinforced Dundonald with artillery and then with infantry, he 'would have achieved the immediate objective of turning the Boer flank, and the road which led direct to Ladysmith would have been open to him.'[17] Amery considered that Warren, 'never for a moment realising the chance of victory Dundonald's trifling success had a second time brought victory within his grasp,' merely regarded it as an unfortunate complication.[18]

The movements of the various elements of Warren's force on 19 January did not take the advance very much further. At 6.00 a.m. Hildyard's brigade marched to Venter's Spruit in accordance with Warren's briefly held view that the cavalry might need support; it was accompanied by a huge wagon train. It proved impossible to get the bulk of this over the spruit, so Hildyard, after spending the day waiting for this, returned to the east of the spruit to bivouac

15 Ibid., p. 632.
16 Pemberton, *Battles*, p. 157.
17 Symons, *Campaign*, p. 200.
18 *Times History*, vol. III, p. 223.

for the night. Meanwhile, Hart and Woodgate, whose brigades had not moved for 36 hours, also headed for Venter's Spruit. Woodgate reached a point near to Fairview Farm, while Hart paused at the crossing of the Spruit.

On the evening of 19 January, Warren convened a council of war of his senior officers, to which, pointedly, Dundonald was not invited. Warren had been north of the Tugela for 60 hours, but only now regarded himself as ready to advance against the Boer position. He explained the conclusions which he had placed before his officers in a message to Buller sent at 7.45 p.m., after the meeting had broken up. Warren's reputation for irascibility ensured that if any of his officers had any doubts about the conclusions reached, they did not express them. Warren wrote:

> I find there are only two roads by which we could possibly get from Trickhardt's Drift to Potgieter's Drift on the north of the Tugela, one by Acton Homes, the other by Fairview and Rosalie. The first I reject as too long: the second is a very difficult road for a large number of wagons, unless the enemy is thoroughly cleared out. I am, therefore, going to adopt some special arrangements which will involve my stay at Venter's Laager for two or three days. I will send in for further supplies and report progress.[19]

Warren was choosing between two entirely different kinds of operation; a flanking movement which might overlap the right of the Boer position, and a direct assault in the middle of it. The special arrangements which he had in mind involved an attempt to push the Boers off the Tabanyama heights before marching north up the Fairview road.

Even before receiving this message from Warren, Buller had been feeling increasing concern about the lack of progress being made. He had not, it must be said, done very much about it. Later, he blamed himself for not taking any action:

> I ought to have assumed command myself … I blame myself now for not having done so. I did not, because I thought that if I did I should discredit General Warren in the estimation of his troops; and that if I were shot, and he had to withdraw across the Tugela, and they had lost confidence in him, the consequences might be very serious.[20]

This was a typical piece of tortuous rationalisation by Buller in an effort to justify himself, and it was nonsense. There was no reason at all why he could not have involved himself more closely in the operations to be undertaken; as it was, he assented to Warren's proposals, and to the inevitable delay that they involved.

By 20 January, the time so wastefully given to the Boers meant that an assault on the Tabanyama heights would prove to be a much more difficult operation than it would have been previously; when Warren had begun to cross the Tugela, there were no more than 500 men in position there. The news of Warren's crossing at Trickhardt's Drift, and the obvious threat it presented, caused the Boer leadership serious concern. Once more, however, Botha rose to the occasion, making his way at once to the threatened sector. Both Kruger and Joubert felt that he should exercise overall command on the Tugela front, but Botha was of course, much junior to Lukas Meyer, who had returned to Colenso, and also to Schalk Burger, and he was reluctant

19 *Official History*, vol. II, p. 633.
20 Symons, *Campaign*, p. 202; Elgin Commission, *Minutes of Evidence* vol.. I.

to offend them. He therefore agreed to conduct operations without a formal appointment, and this, perhaps surprisingly, caused no difficulties; this was due to the great respect in which Botha was held by the burghers.[21]

As soon as he arrived, Botha set to work to dig in along the long summit of Tabanyama, taking advantage of the commanding field of fire down the slope to the false crest between 600 and 2,000 yards away, below which Warren was assembling his forces for his planned assault. Even now though, Botha had no more than 1,800 men to defend the position, together with three guns, which he located out of sight behind the summit. The Boers occupied a line of trenches running from the Green Hill, adjoining Spion Kop, to the hill north of Bastion Hill.

Warren issued his orders during the night of 19/20 January. The operation would be conducted by Clery's division, consisting of Hart's 5th Brigade and Woodgate's 11th Brigade, with six batteries of field artillery and three squadrons of cavalry. Hildyard remained with the wagon train at the crossing over Venter's Spruit. Clery's objective was to seize the spurs and re-entrants which formed the southern crest of the Tabanyama heights and to locate suitable positions from which the artillery would thereafter be able to shell the strong Boer positions on Green Hill and Spion Kop.[22]

The troops moved off at 3.00 a.m., led by two of Woodgate's battalions, the 2nd Royal Lancasters and the 1st South Lancashires, which occupied the long spur which fell towards Fairview Farm and Three Tree Hill, without opposition. The artillery was now sent up to Three Tree Hill, but its summit was found to be too small for six batteries, so three of them were located in a mealie field to the east. Hart, meanwhile, had moved up on the west of Three Tree Hill where he absorbed Woodgate's two battalions and from there, moved forward to the assault of the Boer position under the cover of a heavy artillery bombardment.

The advance, along the summit of the western spur, was directed against the Boer trenches on the right and was met with extremely fierce rifle fire. There was a certain amount of cover due to the rocky nature of the terrain, and for a while, some progress was made by short rushes. At 1:15 p.m. the Boer artillery finally opened up on Three Tree Hill, before turning its attention to Hart's infantry. These had succeeded in occupying the southern crest of Tabanyama, the Boers falling back to their position on the true crest. Hart, whose force had already suffered total casualties of the order of 300 men, was preparing to launch an assault when a peremptory order from Clery arrived forbidding the advance; the latter, realising that the artillery could give little support, had declined to attempt a frontal assault. In this he was supported by Warren, who sent him a message that he entirely concurred; a frontal attack, he said, was simply playing the Boer game.[23]

Meanwhile, Dundonald had been active. Following an order from Warren to keep close touch with the main body and which told him of a possible enemy concentration on the Acton Homes road, he set about the capture of Bastion Hill which appeared to him not to be occupied. This was taken by a dismounted squadron of the South African Light Horse, supported by Thorneycroft's Mounted Infantry; the latter was in fact no longer under Dundonald's command. The Boer artillery attempted unsuccessfully to drive them off Bastion Hill. Hildyard's 2nd Brigade now moved up two battalions to support both Hart and Dundonald, the rest of the brigade remaining at Venter's Spruit to guard the wagons.

21 Trew *Generals*, p. 147.
22 *Official History*, vol. II, p. 366.
23 Ibid., p. 634.

Overnight, the Boers continued to strengthen their entrenchments rendering them almost impregnable. The next day, Hart extended his line to his left, occupying a further section of the crest line. An attempt by Colonel Kitchener to launch a flank attack in accordance with the intentions of Warren and Clery, however, failed with not inconsiderable loss, and was abandoned by 11.00. Total British casualties during the day amounted to 158 killed, wounded and missing.[24]

That morning, Buller rode over to see Warren and made clear that he was unimpressed with the way in which matters had been dealt with. In particular, he criticised the positioning of Warren's batteries on the inner flank; two of them were accordingly relocated to the left of the position taken up by Hildyard. After Buller's departure, Warren rode round to inspect the left flank beyond Bastion Hill to see if an attack could be resumed there; he decided it could not and instead, proposed an assault for the next morning on the Boer trenches opposite Three Tree Hill. Before launching this, he planned a heavy bombardment of the enemy positions. He also sent a message to Buller asking for the 10th Brigade (Coke), a howitzer battery and naval guns. The infantry and four howitzers were duly released to him. That night, Warren reported to Buller that he fancied that the Boers were fighting more to protect their communications than to prevent their getting to Ladysmith.[25]

In fact, notwithstanding prolonged exchanges of fire, not much happened on 22 January. Both sides were now so well entrenched that few casualties were suffered and Warren was, in any case, awaiting the arrival of Coke's brigade. At 10.00 a.m., having previously sent a message warning of a possible counter-attack, Buller arrived at Warren's headquarters. He was still extremely dissatisfied with the lack of progress and flatly refused Warren's suggestion of two days' artillery preparation before an assault was launched. Warren, he said, must either attack the Boer right or retreat across the Tugela. Warren wished to advance up the Fairview-Rosalie Farm road but, he said, they could not go that way without first taking Spion Kop. To this, Buller responded by saying that of course he must take it.[26] It was out of this conversation that the hitherto unconsidered plan to attack Spion Kop was born.

Buller then rode off to the left, and Warren subsequently held a meeting with Clery, Hildyard, Woodgate and Coke, the latter having arrived at noon. Warren, after outlining alternative courses of action, announced that he proposed to attack Spion Kop, to which there was no dissent. When Buller, having looked at the left flank, sent over a suggestion for attack at that point, Warren disregarded it. These proceedings were condemned by Amery who noted that Buller, 'by the absurd threat of withdrawing the force, and thus abandoning all the progress made, induced Warren to undertake an operation which neither he nor Warren really believed in.' [27] In all the circumstances, it is difficult to say that this comment is unjust.

The coming battle for Spion Kop would face the same problem that had haunted previous operations and that was the almost total ignorance of the topography. Spion Kop rises 1,470 feet above the Tugela plain. The Tabanyama ridge, which Warren's men had been facing for the last four days, has its eastern end at Green Hill, from where the ground falls away to a deep gully, on the opposite side of which rises Conical Hill, which is the north-western end of Spion Kop. This mountain extends some three miles eastward, along the saddle at the end of

24 Ibid., p. 371.
25 Ibid., p. 634.
26 Pemberton, *Battles*, p. 160; Symons, *Campaign*, p. 208.
27 *Times History*, vol. III history, vol. III, p. 239.

which it rises to two commanding heights known as Twin Peaks. Immediately south-west of the summit of Spion Ko,p there is a height known as Aloe Knoll. Spion Kop could be approached by two tracks, one from Three Tree Hill and one much longer, from Trickhardt's Drift up the northern spur. Notwithstanding the lack of knowledge of the ground, Warren had it in mind to launch the assault during the night of 22/23 January, but Coke, two of whose battalions were to conduct the assault, asked for more time to reconnoitre, and it was scheduled for the following night. Warren rode out at dawn on 23 January to examine the approaches to Spion Kop; then, returning to his headquarters he again met Buller, who reiterated his demand for either an immediate attack, or a retirement, adding that he still preferred an assault on the right of the Boer position.

Buller, in his subsequent report to Lansdowne, explained his reasons for the ultimatum which he gave to Warren, observing that he had received no reports from him about the special measures which he contemplated; he went on:

> For four days he had kept his troops continuously exposed to gun and rifle fire on the edge of an almost perpendicular precipice; that this position admitted of no second line; that the supports and reserves were huddled up close behind the firing line in a formation which admitted of no defence, and that a panic or sudden attack by the enemy might throw the whole mass in disorder off the heights at any moment. I maintained that the situation was too dangerous to be persisted in any longer, and that Warren must either attack or withdraw his troops.[28]

A clearer admission of Buller's own failure to exercise his command properly can hardly be imagined. If he considered that the situation was as bad as he described, he had only to issue a direct order to Warren to carry out the assault on the Boer right which he favoured. Instead, he weakly assented to Warren's wish to go through with the attack on Spion Kop. When shown Warren's orders for the attack, he made no comment save to require Woodgate to command the actual assault, as Coke was still recovering from the effects of a broken leg.[29] Warren had had in his mind that he should lead the assault himself, but Buller had expressly forbidden this.

Buller provided Woodgate with the services of Colonel Charles à Court, from his staff. When Buller was briefing him, à Court asked what the column was to do when it had taken the hill, to which Buller replied: 'It has got to stay there.' A Court said that guns would be required, so the mountain battery which had been left at Frere was sent for. A Court asked that Buller point out the exact point that was to be taken as the maps were so bad. Commenting later, à Court wrote: 'There was no plan except that we were to take the hill and stay there. Some 1,700 men were to assault a hill 1,470 feet high in the centre of the Boer position, and the rest of Buller's 20,000 men were to look on and do nothing. '[30]

Warren issued a set of general orders for the operation after Buller had left, dividing his force into a Right Attack under Coke, and a Left Attack, under Clery. Coke, in turn issued his orders to Woodgate, prescribing that he should attack with two battalions from his brigade to which Thorneycroft's Mounted Infantry (about 200 strong), and half a company of Royal Engineers, would be attached. The men would carry 150 rounds of ammunition, together with water bottles

28 *German Staff History*, vol. II, p. 133.
29 *Official History*, vol. II, pp. 175, 636.
30 *Symons, Campaign*, p. 211.

and a day's rations. The battalions selected by Woodgate were the Royal Lancashires and the 2nd Lancashire Fusiliers, which were to assemble at White's Farm at 7.00 p.m. The rest of Coke's command were to support the attack from Three Tree Hill; Clery was to use his discretion about opening fire on his front.[31] Before setting off, Thorneycroft and Colonels Crofton and Hill, the battalion commanders, spoke briefly to their men. There was to be no noise, no talking, no smoking and no shooting; it was to be bayonet work. The honour of the regiment was in their hands.[32]

Soon after 9.00 p.m. the ascent began, from time to time in drizzling rain. At first, the column was led by the Lancashire Fusiliers, but after about half a mile, Thorneycroft, who had just before nightfall made a sketch of several landmarks on the route to be taken, offered his services as a guide; Woodgate halted and asked Thorneycroft to take his men to the front. Alec Thorneycroft had been one of the special service offices sent out to South Africa by the War Office when it appeared entirely possible that hostilities might break out, with a brief to organise locally raised volunteer units. Thorneycroft's Mounted Infantry so far had played a valuable role, and he had impressed Buller with his leadership qualities.

By midnight, about a third of the ascent had been covered, moving past Thorneycroft's landmarks in succession. The climb continued, not without difficulty (but without incident) to a grassy slope, fringed with trees which led directly to the summit. Spion Kop was clothed in a dense fog; when Thorneycroft's men reached the edge of the open plateau they crept forward over the crest, followed by the Lancashire Fusiliers. Suddenly, a loud challenge in Dutch rang out, followed by a burst of rifle fire from the picket consisting of a dozen or so Boers. These disappeared into the fog; the rest of the Boer outposts, about 70 men, also rapidly retreated and by 4.00 a.m. the summit of the mountain was in Woodgate's hands. He at once gave orders for the engineers to lay out a system of entrenchments.[33]

The prominent central position of Spion Kop in the Boer line, and the consequent importance attached to its possession, make it surprising that it had been held by so small a force. The Official History, noting that the Boers had raised no *schanzes* there, suggests that they had it in fact realised that 'it was untenable by friend or foe. A glance northward, and at either side … would have shown that Spion Kop was but a cape projecting into the enemy's position.' The loss of the hill, therefore, at this point did not dismay the Boers, since it appeared to them that it 'did not gravely threaten their own commanding and enveloping positions.'[34]

However, when the news of its abandonment reached Botha, he at once decided that it must be retaken. His headquarters were on a small kopje some 2,000 yards north of Spion Kop, and from here he began ordering every man and every gun at his disposal into the best position from which to recapture the hill. He located a 75mm Krupp gun and a pom-pom behind Green Hill and two Creusots about three-quarters of a mile further back. He ordered Commandant Opperman with 300 men, to climb the north-west slope of Spion Kop. Meanwhile, at Schalk Burger's camp below the Twin Peaks, Commandant Hendrik Prinsloo took charge of the counter-attack from that direction, locating a 75mm Krupp gun on the north-west slope of the Twin Peaks and a pom-pom on the ridge to the west. Even more importantly, he sent a force of 50 men to occupy Aloe Knoll, a small kopje 250 yards from the summit of Spion Kop, from

31 *Official History*, vol. II, pp. 636–638.
32 Pemberton, *Battles*, p. 164.
33 *Official History*, vol. II pp. 380–381; *Times History*, vol. III pp. 250–251.
34 Ibid., pp. 383-384.

which rifles could bear upon the British trenches. The existence of this particularly grave threat was quite unknown to the British. Prinsloo now set off to climb the north eastern slope of Spion Kop with 65 men. All this time, the thick mist continued to shroud the heights, concealing the Boer activity.[35]

While the Boers were thus reacting to the British arrival on the summit, the work of entrenchment had begun, though not without serious difficulty. There were inadequate tools available and it was soon found that there were only a few inches of soil before hard rock was struck. The parapet and trench combined was no more than 18 inches in height. The Royal Engineers had laid out a trace for the defence work, the front of which facing north was some 300 yards long, with shorter arms thrown back on right and left.[36]

When the fog lifted for a while, it soon became apparent that the trench had been dug in the wrong place. Although traversing the top of the hill, which in its front shelved downwards, it then dropped so suddenly and steeply after about 200 yards that the ground below was totally dead ground in which the enemy could concentrate undisturbed. Realising this, Woodgate sent forward parties of troops in an effort to entrench what was effectively the true crest of the hill.

Posting the rest of his troops for defence, Woodgate located four companies of Lancashire Fusiliers on the right flank, Thorneycroft's Mounted Infantry in the centre and the Royal Lancashires on the left. At 7.15 a.m. he sent à Court down to Warren reporting his success in taking the summit. By 8.00 a.m. however, the fog began to lift, and the Boers opened fire from their positions near the crest of the hill and from the Twin Peaks. The fire from Aloe Knoll was particularly galling and continued so throughout the day, inflicting heavy casualties on the troops on the right of the British line. The Boer artillery now began to shell the summit. Woodgate for the moment, pulled back the troops on the forward crest, leaving sentries posted there to warn of any movement by the Boers, who now had 500 men available to assault the summit, some in position only 50 yards below the forward crest. As the Boer fire intensified, Woodgate again sent forward parties of troops to the crest to support the sentries that had been left there. Then, at 8.30 a.m., he was mortally wounded by a shrapnel ball; Crofton, the commanding officer of the Royal Lancashires, assumed command, and sent a signal to Warren. This, somewhat garbled by the signaller, read: 'Reinforce at once or all is lost. General dead.'[37]

Warren, who received this at 9.50 a.m., was astounded. Half an hour earlier, the 2nd Dorset and 2nd Middlesex battalions and the Imperial Light Infantry from Coke's brigade, had already started for Spion Kop, and Warren ordered Coke to send at least one battalion to the summit. In response to this, the Middlesex battalion and the Imperial Light Infantry continued upwards. Warren passed on the news about Woodgate to Buller and to Lyttelton, and he followed this up with a direct request to the latter for assistance from Potgieter's Drift. Lyttelton sent across the 2nd Scottish Rifles and two squadrons of Bethune's mounted infantry to the foot of Spion Kop. To Crofton, Warren sent a message that reinforcements were on their way, adding that he should hold on to the last and that there should be no surrender.[38]

Pondering the command situation disclosed by Crofton's message, Warren decided that Coke, whom he had previously wished to lead the assault, should take over on the summit, and he rode over to where Coke was stationed at the foot of the hill to tell him so. Coke set off to

35 Trew, *Generals*, pp. 147-148.
36 *Official History*, vol. II, p. 381.
37 Ibid., p. 385.
38 *Times History*, vol. III, p. 260.

climb the hill with the Dorsets at 11.00 a.m., with Warren's injunction that there must be no surrender ringing in his ears. On Mount Alice, Buller had been watching the assault; he was joined there by à Court, who told him that the position held on Spion Kop was splendid and that Crofton must have lost his nerve. Buller accordingly sent Warren a heliograph, which was received at 11:40 a.m.: 'Unless you put some really good hard fighting man in command on the top, you will lose the hill. I suggest Thorneycroft.'[39] Warren at once sent a signal to Crofton that Thorneycroft was to command on the summit with the local rank of Brigadier General, but he failed to tell Coke, who was still on his way up.

The troops on the summit were still subject to ceaseless fire, both from the Boer riflemen around the crest and on Aloe Knoll, and from the Boer artillery, which the British gunners had been unable to locate. The naval guns south of the river were however able to see the Boer infantry on Aloe Knoll, and concentrated their fire here until receiving a message from Warren to tell them that they were firing on his men who occupied the whole summit.[40] The Official History graphically described the scene on Spion Kop:

> The intense rifle fire, coming from and falling at all angles and ranges, the long-range bullets dropping over the low walls, those fired from a few yards tearing a way through the interstices of the stones, or sweeping from end to end of the trenches, the shrapnel which rained incessantly upon every quarter and sought out every nook, the flights of little shells from the pom-poms racing in procession of explosions across the plateau, these were dangers which the soldiers would willingly have exchanged for close combat, for these it was impossible to avoid, to deal with in return, or for long to survive.[41]

During the morning, the fire from Aloe Knoll had been so intense that a charge was made by a party of Thorneycroft's men in an unsuccessful effort to clear the position. When the Boers closed in still further, Thorneycroft himself led a further charge towards the northern crest line which was also driven back with heavy loss. However, parts of this crest did remain in British hands and by noon, the reinforcements sent up had begun to take their place in the firing line. Soon after this, Thorneycroft learnt of his promotion; Coke, who had now reached a point near the summit, still remained in ignorance of this. He reported to Warren at 12.50 p.m. his understanding that the top of the hill was crowded with men who were holding out well.

This was an extremely over optimistic report; although there were now some 1,800 men on the summit, most of the officers and very many men had been killed or wounded, and those that had not, had endured many hours in the blazing sun without food or water. By 1.00 p.m. the situation had become all too much for some of the Lancashire Fusiliers on the right of the line and about 170 of them rose to their feet from their trenches displaying a white flag. A number of Boers came forward to accept their surrender. De Kock, from a Transvaal commando, described what happened next: 'The English were about to surrender, and we were all coming up, when a great big, angry, red-faced soldier ran out of the trench on our right and shouted, "I am the commandant here; take your men back to hell, sir! I allow no surrenders." '[42]

39 *Official History*, vol. II, p. 388.
40 Symons, *Campaign*, p. 220.
41 *Official History*, vol. II pp. 387-388.
42 Pakenham, *Boer War*, p. 298.

This was the imposing Thorneycroft, hobbling with the aid of a stick having sprained his ankle. He then withdrew, taking with him the men who would listen to him, and called on them to take cover behind a line of rocks and open fire. The Boers retreated, taking their prisoners with them, forced back by a desperate charge from a company of the Middlesex.

At 2.30 p.m., Thorneycroft sent a message to Warren, reporting that he was hanging on, that some of the Middlesex had arrived and that the Dorsets were coming up, but that his force was inadequate to hold such a large perimeter. He asked what reinforcements would be sent up to hold the hill and added that they were badly in need of water.[43] This note reached Warren at about 4.00 p.m.; it had passed through Coke's hands, who had added a comment of his own, to the effect that he had ordered the Scottish Rifles and the King's Royal Rifles to reinforce, and that 'we appear to be holding our own.'

Lyttelton, looking across to Spion Kop, had noticed the arrival of the Middlesex's, and it seemed to him that one of the two battalions he had sent to support the assault might be better employed in an attack on the Twin Peaks in an effort to silence the Boer fire from this point. At 2.00 p.m., the King's Royal Rifles forwarded the river at Kaffir Drift and advanced to the assault. Moving quickly under heavy rifle fire up the long undulating incline which led to the foot of the Twin Peaks, they then climbed the steep slope, covered by the fire of the naval guns, and by 5.15 p.m., both peaks had been carried. The 200 or so Boers who had been holding the position, retreated rapidly in considerable disorder down the far side of the heights.

Throughout the afternoon, Warren had had no information until he read Thorneycroft's note of 2:30 p.m., with Coke's addendum, which led him to discount the gravity of the situation. By 5.50 p.m., however, Coke had become aware that the situation was indeed critical, as he reported to Warren. When the latter received it two hours later, he ordered Coke to come to him to report. This he did, though much later, setting off at 9.30 p.m. and then becoming lost before reaching Warren at 2.00 a.m. At 6.30 p.m. Thorneycroft sent a detailed report to Warren which reached him at much the same time as Coke's report. In this, Thorneycroft reported that the troops of the original assault force were 'quite done up.' They had no water, and ammunition was running short. He considered that even with the reinforcements it would be impossible to hold Spion Kop while the enemy's guns could sweep the plateau. Casualties had been very heavy. He asked for instructions; the situation, he said, was critical.[44]

There had been little remission in the ordeal of those on the summit, as Thorneycroft made clear. Although the taking of the Twin Peaks had offered some relief from that quarter, Boer fire from elsewhere seemed if anything, to have intensified. As the evening wore on, it became increasingly clear to Thorneycroft that there was a serious risk of all or a large part of his force being trapped on the summit. He had no news or instructions from Warren, save for a note urging him to hold on. Warren did not let Thorneycroft know that at 9.00 p.m. he had belatedly given instructions for a working party of 1,400 men to go to the summit so that emplacements could be dug for the two naval guns and the mountain battery, as well as improving the defences of the British position. At this point, Winston Churchill, who had made his own way partly up the route to the summit before turning back to tell Warren what he had seen, appeared at the general's headquarters. Churchill later described his experience:

43 Ibid., p. 299.
44 *Official History*, vol. II, p. 640.

> We passed through the ambulance village, and leaving our horses climbed up the spur. Streams of wounded met us and obstructed the path. Men were staggering along alone, or supported by comrades, or crawling on hands and knees, or carried on stretchers. Corpses lay here and there. Many of the wounds were of a horrible nature. The splinters and fragments of the shell had torn and mutilated in the most ghastly manner. I passed about two hundred while I was climbing up. There was, moreover, a small but steady leakage of unwounded men of all corps. Some of them cursed and swore. Others were utterly exhausted and fell on the hillside in stupor.[45]

Warren gave Churchill a note to Thorneycroft to tell him about the working party and the guns, and Churchill set off again to the summit. When he got there, he found Thorneycroft in a state of shock:

> He was sitting on the ground surrounded by the remnants of the regiment he had raised, who had fought for him like lions and followed him like dogs. I explained the situation as I had been told and as I thought. Naval guns were prepared to try, sappers and working parties were already on the road with thousands of sandbags. What did he think? But the decision had already been taken. He had never received any messages from the general, had not had time to write any. Messages had been sent him, he had wanted to send others himself. The fight had been too hot, too close, too interlaced for him to attend to anything, but to support this company, clear those rocks, or line that trench. So, having heard nothing and expecting no guns, he had decided to retire. As he put it tersely: 'Better six good battalions safely down the hill than a mop up in the morning.'[46]

Thorneycroft called a brief council of war; Hill, the Middlesex's commanding officer who was the most senior of the colonels, did not accept that Thorneycroft was in command, but Thorneycroft overrode this and with the reluctant assent of the others, gave orders for the retirement. He gave Churchill a note to Warren telling him this. On the way down, Thorneycroft met engineer Lieutenant Colonel Sim, at the head of the working party, who was the bearer of Warren's original note to Thorneycroft telling him to hold on. 'I have done all I can,' said Thorneycroft, 'and I am not going back.'[47] He finally reached Warren about 2.00 a.m., at much the same time as Churchill. The battle for Spion Kop was over. Soon after dawn next day, the handful of Boers remaining below the northern crest were amazed to discover that the British had gone.

The one outstanding success for Buller's army had been the taking of the Twin Peaks, which was, or could have been, a serious threat to the whole Boer position. This, however, was barren of result, for Buller, apparently doubtful of the wisdom of Lyttelton's splitting of his force, gave insistent orders that the King's Royal Rifles withdraw at once from the position which they had occupied. This, although waiting until darkness had fallen, they did in perfect order.[48]

It had nearly been a famous victory. Many of the Boers had also been coming to the end of their tether. It was only the resolution of Louis Botha, confident that the British would abandon the hill, that kept his army in the fight. He was determined that the effort to take the hill

45 Churchill, *Boer War*, p. 138.
46 Ibid., pp. 139-140.
47 Pakenham, *Boer War*, p. 305.
48 *Official History*, vol. II, p. 398.

should be continued on the following day and had sent encouraging messages to Kruger and Joubert. To Schalk Burger, who had abruptly retreated from behind the Twin Peaks he wrote sternly: 'let us struggle and die together. But, brother, let us not give way an inch more to the English.' Botha did not know then that Burger's nerve had gone and that he was in full retreat to Ladysmith.[49]

At 6.00 a.m. the next morning, Buller rode over to Warren's headquarters. He dismissed the latter's suggestion that a fresh attempt might be made on Spion Kop. He already had another plan in mind and he accordingly gave orders for the retreat of the whole army behind the Tugela. Churchill gave an account of this operation which the army, he wrote, believed might come to 'a bloody and even disastrous rearguard action:'

> But now, when things had come to this pass, Buller took personal command. He arrived on the field calm, cheerful, inscrutable as ever, rode hither and thither with a weary staff and a huge notebook, gripped the whole business in his strong hands, and so shook it into shape that we crossed the river in safety, comfort, and good order, with most remarkable mechanical precision, and without the loss of a single man or a pound of stores. The fighting troops stood fast for two days, while the train of wagons streamed back over the bridges and parked in huge black squares on the southern bank. Then, on the night of the 26th, the retreat began. It was pitch dark, and a driving rain failed all lights. The ground was broken. The enemy near. It is scarcely possible to imagine a more difficult operation. But it was performed with amazing ease.[50]

The Boers, happy to see the British go, made no attempt to interfere with their departure. It should be added that Owen Coetzer, not perhaps the most dispassionate of historians, claims that the withdrawal operation was in fact, conducted by Warren, a view which Symons shares. Buller's demeanour as he met with Warren occasioned a particularly virulent attack by Amery, in a spiteful description of Buller's reaction to the battle. He observed that the general 'could scarcely conceal his satisfaction at the turn of events.'[51] As has been seen, Buller was almost excessively considerate of his men and extremely sensitive to casualties; it is inconceivable that his dislike or contempt for Warren could have led him to feel any satisfaction at the outcome of the battle and the losses his army had suffered.

Amongst Buller's senior commanders, there were a number who now doubted their supreme commander: Lyttelton wrote home that he had lost all confidence in him 'and I am sure he has himself.' However, as previously, such feelings were not shared by Buller's men, who were greatly cheered by the speech which he made them after the retirement had been completed.

Throughout the Spion Kop operations (17-24 January), the army had suffered a total of 1,733 casualties: 412 killed, 1,034 wounded and 287 missing. The officers had suffered disproportionately; 42 had been killed and 65 wounded. During the fighting on Spion Kop itself, on 24 January some 900 officers and men had been killed or wounded; Boer losses on that day had been estimated to have been no more than a quarter of this number.[52]

49 Pakenham, *Boer War*, pp. 301–302.
50 Churchill, *Boer War*, p. 153.
51 *Times History*, vol. III, p. 2944.
52 *Official History*, vol. II, p. 597.

In the end, the outcome of the battle had come down to the decision of one man. It is difficult not to feel sympathy for Thorneycroft after all that he had endured during an appallingly difficult day. Leo Amery, however, was fiercely critical of his action in retiring from the summit:

> On no theory of military conduct is it possible for an instant to justify Thorneycroft's action. He had been put in command to hold the position which, he knew, was, rightly or wrongly considered important by his commanding officer. To decide for himself that the position was not worth holding was an assumption of authority which there was nothing in the circumstances to warrant … It is not as an error of judgement, nor as a collapse under excessive strain, but as an act of deliberate disobedience that Thorneycroft's decision must be judged.[53]

Immediate reactions from Thorneycroft's superiors were perhaps predictable. Buller considered that Thorneycroft had been wise to order the retirement and offered no criticism of him for doing so. Unsurprisingly, when it came to apportioning blame, he was sure that the outcome of the battle was Warren's fault: 'We had really lost our chance by Sir C. Warren's slowness. He seems to me a man who can do well what he can do himself, but you cannot command, as he can use neither his staff nor subordinates. I can never employ him again on an independent command.'[54] When Roberts received this report and sent it on to Lansdowne, he would have none of this. He felt that the principal blame must fall on Buller as he was present and was in chief command:

> If, however, it was his opinion that his instructions were being incorrectly carried out, it was, as I judge, his manifest duty to interfere, as soon as he had reason to believe the success of the operation was endangered. His reasons for not interfering can hardly be deemed relevant … Whatever may have been Sir Charles Warren's shortcomings, the want of success must also be ascribed to the disinclination of the general commanding in chief to exercise his authority and to keep matters in the right groove.[55]

Pemberton, noting that Roberts also criticised Thorneycroft's decision as 'an inexcusable fault,' describes this comment as unfeeling, and as having been made 'without a first-hand knowledge of the circumstances.'[56] The Official History, as usual, carefully avoided criticism altogether, assigning no blame to any individual and leaving the facts as recorded to speak for themselves. Among other historians, Owen Coetzer, of course, sets out at length his passionate defence of Sir Charles Warren, relying not only on Warren's evidence to the Elgin Commission but also on the detailed account which he later gave of the operations.

In London, *The Times*, along with the rest of the British press, was dismayed but not overcome by the news of Spion Kop. Its first reaction, on 27 January, reflected the national determination, as it had done previously:

53 *Times History*, vol. III, pp. 289–290.
54 Symons, *Campaign*, p. 241.
55 *German Staff History*, vol. II, pp. 180-185.
56 Pemberton, *Battles*, p. 194.

> Again an apparently real success has been quickly followed by an unquestionably real reverse … This attempt has received a serious check, necessarily unfortunate, but incapable of being estimated at its real importance in the absence of information. There are evident reasons for reticence at this juncture, but the extreme brevity and the vagueness of the published official despatches must tend to create deep and widespread anxiety. The government must prepare fresh reinforcements for South Africa, and whatever Lord Roberts demands will have to be supplied. The nation is united in the determination to bring the war to an honourable conclusion, and the reverse at Spion Kop, whatever may be its effects, must be treated as a phase – important and disagreeable, but temporary – in the difficult task to which we stand committed.[57]

Two days later came a hint of dissatisfaction with Buller:

> The public will not be slow to appreciate the gravity of the situation revealed by the despatch from General Buller which the War Office issued yesterday. The most carefully planned and executed movement of the present campaign has entirely failed. If, as Sir Redvers Buller remarks, with the same strange air of detachment which characterised certain of his dispatches in Friday's Gazette, the unmolested withdrawal across the Tugela of an army for which there was to be 'no turning back,' proves that the enemy has been taught to respect the fighting powers of our soldiers, the public which has never doubted them will hardly find in that opinion much consolation for the failure of our generals to effect the relief of Ladysmith.[58]

This article went on to reflect on the reasons for the failure to relieve Ladysmith and considered the possibility of its fall:

> It is now clear that the force was not adequate to the difficult task to which it was committed. One of the undoubted lessons of the war is that modern weapons confer special advantage upon the defence in such a rugged country as Northern Natal. It need not, therefore, cause surprise that a British force, which would have defeated three times its number of Boers in the open veldt, has been successfully resisted by a somewhat greater number than itself among the rocky fastnesses which our correspondents have described. The violation of strategic principles which has characterised the campaign exacts the inevitable penalty. Sir Redvers Buller has made a strong effort. His plan was probably the best possible; it has failed, and we are now face to face with the painful contingency of the fall of Ladysmith … Strategically the effect would not entail great disadvantage. Politically and morally the result would be exceedingly serious. In our history only the surrender of 7,000 men at Yorktown in August 1781, presents a parallel humiliation.[59]

57 *The Times*, 27 January 1900.
58 Ibid., 29 January 1900.
59 Ibid.

18

Val Krantz

In his search for a point at which he might break through the barrier which had thus far proved impenetrable, Buller had come to the conclusion that this was to be found at the Vaal Krantz ridge. Here the ridge came down to the riverbank. It was of no great height, but if it was taken, any Boer guns trained on it would themselves be dominated from Mount Alice and Zwart Kop, where Buller planned to locate heavy batteries. It appeared that the top of Vaal Krantz would be practicable for artillery which from there, could command the plain and the tracks leading to Ladysmith. However, the town was still 12 miles away, and behind Vaal Krantz it was reported that the Boers had strongly entrenched a position at Roodepoort, while the left flank of an attack on Vaal Krantz was exposed to the strong Boer position between Spion Kop and Brakfontein.[1]

Work had been put in hand as early as 27 January to create a slide up the southern slope of Zwart Kop up which to haul the naval guns. It was attempted, unsuccessfully, to conceal the work from the Boers; it was also hampered by stormy weather. By 2 February, however, the work been completed. Six naval 12-pdrs, two guns of the 64th Field Battery and the six guns of the 4th Mountain Battery were installed on the top of Zwart Kop. Two 5-inch guns, which could not be hauled up the slope, were located on a spur to the west. A 4.7-inch naval gun was posted on each of Naval Gun Hill and Mount Alice, and two naval 12-pdrs on the plateau to the north of Mount Alice.[2]

In advance of the coming attack, Buller made a number of organisational changes, appointing Colonel Wynne, his chief of staff, to command Woodgate's 11th Brigade, and splitting his cavalry into the 1st Cavalry Brigade (Burn-Murdoch) of regular troops and the 2nd Mounted Brigade (Dundonald) largely composed of volunteers. On 3 February, Buller held a conference with his senior officers and later that day, issued his orders for the operation. Lyttelton's 4th Brigade was to carry out the attack, supported by Hildyard's 2nd Brigade and Hart's 5th Brigade. These brigades would be under Clery's command. A feint attack was to be carried out between the two loops of the Tugela against Brakfontein by an advance on the Maconochie Kopjes by Wynne's 11th Brigade with six batteries of field artillery and the howitzer battery. It was hoped that the assembly of the brigades to assault Vaal Krantz would be taken by the Boers as a movement in support of that on Brakfontein.

1 *Official History*, vol. II pp. 404-405.
2 Ibid., p. 406.

Amery, reviewing the plan for the attack on Vaal Krantz, wrote that the general idea was sound enough, 'but the way in which it was worked out in the orders was unnecessarily complicated in detail, though no doubt ingenious; it was seriously defective in the points that really mattered.' The fundamental problem was that if the Boers were given time to occupy Doorn Kloof and Doorn Kop, it would become in effect, a frontal attack: 'Rapidity and surprise were therefore conditions indispensable to the success of Buller's plan.'[3] Roberts, himself planning to commence operations in the west to invade the Orange Free State by 5 February, told Buller that unless he felt 'fairly confident' of success, he should maintain a bold front but not attack until the effect of his own operations should be felt. Buller, though, was becoming increasingly concerned about the situation of Ladysmith and he wrote to White on 28 January to tell him of Roberts's views:

> Roberts says … that if you will wait till the end of February he will by then be in Bloemfontein and will have relieved Kimberley, which will, he says, reduce the pressure on Ladysmith. I doubt Roberts' forecasts coming off and think I had better play my hand alone. What do you think?[4]

Meanwhile, Roberts had himself, on 28 January, sent a message to White, which cheered that gloomy commander, as well as a message to Buller asking his plans, but still urging a defensive stance in the absence of a reasonable prospect of success. In reply, Buller told him that he planned to attack on 31 January and that he was fairly confident, and it was in this frame of mind that he had prepared his attack.

The Boer units that would face this assault were led by Commandant Ben Viljoen and were about 800 strong. It was apparent to him that the British were preparing for an attack on his position, but his appeals for reinforcement fell on deaf ears. Botha had gone to Pretoria for a few days' leave after Spion Kop, while Joubert thought that Viljoen was unduly nervous, and sent Lukas Meyer to ride over from Colenso to put some backbone into him. Meyer did, however, recommend that the 'Long Tom' be sent from Ladysmith to be mounted on Doorn Kop. Schalk Burger and A. P. Cronje were both apparently unwell, and President Steyn proposed that the Free Stater Martinus Prinsloo be placed in command on the Tugela; Kruger did not think this a good idea, but Joubert agreed and Prinsloo went down to the Tugela on 5 February. In the operations that had by then already begun, Botha, who had returned to the scene, effectively took command on the following day.[5]

At 6.00 a.m. on 5 February (three hours too late in Amery's opinion) Wynne's brigade began moving out from the Maconochie Kopjes, supported by the six field artillery batteries under Colonel Parsons. These guns opened a heavy fire from 7.00 a.m. on the Boer position on Brakfontein and under cover of this, Wynne's men advanced in broad lines. There was, however, no response from the Boers until one battery had moved to cover the construction of an additional pontoon bridge on the western side of the loop of the Tugela due south of Vaal Krantz. At 11.45 a.m., the Boer artillery, consisting of three guns and a pom-pom located between Spion Kop and Brakfontein, opened a heavy fire. The troops lay down; the batteries were exposed but suffered relatively little loss. At 12.20 p.m., Parsons ordered his guns to prepare to move

3 *Times History*, vol. III, p. 304.
4 Ibid., p. 307.
5 Trew, *Generals*, p. 149.

to the flank, just as the third pontoon bridge was completed. At 1.30 p.m., Wynne gave the order to his infantry to retire, a movement which prompted heavy rifle fire from Brakfontein, again without causing much loss. For what it was worth, the feint attack had been carried out extremely efficiently. Amery wrote that 'it provided a magnificent spectacle to the rest of the army and reflected credit on the previous company and battery drill of the troops engaged in it. As a military operation it was ludicrous.'[6]

At 2.00 p.m., Buller ordered Lyttelton to commence his advance against Vaal Krantz, which all this while had been heavily bombarded; its garrison of no more than 95 men had suffered considerably. Two of Lyttelton's battalions, the 1st Durham Light Infantry and the 1st Rifle Brigade, crossed the bridge as rapidly as possible and then moved upstream sheltered by the 20-foot-high left bank of the river. After half a mile, this cover was no longer afforded to them and they began to suffer casualties as they swept up the slopes of Vaal Krantz. What was left of Viljoen's troops retreated down the far side of the hill; only the personal intervention of Viljoen himself saved the pom-pom gun, which had been located there, from capture.[7]

Thus, the first objective had, by 4.00 p.m. been attained. However, it soon became clear to Lyttelton that Vaal Krantz was not as valuable a prize as it had seemed: 'Immediately to the northward, and separated only by a deep and narrow saddle, the grassy downs of Brakfontein and Krantz Kloof ended in a bold hill (Hill 360). This was seamed with trenches, and though it had been earlier set ablaze by shells, was still strongly held.'[8] From here and from the heights to the west, the Boers could pour a heavy rifle fire on Vaal Krantz, and from Spion Kop, Brakfontein and Green Hill, the crest of the hill was exposed to heavy artillery fire. In addition, no way had yet been found to bring artillery up to the crest, which was the principal object of taking Vaal Krantz. Lyttelton, for the moment, could do no more than order his men to entrench the position which they had won, a task which had to be carried out under heavy artillery and rifle fire. As the sun went down, Lyttelton had three battalions on Vaal Krantz, while the 2nd Devonshire Battalion of Hildyard's brigade was on his right at Munger's Farm; its objective was Green Hill and from behind low stone walls, it exchanged fire with the Boer riflemen there.

During the evening Buller sent à Court to Lyttelton in order to assess the situation. When he returned, it was to advise an attack on Green Hill at dawn, with artillery moving up on the left to support Vaal Krantz, and that an additional bridge should be constructed at the foot of the hill. Buller decided to defer further action until the morning; his objective in securing Vaal Krantz was to use it as a position for his artillery but in the meantime, he recognised that he would have to take action against Hill 360. The suggestion of a night attack appears to have been put forward to Buller, but he rejected this out of hand.

Meanwhile, the Boers had reacted strongly to the attack on Vaal Krantz. Botha had returned from Pretoria and supervised the establishment of a formidable gun line. This was based on the arrival from Ladysmith of the Long Tom which was located on Doorn Kop; two guns from Krantz Kloof were brought to the northern slopes of Doorn Kloof, and one of the Krupp guns from Spion Kop was situated at a point 3,000 yards north of Vaal Krantz. The pom-pom rescued by Viljoen was placed on the northern slopes of Green Hill.

The German Staff History is severely critical of Buller at this juncture:

6 *Times History*, vol. III, p. 317.
7 *Official History*, vol. II, p. 411.
8 Ibid., p. 412.

> On the morning of February 6 a condition of absolute helplessness prevailed at British headquarters. The hopeful spirit which Buller had expressed in his telegram had changed to the exact opposite when the difficulties of breaking through had been more clearly recognised the day before.[9]

It is a fair comment. Buller began the day with the idea that he could clear the northern end of Vaal Krantz with artillery, and he sent a message to Lyttelton to this effect. Then at 6.45 a.m., in reply to a suggestion from Lyttelton that there should be a bridge at the foot of Vaal Krantz to assist a withdrawal should this become necessary, he agreed with the proposal, but went on to seek Lyttelton's opinion of another plan which he had in mind. This was to advance another brigade along the western side of Vaal Krantz – that is, behind Lyttelton – to attack Hill 360. Lyttelton replied that this stood little chance, preferring to see an advance on the eastern side. Next, later in the morning, Buller enquired whether Lyttelton could hold his position until sundown, as he wished to 'watch developments.' Yes, said Lyttelton, provided the Boers brought up no additional artillery. One thing had now become certain, and that was that there was no prospect of getting any guns to the top of Vaal Krantz; this, of course, had been the object of seizing it.[10]

Still vacillating, Buller now turned to a way to pass responsibility for the next step to Roberts, sending a telegram to him during the morning to say that he had pierced the enemy's line, and held a hill which divided their position and which, if he could advance, would give him access to the Ladysmith plain:

> But to get my artillery and supplies onto the plain, I must drive back the enemy either on my right or on my left. It is an operation which will cost from 2,000 to 3,000 men, and I am not confident, though hopeful, I can do it. The question is how would such a loss affect your plans and do you think the chance of the relief of Ladysmith worth the risk? It is the only possible way to relieve White; if I give up this chance I know no other.[11]

Since Roberts's injunction to him had been to stand on the defensive, Buller may well have been expecting to be instructed to discontinue the operation. Roberts, however, disappointed him, replying:

> Ladysmith must be relieved, even at the loss you anticipate. I would certainly persevere, and my hope is that the enemy will be so seriously punished as to enable White's garrison to be withdrawn without great difficulty. Let your troops know that the honour of the Empire is in their hands, and that I have no possible doubt of their being successful.[12]

During 6 February, there had been a more or less continuous exchange of artillery fire, which generally, had not been very effective, save a lucky shot from one of the naval guns on Signal Hill that blew up the ammunition wagon of one of the Boer guns on Doorn Kop, putting it out of action for several hours. At about 3.00 p.m., however, Botha launched an infantry assault on the northern end of Vaal Krantz, which drove back the advanced posts of the Durham Light Infantry but which in its turn, was then driven back to its start line; this action had only occupied

9 *German Staff History*, vol. II, p. 213.
10 *Official History*, vol. II, p. 415; *Times History*, vol. III, p. 322.
11 *Times History*, vol. III p. 323; Symons, *Campaign*. p. 253.
12 Ibid., pp. 323-324.

10 minutes. At the end of the afternoon, Hildyard's brigade began to cross the river by the new bridge, in order to relieve Lyttelton's brigade, an operation which was completed by 9.00 p.m. The Devonshires were relieved at Mungers Farm by the Connaught Rangers from Hart's brigade.[13]

Lyttelton, with Henry Wilson, his brigade major, returned to report to Buller, who was at dinner. He asked what sort of time they had had. 'Very bad,' said Lyttelton. 'Shot at day and night from nearly all sides.' Buller's response was to serve them with champagne, which they later said was 'the most refreshing drink they had ever tasted.'[14] Buller was still uncertain about his next move. The following morning, he made a personal inspection on horseback with Warren which provided him with no clear indication of what he ought to do. In the hope that a further demonstration of his strength might induce the Boers to go away, he marched Warren's two brigades round from Potgieter's to Zwart Kop. Hildyard, meanwhile, sent Buller a report suggesting that an attack might be made at dusk to seize Hill 360; but fortification of the position would be difficult, and it would be enfiladed on both flanks at closer ranges than Vaal Krantz. It was clearly not a good idea.[15]

As the day wore on, the Boer artillery continued to dominate the whole of the position occupied by the British Army. Buller accepted Warren's offer to make a further inspection from the top of Vaal Krantz, where the general made a number of sketches and notes. He brought these back to Buller, who evidently found no inspiration in them, for at 4.00 p.m., he called a meeting in Clery's tent to discuss the situation. Warren, Clery, Lyttelton, Hart, Wynne and Colonel Miles, the new chief of staff, attended. Buller told them that Roberts considered that the attack should be continued and asked them for their views. Lyttelton, Wynne and Clery favoured retirement; Hart argued that the attack should be continued. Of this latter view, Warren wrote that 'Hart was splendid. Nothing would induce him to retire except a direct order.' Warren himself was of the same opinion; they should go on, he thought, unless Buller had a better alternative. That, he suggested, might be to advance by Hlangwane. Buller thereupon decided that this would indeed be the better option, and it was agreed to adopt it.[16]

Consistently with his previous comments, Amery roundly condemns Buller's proceedings at Vaal Krantz, which he describes as 'one of the feeblest performances in the history of war:'

> There can be little doubt that, in spite of the futility of the feint attack and of the waste of time on the 5th, the original plan would have succeeded at any time up to the morning of the 6th, as, indeed, almost any reasonably planned attack anywhere along the Tugela line would have succeeded if pushed with the least promptitude and resolution … The Vaal Krantz performance must be reckoned as even inferior to Spion Kop. That it was not so disastrous was due to other causes than better generalship at the head.[17]

The operation cost the British 27 killed and 306 wounded; the Boer losses were very slight.[18]

Having received from his senior officers the answer which it may be supposed was what he wanted, Buller at once reported to Roberts and Lansdowne the decision to retire, and issued

13 *Official History*, vol. II, p. 417.
14 Symons, *Campaign*, p. 255.
15 *Official History*, vol. II, p. 417.
16 Symons, *Campaign*, p. 256; *Official History*, pp. 418-419.
17 *Times History*, vol. III, pp. 326–327.
18 *Official History*, vol. II p. 598.

orders for this at 5:45 p.m. This was, as the Official History pointed out, a delicate operation, requiring the profoundest secrecy if the 2nd Brigade was safely to abandon the crest of Vaal Krantz, together with great courage on the bridge at its foot: 'An attack in rear whilst so doing would delay, if not altogether confuse, the whole movement; an attack on the pontoon itself, which was not impossible, might block it altogether.'[19]

In the event, the retirement was skilfully managed; by the evening of 9 February, the army, with all its stores and artillery had, under Warren's supervision, reached Springfield and Chieveley. The Boers made no attempt to interfere, to Botha's extreme frustration; he had advocated a move to cut off the British retreat to Chieveley, but the council of war held on 8 February postponed a decision until it was too late. As the British troops retired after yet another reverse, it might have been expected that the confidence they had in Buller could have been dented, but this was not the case. Winston Churchill reflected their mood when he wrote that if Buller could not relieve Ladysmith with his present force 'we do not know of any other officer in the British service who would be likely to succeed.'[20] and the Official History referred to 'their utter disregard of fatigue and defeat in the determination to achieve their seemingly impossible purpose,' which showed that Buller, as 'the leader of such troops, aided by a fine climate, had nothing to fear either from the rigour or the disappointments of campaigning.'[21]

Such upbeat sentiments were not, however, held elsewhere. Both in Whitehall and in Ladysmith, the failures at Spion Kop and Vaal Krantz had caused such immense concern that Wolseley and White both addressed the possibility that the time had come for the Ladysmith garrison to make a desperate attempt to break through the Boer siege lines. Wolseley's anxieties had been sharpened by the two telegrams which Buller sent to Roberts on 9 February. He told the Field Marshal that he had seriously overestimated the ability of the Ladysmith garrison to detain Boer forces and thus prevent them joining those facing his army. He went on to say that with reinforcements, he might be able to progress but that otherwise, he had little chance of success. In his second telegram he wrote: 'It is right that you should know that, in my opinion, the fate of Ladysmith is only a question of days, unless I am very considerably reinforced.'[22] He went on to complain that he had not received the reinforcements which he had been promised, and that all forces arriving at the Cape should have been sent to Natal. He concluded with the statement that if it was felt that anyone could do better, he would willingly be sacrificed.

Roberts replied, patiently enough, on 14 February, asking that Buller should show a bold front but otherwise remain on the defensive. When Buller protested, Roberts agreed that he should continue to harass the Boers, and that he might act as he thought best so long as he did not compromise his force.[23]

Roberts had, as requested, forwarded Buller's telegrams of 9 February to London. Wolseley was dismayed, and wrote to his wife of his disillusionment with Buller:

> I have been thoroughly disappointed in him, for he has not shown any one of the characteristics I had attributed to him; no military genius, no firmness, and not even the obstinacy

19 Ibid., p. 419.
20 Churchill, *Boer War*, p. 163.
21 *Official History*, vol. II, pp. 421-422.
22 Symons, *Campaign*, p. 259.
23 *Times History*, vol. III, p. 329.

> which I thought he possessed when I discovered he had no firmness. He seems dazed and dumbfounded when he loses men.[24]

Given Buller's propensity to send panicky telegrams which overstated the extent of his difficulties, it is hardly surprising that Roberts, Lansdowne and Wolseley should each be reaching the conclusion that Buller had completely lost his nerve.

Outwardly, the government continued to put on a bold front. Salisbury as usual was contemptuous of the stupidity of Britain's officers, privately comparing them unfavourably with their German counterparts. This was due, he thought, to the fact that there, the entire Junker class was compelled to go into the army, so that it received a good cross-section of intelligence, 'whereas here the clever members of the upper classes are very apt to go into other professions.'[25] Salisbury frankly accepted responsibility for Buller's appointment, but in the House of Lords on 15 February he said firmly: 'I am shut off from discussing those questions altogether.'

Balfour had been the first member of the Cabinet to make any statement on the events of Black Week. In two speeches in Manchester on 8 and 9 January, he admitted no mistakes on the part of the government, defending Lansdowne and the War Office and blaming the British people and Parliament for the lack of military preparation. This failure to respond to national anxiety on the part of the Prime Minister and his deputy represented a serious failure to grasp the state of public opinion. *The Times*, however, which was becoming accustomed to the need to keep up the morale of the British people, wrote after the first news of the latest setback at Vaal Krantz:

> With the exception of a casualty list, nothing has been issued by the War Office which must, apparently, have received frequent reports from Sir Redvers Buller. The news that the attempt had failed and that the British troops had withdrawn across the river came from Boer sources, but has since been confirmed as we anticipated ... The complete absence of all official information throughout last week seems most remarkable, considering the natural anxiety felt in all quarters. The third attempt, unlike the first, has been characterised by careful handling and judicious dispositions of the troops, by which serious losses appear to have been happily avoided. The decision to elevate the relief of Ladysmith into the position of a primary strategic object conferred the greatest possible advantage upon the Boers, who have thus been enabled to employ their best force continuously in a country exactly suited to its fighting capacity ... We must be prepared for the fall of Ladysmith, with the painful humiliation and the moral consequences necessarily entailed. It may be some consolation to reflect the great efforts have been made to succour the gallant garrison, which deserves everything at the hands of its countrymen; but these efforts have already cost at least 3,200 casualties, and the initial strategic mistake has not yet been wholly expiated. It is now clear that, although we possessed a certain number of fine troops, there was no field army, and that the creation of an organised and adequately equipped force had to be undertaken after the outbreak of war. In other words, we have sought and we are still seeking to remedy a dangerous condition of military affairs by improvisation, and after four months of war the effect of the remedy thus applied is still awaited.[26]

24 Symons, *Campaign*, p. 259.
25 Roberts, *Salisbury*, p. 755.
26 *The Times*, 12 February 1900.

19

From Defeat to Victory

The retreat from Vaal Krantz concluded the cycle of defeats that had begun with Black Week. There were still calamities to come, and the war would continue for far longer than could have been foreseen, bringing with it appalling misery. In the end, though, the complete victory which British public opinion had never doubted, ultimately arrived. A modern historian has written:

> The confrontation at Vaal Krantz and Doorn Kop marked the end of the opening British operation in one important sense: it was to be the last set piece action in the old Black Week style. Even General Buller seemed finally to realise that something was going badly wrong, and that the successful resumption of a British advance required other ways of securing and retaining the initiative.[1]

The suggestion that Buller had finally grasped what he was doing wrong may perhaps flatter him; but the events which followed the failure at Vaal Krantz did at last, begin to show that the enormous British numerical supremacy would in the end, be decisive.

It was in the western sector, however, where the first indications were that the tide was turning. Roberts and Kitchener had secretly left Cape Town on the evening of 6 February and made their way to Methuen's camp on the Modder River, where they had, for several days, been assembling the force with which Roberts proposed to take the offensive. He had, since he arrived in South Africa, been considering the lessons to be learnt from the events of the campaign to date. It was plain to him that there must be changes in the tactics to be employed against an enemy which he recognised was formidable, and he issued two detailed memoranda on the subject. In particular, he rejected the idea of the frontal attack:

> We have to deal with an enemy possessing remarkable mobility, intimately acquainted with the country, thoroughly understanding how to take advantage of ground, adept in improvising colour, and most skilful in the use of their weapons. Against such an enemy any attempt to take a position by direct attack will surely fail. The only hope of success lies in

1 Nasson, *Boer War*, p. 165.

> being able to turn one or both flanks, or what would in many instances be equally effective, to threaten to cut the enemy's line of communication.[2]

With these considerations in mind, Roberts planned a flank march with Bloemfontein and Pretoria as his objective, but instead of the original plan for an advance in the centre into the Orange Free State, he concentrated his army at Orange River Station. He sought to persuade his enemy that he would advance by the direct route across Norvals Pont with a view to relieving Kimberley from the south-west. Instead, though, on 11 February he marched eastward and then north; with Cronje maintaining his position at Magersfontein until too late, Roberts's move threatened to cut him off not only from Bloemfontein but also from his line of retreat into the Transvaal. Meanwhile, Roberts sent his cavalry under French, with orders to outflank Cronje and head with all speed to the relief of Kimberley, an operation that was completed on 15 February.

Cronje finally began to pull out of his position at Magersfontein on 16 February, but he had tarried too long. Retreating across the front of the advancing British Army, he was caught at Paardeberg on the Modder River, where he was surrounded. Hastily entrenching his position there, he faced a frontal assault ordered by Kitchener in the absence of Roberts, who was ill. It was an unnecessary attack, which Cronje was able to repel, inflicting 1,200 casualties; but his position was hopeless, and on 22 February, he surrendered with some 4,000 men.

Meanwhile, Buller had embarked on his fourth attempt to relieve Ladysmith by attacking the left flank of the Boer position on the Tugela. He succeeded in capturing key hills at Cingolo and Monte Cristo on 17 and 18 February, after which the Boers retreated from their position on Hlangwane. Following up this success, Buller pushed on, although slowly, and the Boers established defensive positions on the left bank of the Tugela from Red Hill to Pieters Hill. Heavy fighting ensued over the next few days, culminating in the battle of Pieters Hill on 26 February, when the Boer line collapsed. On 28 February, Dundonald's mounted brigade rode into Ladysmith. In March, Botha began to establish a new defensive line on the Biggarsberg.

In the west, Cronje's surrender had left Roberts with little opposition to face on his march to Bloemfontein, which he entered on 18 March. It was, however, seven weeks before Roberts could resume his advance, which had Pretoria as his next objective. For this, he had approximately 100,000 men, moving in a three-pronged attack from Kimberley, Bloemfontein and northern Natal. Botha, who had formally succeeded to the chief command following the death of Joubert on 27 March, had no more than 30,000 men to resist the British advance, and these were scattered in a number of separate groups. It was plainly impossible to continue the siege of Mafeking, which was relieved on 17 May, leading to an extraordinary outpouring of emotion on the part of the British public.

When Roberts was finally able to resume his advance from Bloemfontein, he headed for Kroonstad. There, Botha had some 8,000 men and 20 guns, but he had little hope of resisting the British Army that opposed him of 38,000 men and 100 guns. Inevitably, the Boers fell back from Kroonstad on 11 May. After a brief pause, Roberts crossed the Vaal on 27 May; this was the last of the five rivers that lay between Bloemfontein and the Transvaal. Before this, he had on 24 May, officially proclaimed the annexation of the Orange Free State.

2 Elgin Commission, *Appendix* H p. 532.

Botha next made a stand outside Johannesburg at Doorn Kop, the place where Dr Jameson had surrendered in 1896, but the force of the British advance had become obviously irresistible. On 29 May, Kruger and Francis Reitz, his State Secretary, left Pretoria for Machadodorp, 140 miles to the east, carrying on the business of the government there from a group of railway carriages. The fall of Pretoria – which occurred on 2 June – was inevitable, and to Roberts and many others, it seemed that the war was about to end. This was not, however, the unanimous view among the headquarters staff; the perceptive Colonel Henry Rawlinson had written on 13 May: 'It looks to me as though the war could last for a good many months more. The enemy will, as I have always said, break up into small parties and take to guerilla war, which will take much time and blood to conquer.'[3] It was a forecast that was to prove painfully accurate.

On 1 June, a number of Boer generals, recognising that the fall of the capital was imminent, had met in Pretoria and resolved to send a telegram to Kruger suggesting that the war should now come to an end. Kruger consulted Steyn, who was adamant that there should be no surrender. The next day, the generals attended a *krigsraad* to consider what steps should be taken for the defence of Pretoria; only Botha, Smuts and one or two others had seen Steyn's impassioned reply. The tone of this was matched, however, by a number of the younger Transvaal commanders who attended the meeting and it was ultimately agreed that the war must go on, and the immediate policy should be a fighting retreat.[4]

After the relief of Ladysmith, Buller's force was tasked with breaking through the Boer position on the Biggarsberg. Advancing from Ladysmith on 7 May, Buller moved so rapidly that the Boers were taken by surprise. By 13 May, he had penetrated well into the range, and the Boers, fearful of a threat to their line of retreat, abandoned their entire position. Buller was pleased with himself, as on this occasion he had every right to be; he wrote to his wife to tell her of his success: 'I have surprised and outmanoeuvred the Boers and have got a considerable force out of an enormously strong position, with very small, and indeed infinitesimally small loss.'[5]

Behind the scenes, Roberts was anxious to be rid of Buller, as he made clear in his correspondence with Lansdowne, but the latter considered that this would be unwise. Buller was, he pointed out, very popular with a large section of the army and to public opinion,, he was a dogged soldier who after great difficulties, had succeeded. His supersession, Lansdowne believed, would be received with indignation, while he did not like 'the idea of washing all our dirty linen in public and before the eyes of a foreigner.' He left the decision to Roberts but said that the Cabinet would have 'little doubt that you will leave Buller where he is.'[6]

After forcing the Biggarsberg, Buller went on to turn the Boers out of their extremely strong position at Laing's Nek, followed by a hard-fought battle at Alleman's Nek on 11 June. It cost him 150 casualties but in the end, the Boers retreated and Buller had succeeded in clearing Natal of the invaders. In letters home he wrote that he 'was really rather pleased;' it was a further indication that he had restored his lost self-confidence.

Roberts, meanwhile, had moved out of Pretoria to attack Botha in the position which the latter had taken up with 6,000 men and 23 guns along a series of ridges to the east of the city. Fought over two days on 11–12 June, the battle was indecisive; Roberts had 16,000 men, but his conduct of the battle was ineffective, although at least he had succeeded in driving Botha

3 Pakenham, *Boer War*, p. 421
4 Trew, *Generals*, p. 153.
5 Ibid., p. 182.
6 Powell, *Buller*, p. 181.

away from the capital. For the Boers however, it was an engagement which lifted morale; Smuts wrote that it had 'an inspiring effect which could scarcely have been improved by a real victory.'[7]

Although the advance of the British had, it seemed, brought the war almost to an end, Roberts faced an immediate threat to his lines of communication, and he was anxious that Buller should continue his advance so that, with the clearing of the blocked railway tunnel at Laing's Nek, the railway line through Natal should be available as a supply line. There remained, though, the danger to the railways from the mobile commandos, which scored a number of successes against isolated British units. Meanwhile, Buller himself arrived in Pretoria by rail on 7 July for what proved a reasonably cordial meeting with Roberts.

The principal threat to the lines of communication had come from the presence of about 5,000 Free Staters concentrated in the Brandwater Basin. By the end of July, however, the bulk of these had surrendered and Roberts was free to move against Botha, who had taken up a position covering the Delagoa Bay railway line west of Machadorp. Buller was ordered by Roberts to move there with an infantry division and two mounted brigades and he set off on 7 August on what would be a march of about a 100 miles via Carolina. A week later, he was able to replenish supplies at Middelburg, a supply base held by French. After a delay ordered by Roberts which greatly annoyed him, Buller moved forward again on 21 August. The two men met again at Belfast on 28 August and the next day, Buller advanced against the Boer positions, which he took at the cost of 120 casualties.

On 1 September, Roberts formally proclaimed the annexation of the Transvaal and in the following days, the continued advance of the British suggested that organised resistance was now at an end. On 24 September, Pole-Carew occupied Komati Poort, which finally closed the route into Portuguese East Africa; Kruger had previously made his way to Lourenco Marques and from there he sailed for Europe on 19 October, having been invited to take up his residence in the Netherlands.

In London, the Cabinet had resolved to go to the country to take advantage of the apparently successful conclusion of the war. In the ensuing election, the government was returned to office with a majority which was only slightly less than Salisbury's landslide victory of 1899. Known as the 'Khaki Election', it inevitably gave a divided opposition considerable difficulty, since naturally it was the war that was the dominant issue, and the government made the most of the patriotic mood of the country.

Buller, feeling that his work in South Africa was done, asked to be relieved and on 24 October, he sailed for England, arriving at Southampton in early November to a hero's welcome. He paid a visit to the Queen at Windsor. Evidently realising what might lie ahead, she wrote in her diary: 'When I urged that there should be no recriminations, Sir Redvers said there would be none from him.'[8] Buller now returned to his previous post in command at Aldershot.

On 29 November, confident that the war had effectively ended, Roberts handed over command to Kitchener, sailing home from Cape Town on 10 December. Before he left, there was a triumphant dinner, about which Milner, who did not share his view that the war was over, had mixed feelings: 'We have all shouted ourselves hoarse over him, and I am glad for his sake … But I must own that, apart from him, there is something ill-omened, and bizarre and almost repulsive

7 Pakenham, *Boer War*, p. 434.
8 Powell, *Buller*, p. 192.

in all this triumphing and congratulations in the middle of war.'[9] When Roberts returned to England in early January, he was rewarded with the earldom and a grant of £100,000.

The war, however, was far from over. When Kitchener assumed the command, it still had 17 months to run, in the course of which the Boer guerillas continued to inflict embarrassing defeats on isolated British units and to mount invasions of both Cape Colony and Natal. The struggle became increasingly bitter, with the burning of Boer farmsteads and the establishment of concentration camps for their displaced inhabitants, in which large numbers of Boers, especially women and children, perished. The erection of an enormous series of blockhouses across the veld, some 8,000 in number, played an important part in checking the mobility of the gorillas. Eventually, however, the long campaign against the guerillas came to an end, and peace was signed at Vereeniging on 31 May 1902.

Black Week may have seemed a long time past, but it cast a long shadow. In the military context it had two particular echoes. At the end of March 1900, Christiaan de Wet had won a striking victory at Sanna's Post, when he captured the waterworks pumping station on the Modder River that supplied Bloemfontein with its water. Immediately after his victory, de Wet had ridden off in the direction of Dewetsdorp (a village that had been named after his father, which lay about 40 miles south-east of Bloemfontein), where he found another opportunity of which he determined to take advantage. On 28 March, Roberts had told Gatacre, still in command of the attenuated 3rd Division (it was only four battalions strong and was on line of communications duty) that if he had enough troops at his disposal he wished him to occupy Dewetsdorp. Gatacre took this to be an order and sent a force of about 500 infantry under the command of Captain William M'Whinnie. On the night of 31 March/1 April, learning how small was this force, Roberts sent an order that it be withdrawn; Gatacre passed this on to M'Whinnie, but though he had been told of the battle at Sanna's Post, he gave no information to M'Whinnie of the danger.

M'Whinnie marched his force towards Reddersburg, some 20 miles to the west of Dewetsdorp. On 3 April, four miles to the north-east of his destination, he became aware that he was being followed by a substantial Boer force and he hastily occupied a ridge called Mostert's Hoek and did his best to prepare a defensive position there. It was de Wet who pursued him, having called up 1,500 infantry and three guns, and he called on M'Whinnie to surrender, which he refused. As night fell, the Boers closed on the British position.

At 7.00 that evening, both Roberts and Gatacre became aware of the problem and the latter was ordered to go to the relief of M'Whinnie. Roberts sent five companies of Cameron Highlanders by rail from Bloemfontein to Bethanie, 12 miles west of Reddersburg, instructing Gatacre to hasten with them and any other available troops to the rescue of M'Whinnie's force. Early on 4 April, the scouts and a company of mounted infantry reconnoitring towards Reddersburg, set off at 6.00 a.m. and an hour later, reported that they could hear firing. As soon as the Cameron Highlanders arrived, Gatacre set off to Reddersburg, but at 9.30 a.m., received a report that the firing had stopped. He marched on until he was five or six miles from the village; then, at about 11.00 a.m., he learnt that M'Whinnie had surrendered.[10] He halted for an hour, and then decided to retire on the railway; after marching back 4 miles, he received orders to occupy Reddersburg which he did, only to receive at midnight, orders to return to Bethanie.

9 Pakenham, *Boer War*, p. 458.
10 Gatacre, *Gatacre*, p. 256.

De Wet had resumed his attack on M'Whinnie at dawn; by 8.00 a.m., the Boers had forced their way on to the ridge itself, which compelled the British to retire to a position which was impossible to defend for long, and at 9.00 a.m., the white flag was raised. De Wet took 546 unwounded prisoners; in addition, M'Whinnie had lost 10 killed and 33 wounded.[11]

The immediate consequence of this unfortunate affair was that Roberts relieved Gatacre of his command and sent him home, sending a report on 16 April of his reasons for doing so. He explained that he might have superseded Gatacre for his conduct at Stormberg, but did not do so, to avoid the slur to his reputation. Reviewing the conduct of Gatacre's operations around Reddersburg, he concluded that he had 'shown a grave want of judgement which must necessarily shake the confidence of those units under his orders and have a bad effect on the morale of his troops.'[12] This decision was a little hard; the problem had occurred because Gatacre interpreted the ambiguous telegram about the occupation of Dewetsdorp as an order, while having no information before him about any risk from de Wet.

There was another reminder of Black Week when Lord Methuen, much later, as the war neared its end, again encountered his nemesis Koos de la Rey, the architect of his defeat at Magersfontein. After Black Week, the government had decreed that both Gatacre and Methuen should be superseded at once, but Buller, himself soon to be superseded by Roberts, had refused to do so, and both men continued in active commands. Buller objected to being told how to employ his subordinates and in Methuen's case, had some sympathy with his difficulties; in any event, since Warren was to be diverted to Natal, there was nobody suitable to take over from Methuen.

After Magersfontein, Methuen had remained on the Modder River on the defensive during the rest of December and January. He met with Roberts on 8 February before the latter's flank march began; the meeting did not go well, but Roberts declined to accept Methuen's offer of resignation. Methuen had a considerable dislike of Kitchener, whom he suspected of 'running the whole show,' and he heard the news of Kitchener's setback at Paardeberg with undisguised satisfaction.[13]

During the course of the next two years, Methuen enjoyed some success, although largely in small-scale operations. He wrote of this to his wife, saying that many generals would be very angry, but that he was beyond that now. Nevertheless, this work went a long way to restoring his reputation. He was one of only three senior British commanders who served throughout the war, the others being Lyttelton and French. He was still nominally in command of the 1st Division, but this had been greatly reduced in size. In August 1900, there began a prolonged and complicated attempt to catch Christiaan de Wet, in which Methuen took an important part. Thereafter, he conducted a series of operations, about which Roberts, on leaving South Africa, wrote to congratulate him.[14]

Under Kitchener, Methuen was, perhaps surprisingly, given a much greater degree of independence and throughout 1901, he was operating in the Western Transvaal, where he was extremely active. With only a relatively small body of troops, he had to deal with Boer guerilla attacks over a huge area. During this time, he became increasingly sympathetic to the sufferings of the civilian population and personally favoured a humane policy to restore goodwill between the two peoples.

11 *Official History*, vol. II, p. 310.
12 Ibid., pp. 614-615.
13 Miller, *Methuen*, p. 191.
14 Ibid., p. 216.

Towards the end of 1901, Methuen's principal objective was to catch de la Rey. Kitchener wrote to him on 17 September: 'De la Rey is very nearly done. He has been much hustled lately and a little more would result in collapse in the whole Western Transvaal. I hope you will give him the little more necessary and give him no rest.'[15]

However, De la Rey was not done. Methuen was anxious that the small forces available to him were inadequate and his concerns were justified when in February 1902, de la Rey, with a force 1,300 strong, ambushed and captured a convoy under von Donop, taking 700 prisoners. Collecting what forces he could, amounting to no more than 1,300 men, mainly irregulars and many of whom had never seen action, Methuen set off on 2 March to catch de la Rey and his captives before they escaped into the Marico Valley. He was obliged to move to Tweebosch in search of water; he was expecting to meet with substantial reinforcements, but for the moment believed that de la Rey was still to the south.

The Boer commander was, however, close at hand. Aware of Methuen's movements, and with a force now 1,500 strong, he attacked Methuen, whose troops were marching in two columns, at 6.00 a.m. on 7 March. Unusually for the Boers, de la Rey ordered a mounted charge, routing the inexperienced British troops. *The Times History* recorded the débacle: 'The horde of fugitives swept along the left flank of both convoys, crossed the river, sucked into the current of flight the 86th Yeomanry and Cape Specials, who had not fired a shot, and never drew rein till they reached the top of the rise some three miles away.'[16] Practically all Methuen's gunners were killed or wounded; he stayed with the guns, but was himself wounded twice and his horse was shot beneath him, falling on him and breaking his leg. At 9.30 a.m., the white flag was raised.

The catastrophe occasioned widespread alarm; the new Secretary of State for War, William St John Brodrick, described it as the worst disaster since Colenso. Methuen's biographer has pointed out, however, that while blame was attached to the War Office for the poor quality of the troops assigned to Methuen, and Kitchener was blamed for the weakness of the forces in the Western Transvaal, almost no one blamed Methuen. He received many public and private tributes; H. W. Wilson wrote: 'No officer had more endeared himself to the British nation, and there were none whose efforts it would have preferred to see crowned with victory; for, of all those in high command, he alone remained to the last.'[17] And de la Rey wrote to de Wet to say that Methuen's conduct 'was beyond praise.' De la Rey treated Methuen with great kindness and respect; his wife, whom Methuen had encountered earlier in the war, when he had spared her farmhouse from burning, visited him and prepared a meal, and sent a telegram to Lady Methuen to say that her husband was in no danger. Methuen was released on 13 March and returned to England in June. Unlike poor Gatacre, who never held another command, Methuen's career continued to prosper, and he rose in due course to the rank of Field Marshal.

These setbacks illustrated the problem, which beset the British Army throughout the war, of collecting reliable intelligence about the movements of a highly mobile enemy. Indeed, it could be said that the failure to accord sufficient priority to the whole issue of military intelligence had been one of the most significant failings of the British Army before it entered on war in South Africa.

15 Ibid., p. 223.
16 *Times History*, vol. V, p. 506.
17 H.W. Wilson, *After Pretoria*: *The Guerilla War* (London: Amalgamated Press, 1902) p. 956.

In Britain, the causes of the early setbacks in the war were at the front of everyone's mind. There was a burgeoning debate about who or what was to blame, a debate that would continue until long after the war had ended. In the autumn of 1900, one key question was easily resolved – that Roberts should succeed Wolseley as commander-in-chief. The latter's term of office was due to end of 31 October, but he agreed to stay on for a further month while Roberts made his way back to England. Wolseley left office with the bitterest of feelings. Of Lansdowne, he wrote that he was 'very civil and grinning, but never says he regrets my departure or is obliged for my work.' He was particularly angry with Salisbury, who had written a letter saying he looked back on their relationship with pride and pleasure; Wolseley remarked that it was 'from either a dis-remembering humbug or from a man whose mind is either going or gone.' When he left the War Office, Wolseley went to say goodbye to St John Brodrick, observing later that he 'shook hands with that underhand and tricky prig and bid him goodbye … I hope never to have any relations in life with him again.'[18]

Wolseley left behind him a vigorous debate on what should be the powers and duties of a commander-in-chief. He firmly believed that the position had become untenable as a result of the reorganisation of 1895. Before he left office, the Queen had encouraged him to write a memorandum putting his side of the argument about the responsibility for the initial failures in South Africa and his suggestions for improving the administration of the army. This he did on 12 November. He pointed out that since 1895, the commander-in-chief no longer had direct control of the administration of the army and that the Secretary for War had consequently become its military head. 'It is idle,' he wrote, 'to hope that any civilian, however eminent, can have the professional training and experience required to enable him to control an army.'[19] If control was not restored to the commander-in-chief, he recommended that the office should be abolished, as serving no useful purpose.

Roberts, when he took office, chafed under the same restraints on his authority, finding himself at odds with Brodrick who was no readier than Lansdowne to give up civilian control. In August 1901 Roberts wrote to him:

> I accepted the commander-in-chiefship with no light heart, but with every desire to assist you to the best of my ability in the very difficult task you had before you, but I confess eight months' experience has not made me feel sanguine as to there being any successful result. For some reason or another War Office work is unsatisfactory. It is too hurried, and there are too many ramifications, too many masters … If I am to remain I must feel that I have your entire confidence. I cannot work unless I am trusted, and if this is not to be, I would far rather make way for someone else whom you can trust.[20]

The particular dispute which prompted this was soon smoothed over; within a couple of months, however, the two men had to deal with a very different issue, in which they were at one.

Buller's surrender telegram had never been published, but its existence was widely known, and on 28 September 1901, Amery lit the fuse which was to detonate the explosion. Writing in *The Times* a savage anonymous letter over the pseudonym 'Reformer,' Amery attacked Buller on a number of counts:

18 Symons, *Campaign,* p. 283.
19 Hamer, *British Army*, p. 182.
20 Symons, *Campaign*, p. 287.

> The utter fatuity of Colenso, the unnecessary abandonment of the guns, the message to Sir G. White suggesting the surrender of Ladysmith, the want of decision at Spion Kop, the half-hearted attempt at Vaal Krantz, the costly blundering back into the Colenso deathtrap after the capture of Monte Cristo might have shown the way to the blindest, the inexcusable failure to pursue a demoralised enemy – is this the record for which the government and Lord Roberts, who know all, have chosen the commander on whom the first shock of the next war may fall?[21]

Buller had always had difficulty in controlling his temper, and this was too much for him, and he told a friend that it had made him 'combative and quarrelsome.' On 10 October, he gave a speech at a lunch given by the Queen's Westminster Volunteers. It is possible that Buller had had perhaps little too much to drink. Perhaps his feelings were especially aroused by the sight of Amery in the audience. At all events, he tackled the matter of the letter in *The Times* head on. Amery subsequently published the text of his remarks in *The Times History*; in part they read as follows:

> They attack me, and they say that I wrote a telegram in which I ordered Sir G. White to give up Ladysmith, to destroy his books, and so forth. I wrote a good many telegrams and wrote one telegram that admits partially of that description … I attacked Colenso on December 15. I was unsuccessful; it was a very trying day; I was 36 hours at work; I was 14 hours in the saddle. It was the hottest day we had the whole of the time I was out there, and I had rank bad luck, and I hope to show some day that if I had not had bad luck I had good enough men with me to get in. I attacked Colenso and I failed; and having failed, I had to consider the people in front of me in Ladysmith … I was in command of Natal, and it was my duty to give my support some assistance, some lead, something that in the event of his determining to surrender he would be able to produce and say, 'Well, Sir Redvers Buller agreed.' I, therefore, spatchcocked into the middle of that telegram a sentence in which I suggested if it would be necessary to surrender the garrison, what he should do when he surrendered, and how he should do it.[22]

On any view, it was a fatally unwise speech to make, and played into the hands of those who did not wish him well. These included not only Amery, who made use of the speech to attack him still more vigorously, but also Roberts and Brodrick. These two consulted with Salisbury and Balfour; it was decided that Buller should be dismissed from his post as general officer commanding Aldershot and be put on half pay. Roberts had made it clear that either Buller or he must go. He ignored the advice of Lieutenant-General Thomas Kelly-Kenny, one of his divisional commanders in South Africa, now Adjutant-General, who minuted him that Buller should be no more than censured and cautioned; he pointed out that Buller had not been alone in being indiscreet.[23] Roberts, though, remained adamant. Buller demanded, and was granted, an interview with Brodrick. In the course of this he complained of Roberts, of White and about the way he had been treated in the publication of despatches. He had asked that Robert should not be present at the meeting, but when the latter entered the room, Brodrick had much

21 Powell, *Buller*, p. 197.
22 *Times History*, vol. II, pp. 461-462.
23 Powell, *Buller*, p. 199.

difficulty in keeping the peace. Buller refused to resign and appealed to the King, saying that while he regretted the speech it should not be the ground for 'depriving me of my position, and of driving me from the service which I have served for 43 years.' His appeal fell on stony ground, and the decision to remove him was announced on 23 October.[24] Almost at once, Buller began to receive many hundreds of letters from members of the public regretting his dismissal and expressing unshaken confidence in him.

When Buller came to give his evidence to the Elgin Commission, he was ready to admit that his telegram to White was 'stupid' and that he ought not to have sent it but said that it was sent in a hurry. Pressed to explain what he actually meant by the words 'after which I suggest your firing away as much ammunition as you can and make the best terms you can,' he disclosed in his reply, the bitter resentment which he felt towards White:

> I was face-to-face with a man who had a better force theoretically, a more experienced force, and a larger available force to help himself than I had to help him. In his telegrams he had thrown the whole onus of his relief upon me, he could not come out, he could not go large and could only help me in a particular hole, the most difficult place to get to. As I say, the onus of his relief was thrown upon me, and practically he had got into Ladysmith and was directing me, as he did then and afterwards, to bring the whole forces of the Empire to get him out ... I did not consider that he had much initiative for active fighting, and I thought that the most effective lever I could employ to move him would be the warning that unless he could offer me active assistance he might possibly have to surrender.[25]

It was a brave effort at self-justification but cannot really be said to have been convincing. Taken together, the meaning of his messages still seems entirely clear.

24 Symons, *Campaign*, pp. 289-290.
25 Elgin Commission, *Minutes of Evidence*, vol. II, p. 205.

20

Inconclusive Conclusion: The Elgin Commission

Lord Salisbury's contempt for the military was long-standing and events in South Africa naturally confirmed all his doubts about the competence of the generals. The concept of an inquiry into the conduct of the war was one which had begun to appeal to him as a means of formally shifting the blame for the initial setbacks away from the government and onto the generals. On 4 January 1901, he wrote to Balfour to suggest that an inquiry was 'essential if we are to get out of a rather awkward corner.'[1] When the proposal was put to the Queen, she was at first opposed, believing that it could only help the Boers and foreign countries, but Salisbury and Balfour persuaded her that it would be necessary.

Meantime, on 17 December, Clinton Dawkins had been named as chairman of a committee of inquiry into the organisation of the War Office. This began its hearings on 8 January 1901, and it issued its report on 9 May. In general, it supported the military in respect of their grievances over the preceding 15 years, finding that the War Office had been built up piecemeal and that as a result, there was confusion in administration and an absence of clearly defined responsibility. The reasons for this included the administration of the army by the War Office 'through a vast system of minute regulations, which tend to destroy the responsibility of general officers.' These were too complex. The War Office had been absorbed in directing local affairs and interfering with command functions. The committee recommended that the War Office be divided into well-defined sections, each with a clear responsibility; and that the existing War Office Council and Army Board be abolished, and a permanent army board established to be called the 'War Office Board,' with larger authority than its predecessors. It should institute a number of reforms, intended to simplify the business of the War Office and decentralise routine work.[2] The overall effect of the report was strictly to limit the participation of senior civil servants in the administration of the army.

An Order in Council of 4 November, reduced the status of the Adjutant-General to a position in which he would be controlled by the commander-in-chief; it increased the extent of the duties of the Director of Mobilisation and Military Intelligence, who would exercise some of the functions performed by the chief of staff in foreign armies, and he was to report to

1 Roberts, *Salisbury*, p. 793.
2 Hamer, *British Army*, pp. 187-189.

the commander-in-chief. Pursuant to this change, Sir William Nicholson succeeded Sir John Ardagh as Director.

Before this committee published its report, however, there had been a heated debate in the House of Lords on the question of civil and military authority. The Duke of Bedford complained that it was not known whether the commander-in-chief was the real adviser of the Secretary of State and the real head of the army, nor his position in matters of finance; a detailed investigation was called for. In the course of the debate, the newly retired Wolseley had, naturally, much to say from the crossbenches. He said that his arguments were not directed against individuals, but against the system. He called for a reversion to the pre-1895 system, but wanted the commander-in-chief to have the power to make public any important issue in which his opinion was at odds with that of the Secretary of State.

Lansdowne, in reply, made a speech not only in defence of the War Office but one which incorporated an assault on Wolseley's performance of the duties of commander-in-chief; it was not, he claimed, that the office of commander-in-chief had failed but the man who held the post. This personal attack was, to many members of the House of Lords, extremely shocking, especially to members of the Liberal opposition. When Salisbury spoke at the end of the debate, however, he was emphatic in his view of the matter of civil-military responsibility:

> In speech after speech from military men, men who know the language and spirit of the War Office, it is easy to detect a desire that military problems shall only be solved by military men; but any attempt to take the opinion of the expert above the opinion of the politician must, in view of all the circumstances of our constitution, inevitably fail.[3]

In a subsequent debate on the memorandum which Wolseley had written to Salisbury during the preceding November, he had an opportunity to answer the charges made against him by Lansdowne. He made a spirited speech in his defence, saying that if Lansdowne had been unhappy with his performance, he should have raised it at the time. To show that he had carried out his duties fully, he would have to produce all the memoranda he had written during his term of office. As to the preparations for war, he cited the various memoranda he had written about reinforcements for Natal and the Cape. He admitted that in common with all persons and authorities who had expressed an opinion, he had underestimated the fighting power of the individual Boer.[4] In the end, though, the government's supporters in the House of Lords prevailed and Wolseley's motion was defeated by 62 to 38.

Throughout 1901 and 1902, there was continuing pressure for a more general inquiry into the early setbacks in South Africa. At the same time, Roberts was, as has been seen, unhappy, just as Wolseley had been, with the restrictions placed on his authority. In September 1901, he was contemplating resignation. His relations with Brodrick had become seriously strained. He was criticised in Parliament because of the favouritism he was alleged to show to members of the 'Roberts Ring.' He struggled with his administrative responsibilities, in respect of which he was far less able than, for instance, Wolseley or Buller.[5] At the same time, though, the continuing effect of the Dawkins Report had greatly strengthened the influence of the professional soldiers.

3 Ibid., p. 185.
4 Kochanski, *Wolseley*, pp. 260-261.
5 Symons, *Campaign*, p. 291.

In 1902 the government, not without some reluctance, agreed to appoint a Royal Commission to investigate in particular, the matters raised by Wolseley in his battle with Lansdowne. King Edward had been opposed to this because, as he wrote to Salisbury, he thought that it might do the army harm in the eyes of the civilised world. On the other hand, it would provide, as Salisbury continued to believe, an effective way of passing the responsibility for the early defeats to the soldiers. This appeared in the terms of reference of the Commission:

> To inquire into the military preparations for the war in South Africa, and into the supply of men, ammunition, equipment, and transport by sea and land in connection with the campaign, and into the military operations up to the occupation of Pretoria.[6]

The final limb of the terms of reference was of course intended to ensure that the Commission looked at the performance of the generals who had conducted the operations during the period to be reviewed.

Apart from Lord Elgin, a former Viceroy of India, the members of the Commission were Lord Esher, Sir George Taubman-Goldie, Field Marshal Sir Henry Norman, Admiral Sir John Hopkins, Sir John Edge, Sir John Jackson, Lord Strathcona and Sir Frederick Darley. The Commission sat at St Stephen's House, Westminster, taking evidence on 55 days and hearing 114 witnesses to whom some 22,200 questions were put. The evidence was recorded in two volumes of minutes of evidence; a large number of documents were received, some of which were annexed to the Report itself, and the rest of those considered useful in a separate volume of appendices. The reports of a number of other Royal Commissions and committees were considered, including those of the Hartington Commission and the Dawkins committee.

The Commission began its deliberations in October 1902, the day after the last two members were appointed. The reason for this urgency was that Kitchener, clearly a necessary witness, was on the point of departing for India to take up his post there as commander-in-chief. The three individuals who had held the office of commander-in-chief in South Africa, White, Buller and Roberts, were invited to submit a statement of the matters which they wished the Commission to take into account. Buller, whose statement was much the longest, was assisted in its preparation by the distinguished historian of the British Army, Sir John Fortescue. The Report commented on these in the following terms:

> As expressing the view taken of the events with which they deal by the men who had the chief share in directing the operations, they will be read with interest and attention. Differences of opinion will be found here also, and still more in some statements from other officers which have been admitted; but we hold strongly that their nature entirely justifies our decision not to allow an argumentative discussion on controversial questions to be opened up before us, especially as between individual officers.[7]

The commissioners firmly refused to examine the conduct of operations, observing that it was in no sense their duty to compile a military history of the war:

6 Elgin Commission, *Report*, p. 1.
7 Ibid., pp. 2-3

> No one would employ the machinery of a Royal Commission for that purpose, and certain branches of inquiry were obviously impossible. The Commission were not so constituted as to enable them to pronounce judgement on questions of strategy or tactics, or to review the decision of superior authority on the conduct of individual officers.[8]

Thus, Salisbury and his Cabinet were denied their hope that blame could be laid at the door of individuals for the early setbacks. The Commission published in full, the minutes of evidence of those that appeared before them, leaving what they said to speak for itself; these witnesses certainly could not complain of their treatment by the members of the Commission who, in questioning them, generally treated them very tenderly and with great respect; Esher, though, pressed Buller rather more severely. He kept the King regularly informed of the deliberations of the Commission, in the course of which he frequently expressed criticisms of Buller. However, his overall opinion of him was not entirely unfavourable:

> He did not cut a poor figure, but appeared what he is, a brave and capable soldier, admirably adapted to hold a high secondary command, but unfitted, by his temperament, to be placed in supreme command of an army in the field. He gave excellent evidence upon military questions generally, and upon War Office questions. Lord Esher finally was enabled to understand why Sir Redvers had won the affection of officers who served under him, and of the rank and file. In spite of his great failings, he is a very human figure. Unpleasing in appearance, with no command of temper, he is nevertheless a man of strong sympathies and generous impulses.[9]

Speaking to Esher after giving his evidence, Buller told him that all his life he had suffered from his 'beastly temper.'

Accordingly, it was in consideration of the first of the matters of inquiry that the commissioners entered into the question of responsibility for any shortcomings in the military preparations for the war. They considered what preparations were made, and whether they were made in sufficient time: 'If they were not sufficiently timely and otherwise adequate, it must be further asked who were the authorities responsible, and what defence they have to offer.'[10] When Wolseley was asked what 'great lesson' could be learnt from the Boer War, his reply was succinct: 'We were not prepared for war, and are not prepared for war at all times.'[11]

Having reviewed the course of events prior to the outbreak of war, the commissioners next examined the reports of intelligence officers, both earlier and in particular, in the three years before the war. That done, they proceeded to identify the division of responsibility for the steps taken as a result of such reports. Under the provisions of the Order in Council of 1895, it was the responsibility of the commander-in-chief to arrange for the distribution of the army, and to prepare and maintain schemes of offensive and defensive operations. It was not the function of the Intelligence Department to decide what force was required to meet the dangers which it identified, while the generals on the spot were required to do no more than detail the positions

8 Ibid., p. 2
9 Powell, *Buller*, p. 201.
10 Elgin Commission, *Report*, p. 4.
11 Ibid.

which the troops might best occupy. That being the case, the commissioners looked at the evidence of Wolseley as to the recommendations which he had made.

They considered his note to Buller of 17 July 1899, and their meeting next day with Lansdowne, to be particularly important, together with the ensuing exchanges between Lansdowne and Wolseley. Reviewing the whole of the circumstances, they came firmly to the view that Wolseley had been at fault: 'the special function of the commander-in-chief … viz, "the preparation of schemes of offensive and defensive operations," was not exercised on this occasion in any systematic fashion.'[12] As a result, they considered it 'not altogether remarkable under the circumstances that no plan of campaign ever existed for operations in South Africa.' They were not impressed by Lansdowne's evidence that 'it was by no means the rule that a general despatched on an errand of this kind is furnished with full and precise instructions.' Lansdowne had added that he could not see that anybody was prejudiced by the absence of a definite plan of campaign. The commissioners found it difficult to see the point of imposing a duty on the commander-in-chief to prepare schemes of offensive operations if something of the kind was not intended: 'In no other line of life would an agent be entrusted with a difficult and responsible task without some attempt at precise and careful definition of the object in view, and there seems to be no reason why military duty should be a solitary exception.'[13]

Having thus concluded that Wolseley did not do his job properly, the Commission's Report published the summary of the views of Lord Roberts, without comment, although remarking that almost every officer examined about what should have been done at the outset expressed a different view. The Commission, consistent with its self-denying decision about judging these matters, observed that it was impossible to subject these opinions to any reliable test, 'and the only course that is fair to all is to leave them on the same footing, i.e. on record for the consideration and judgement of the reader.'[14]

The Commission delivered its report in July 1903. By now, an ailing Salisbury had been succeeded as Prime Minister by Arthur Balfour; Lansdowne continued as Foreign Secretary and Brodrick as Secretary for War. The government's general posture with regard to the army and its future was largely unchanged; Roberts continued to be uncomfortable, to an increasing extent, with the limitations on the office of commander-in-chief. The report was, no doubt deliberately, not published until the recess in August; but if this avoided any immediate difficulties in Parliament, it meant it appearing in the 'dead season,' at a time when there was very little else to talk about, as Balfour put it.[15]

Reviewing the Commission's severe criticism of Wolseley, W. S. Hamer thought that the evidence of deficiencies in the staff work of his department seemed 'less to incriminate Lord Wolseley for neglect of his duties than to strengthen the arguments of those who had demanded the creation of a proper staff and to condemn the politicians for their refusal to accept the recommendations of the Hartington Commission along these lines.'[16] The commissioners were not anxious, he noted, to recommend the creation of a general staff or to consider the political implications of the problem. Looking back, in the light of subsequent developments of the issue, the government's reluctance to establish a general staff does seem astonishing. Hamer's

12 Ibid., p. 22
13 Ibid.
14 Ibid., p. 25.
15 Ibid.
16 Hamer, *British Army*, p. 204.

criticism that the Commission's recommendations were 'vague and out of all proportion to the serious nature of the situation which their investigations had revealed' certainly appears to be entirely justified. Nor is it easy to dispute his conclusion that the government ignored its military advisers, which even the Commission acknowledged was the case.

Not only did the Commission not advocate the creation of a general staff; it also made no suggestion that the office of commander-in-chief be abolished. It did, though, call for a modification of the way in which the consultative process worked: 'No defect in War Office organisation has excited more hostile criticism than the want of consultative power which has characterised its administration.'[17]

For his part, Esher wrote a note of dissent from the majority of the Commission, calling for a major reform of the War Office:

> Discussion in the presence of the Secretary of State, if possible agreement, or an acceptance of the decision of the majority, are essential elements in the military administration of the War Office if the Secretary of State for War's policy is to carry, among his colleagues and in Parliament, the weight which attaches to the views of the First Lord of the Admiralty.[18]

In such an organisation, the position of the commander-in-chief would be anomalous, and should be abolished. This was to lead directly to the establishment of the Esher committee in November 1903, which led to the far-reaching reforms which did include the creation of a general staff and the abolition of the post of commander-in-chief.

Once the report of the Elgin Commission was published, it generated widespread comment, much of it critical. Various writers believed that it had fallen into error in casting so much blame on Wolseley rather than the government. England, the *Spectator* wrote, had been forewarned and not forearmed and Lansdowne was to blame for this. A writer in the *Edinburgh Review* complained that the report was too inconclusive and had added to the confusion; it had failed to answer many of the questions it should have considered. W. T. Stead, writing of Chamberlain and Lansdowne, considered that 'never have any two ministers been shown to have failed so utterly in the qualities that are indispensable to those who would be regarded as statesmen of the Empire.'[19]

Replying to an inquiry from Brodrick in September 1903, Balfour thought that there would be 'a considerable row' over the report; but on the subject of reform, he was sceptical. Critics of the War Office, he said, alleged that soldiers were 'wanting in loyalty and administrative capacity. You will not give them either of these useful qualities by modifying the status of their department.'[20] As an argument for doing nothing, this might be employed in opposing most measures of reform, whatever the subject matter.

In the following years, however, the pressure for army reform continued unabated. Although memories of Black Week steadily faded, the defeats in 1899 and early 1900 had left their mark and ultimately, contributed to the introduction of reforms that had been resisted for so long. The establishment of a general staff and the consequent abolition of the office of commander-in-chief, gave the army the chance to take a long stride forward towards matching Continental armies for efficient management. However, in terms of responsibility for the events of 1899–1900,

17 Elgin Commission, *Report*, p. 138
18 Ibid., p. 145
19 Hamer, *British Army*, p. 210.
20 Ibid., p. 211.

there is really no doubt whatsoever that it was the Cabinet, and Lansdowne in particular, who made decisions which meant that Britain was inexcusably unprepared to make war on the Boer republics. The Cabinet consciously dragged its feet in the matter of sending additional men and stores to South Africa.

Lansdowne, in fact, stood condemned in his own words when he told the Elgin Commission that he was convinced 'that if the delay did carry with it any disadvantage, it was worth running the risk in order to avoid prematurely bringing on a war which up to the last we had hoped to avoid.'[21] For a long time it had not only been diplomatic considerations which prompted the Cabinet to delay; financial reasons had also played a considerable part in its deliberations, with the obduracy of Hicks Beach, the Chancellor of the Exchequer, carrying significant weight. Behind this folly lay their belief that, when it came to it, Kruger would not fight; but if this is what the members of the Cabinet thought, the diplomatic argument put forward by Lansdowne was unsound. If they had been right that Kruger was bluffing, a more resolute stance in respect of military reinforcement would have had the desired effect.

One matter which the Elgin Commission did not explore was the question of how individuals were selected for appointment to higher commands. The need to take account of military seniority limited the choice to those that had risen to the top of their profession, so Wolseley, Lansdowne and the War Office as a whole, cannot altogether be blamed for the selections that were made. There were, though, obvious errors of judgement in some of the appointments chosen.

The overall deficiencies of the British leadership in South Africa were carefully reviewed by the German Staff History, which provided an assessment that was at least independent. Among the failings noted was the mistaken belief of commanders in the overwhelming effectiveness of artillery: 'The supposed fire preparation of the attack existed, as a matter of fact, only in the imagination of the British leaders, and the infantry actually advanced to the attack of an absolutely unshaken adversary.' One example of this was Warren's report about the fighting on the Tugela, in which he wrote that the best course would be 'to keep the Boers, as they lay in their trenches, under an overpowering fire of artillery, until they should be disheartened, and till their position should be almost ripe for assault, and that then the infantry should be sent forward to rush them.'[22] This mistaken doctrine arose from inadequate peacetime training in how to conduct an engagement against an enemy armed with modern long-range rifles.

In the view of the authors of the German Staff History, the principal problem was that the army's leaders, superior and subordinate, had 'no mental grasp of the requirements of a modern battle, deploying too late and in too dense a line, and believing that in the end the outcome would be decided by shock action.' As a result, when faced with a series of defeats, British commanders came to believe that the problem of facing modern rifle fire was insoluble, leading to a series of indecisive battles in which both leaders and led 'lost all the strength of will needed to conquer in a battle no matter what the victory might cost.'[23]

It was certainly the case that there were serious weaknesses in officer training. The system provided little incentive for the development of military intellect; it has been described as operating 'on a basis of lengthy periods of idleness interrupted by brief interludes of hectic cramming.'[24]

21 Elgin Commission, *Minutes of Evidence*, vol. II, p. 513.
22 *German Staff History*, vol. II, p. 329.
23 Ibid., p. 337.
24 John Gooch, 'Britain and the Boer War' in George J. Andreopoulos and Harold E. Selesky (eds.), *The Aftermath of War* (London: Yale University Press 1994) p. 45.

Reviewing the performance of the British infantry in South Africa, the German Staff History quoted the criticism made by Roberts, who concluded that at the start of the war, the self-reliance of the British soldier had not been sufficiently developed, as a result of which he lacked understanding of how to use the ground, while his marksmanship was not good. On the other hand, the Staff History also remarked that the 'British soldier, if only he was well and skilfully led, did not fail in the devoted and thorough performance of his duty, and that he understood how to make a forward movement with great dash.'[25] The expression 'lions led by donkeys' could certainly be applied to the British infantry at the start of the war; this phrase has been attributed to General Erich Ludendorff, speaking to General Max Hoffman of the British troops during the First World War, but he was adopting, consciously or unconsciously, a phrase that had been frequently used to describe troops who were not well led.

Certainly, the training received by the British infantry which has been described earlier, proved to be wholly inadequate. Conan Doyle remarked that 'there is only one thing which wins a modern battle, and that is straight shooting. To hit your enemy and to avoid being hit yourself are the two points of the game, and the one is as important as the other.'[26] In neither respect had the British infantry been properly trained, receiving very limited target practice, while receiving none at all in taking cover. In peacetime manoeuvres, lines of infantry stood and fired at each other at short ranges without comment from their officers, while entrenchment was not taught at all. The Boers on the other hand, made the most skilful use of the ground and dug trenches in which they could safely endure the bombardment of the British artillery.

When it came to it, the British artillery was no match for its opponent, either in equipment or in tactical understanding. The British field artillery was far outranged by the Krupp and Creusot guns of the Boers and was insufficiently supplied with ammunition. Nor was that ammunition of the right kind; in battle after battle, the shrapnel ammunition which formed the largest part of that available proved ineffective against Boers dug in to well-constructed entrenchments. The Boers, too, kept their artillery well hidden, while the British gunners, taught to operate in batteries of six rather than being broken up into smaller groups, fought in the open. The disastrous experience of Long's guns at Colenso was never repeated to the same extent, but gun for gun, the Boers had generally much the best of the artillery exchanges.

The mobility of the Boers and the tactical advantage which it gave them, was apparent from the outset. It soon became clear that the British commanders were suffering from a paucity of mounted troops, with an immediate and serious consequence in the lack of effective reconnaissance. The regular cavalry units, imbued with their long-standing traditions, were in any case, frequently less effective than the mounted infantry and the locally raised volunteer units; the continued reliance on lance and sword seems hard to credit, but it is worth remarking that in spite of the lessons of war in South Africa, traditional views of the *arme blanche* school of thought revived in following years. Erskine Childers ended his book on the subject, published in 1910, with the words: 'Let us trust our own experience, shake off this crippling superstition, and start afresh on lines which we have proved to be successful.'[27]

Ultimately, however, in seeking to find responsibility for Black Week, it is necessary to return to the generals in command and their failure to understand how to fight a modern battle. During the three decades that preceded the war, there had been a vast military literature on the

25 *German Staff History*, vol. II, p. 338.
26 Conan Doyle, *Boer War*, p. 516.
27 Erskine Childers, *War and the Arme Blanche* (London: Edward Arnold, 1910), p. 371.

development of modern warfare. This endeavoured to identify the lessons of the wars of German unification and the Russo-Turkish war in particular. All too evidently, though, these lessons had not been properly learnt by the senior officers of the British Army. Perhaps their military experience during the period in which they fought a large number of colonial wars, exerted a greater influence. At all events, the leaders at the start of the war must necessarily bear a large share of responsibility for the initial defeats, in the course of which the shortcomings of Buller, White, Gatacre, Warren and Penn Symons, as well as of junior commanders, were exposed.

The Elgin Commission may have steered clear of commenting on the responsibilities of individuals in relation to military operations and the Official History may have been obliged to avoid direct criticism, but in the enormous literature of the Boer War, there was little such restraint. Most outspoken of all, of course, was Leo Amery in *The Times History*, writing of Buller in particular, in extravagantly hostile terms which have heavily influenced many later historians.

That Buller's was the greatest responsibility is obvious. His readiness to pass the blame on others is regrettable, though in many instances was partly justified. Although Warren, for instance, was not an especially capable commander, he was not as bad as Buller and many subsequent historians, have made him out to be. He has had a vigorous defender in Owen Coetzer. Methuen's reputation has been considerably restored by Stephen Miller's scholarly biography and Gatacre's widow published a biography of her unlucky husband which naturally sought to defend him against the charges of incompetence laid against him by Roberts and others.

White, having lost at Lombard's Kop and then allowing himself to be shut up in Ladysmith, was naturally always going to claim that he had not any thought of giving up the town, and that by taking a conscious decision to remain there, he effectively saved Natal. However, the judgement of history is against him. That decision shaped the early course of the war and he must be accounted one of the principal architects of Black Week.

In some respects, the process of reforming the Victorian army had, by 1899, already begun; but the Boer War, although it ended with the complete victory the British people had expected, demonstrated just how much further the process of reform must go. It was complicated and was invariably controversial; it had scarcely taken full effect by the time of the outbreak of the First World War and a number of tactical lessons had still not been properly learnt. However, the practical experience of fighting a modern war had taken the British Army a long way forward. It has been said of the war that had the army 'gone out to South Africa knowing what it did, and organised as it was on its return, there is little doubt that its duration and its cost in men and money would have been substantially reduced.'[28] As it was, though, the army was to endure a series of demoralising defeats before the tide would turn.

28 Pemberton, *Battles*, pp. 199-200.

Bibliography

Amery, L.S., ed., *The Times History of the War in South Africa* (7 vols) (London: Sampson Low Marston & Co., 1900–1909)

Andreopoulos, George J. and Selesky, Harold E., eds., *The Aftermath of Defeat* (New Haven and London: Yale University Press, 1994)

Barnett, Correlli, *Britain and Her Army* (London: Allen Lane. 1970)

Barthorp, Michael, *The Anglo Boer Wars* (London: Blandford, 1987)

Bourquin, S.B. and Torlage, Gilbert, *The Battle of Colenso* (Randburg: Ravan Press, 1999)

Boyce, D. George, ed., *The Crisis of British Power* (London: Historian's Press, 1990)

Brice, Christopher, *The Thinking Man's Soldier* (Solihull: Helion and Co., 2012)

——, ed., *Forgotten Victorian Generals* (Solihull: Helion and Co 2021)

Carver, Field Marshal Lord, *The Boer War* (London: Sidgwick and Jackson, 1999)

Castle, H.G., *Spion Kop* (London: Almark, 1976)

Chandler, David and others, eds., Military Miscellany II (Stroud: Army Records Society, 2005)

Childers, Erskine, *War and the Arme Blanche* (London: Edward Arnold, 1910)

Churchill, Winston S., *The Boer War* (Longmans Green and Co., 1900)

Coetzer, Owen, *The Anglo Boer War: The Road to Infamy 1899–1900* (London: Arms and Armour Press, 1996)

Corvi, Stephen J. and Beckett, Ian F.W. eds., *Victoria's Generals* (Barnsley: Pen and Sword 2009)

Curtis, L., *With Milner in South Africa* (Oxford: Oxford University Press, 1951)

Danes, Richard, *History of the Boer War* (London: Cassell, 1901)

De Wet, Christiaan, *Three Years War* (London: Archibald Constable, 1902)

Doyle, Conan, *The Great Boer War* (London: Smith Elder and Co., 1900)

Ehrman, John, *Cabinet Government and War 1890–1940* (Cambridge: Cambridge University Press 1958)

Evans, Martin Marix, *The Boer War: South Africa 1899–1902* (Oxford: Osprey, 1999)

Farwell, Byron, *The Great Boer War* (London: Allen Lane, 1977)

Ferguson, Thomas G., *British Military Intelligence 1870–1914: The Development of a Modern Intelligence Organisation* (London: Arms and Armour Press, 1984)

Forrest, Sir George, *The Life of Lord Roberts* (London: Castle and Co., 1914)

Fuller, Major General J.F.C. *The Conduct of War 1789–1961* (London: Eyre and Spottiswoode, 1961)

Gardner, Brian, *Mafeking* (London: Cassell, 1966)

——, *The Lion's Cage* (London: Arthur Barker, 1969)

Gatacre, Beatrix, *General Gatacre* (London: John Murray, 1910)

German General Staff, *The War in South Africa* (2 vols) (Nashville: Battery Press, 1998)
Gooch, John, *The Plans of War: The General Staff and British Military Strategy 1900–1916* (London: Routledge & Kegan Paul, 1974)
Grehan, John and Mace, Martin, eds., *The Boer War* (Barnsley: Pen and Sword, 2014)
Grendell-Milne, Duncan, *Baden Powell at Mafeking* (London: The Bodley Head, 1957)
Gudgin, Peter, *Military Intelligence: The British Story* (London: Arms and Armour Press, 1989)
Hamer, W.S., *The British Army: Civil-Military Relations 1885–1905* (Oxford: Clarendon, Press 1970)
Hannah, W. H., *Bobs: Kipling's General* (London: Leo Cooper, 1972)
Henderson, Colonel G. F. R., *The Science of War* (London: Longmans Green and Co., 1919)
Howard, Michael, ed., *The Theory and Practice of War* (London: Cassell, 1965)
Hunter, Archie, *Kitchener's Sword Arm* (Staplehurst: Spellmount, 1996)
Jeans, T.T., ed., *Naval Brigades in the South African War* (London: Sampson Low Marston & Co., 1902)
Johnson, Franklin Arthur, *Defence by Committee: The British Committee of Imperial Defence 1885–1959* (Oxford: Oxford University Press, 1960)
Judd, Dennis, *The Boer War* (London: Granada Publishing, 1977)
——, and Sturridge, Keith, *The Boer War* (London: John Murray, 2002)
Knox, E. Blake, *Buller's Campaign* (London: R. Brimley Johnson 1902)
Kochanski, Halik, *Sir Garnet Wolseley: Victorian Hero* (London: The Hambledon Press, 1999)
Kruger, Rayne, *Goodbye Dolly Gray* (London: Cassell, 1967)
Le May, G. H. L., *British Supremacy in South Africa 1899–1907* (Oxford: Oxford University Press, 1965)
Lees-Milne, James, *The Enigmatic Edwardian: The Life of Reginald, Second Viscount Esher* (London: Sidgwick & Jackson, 1986)
Lehman, Joseph, *The First Boer War* (London: Jonathan Cape, 1972)
Luvaas, Jay, *The Education of an Army* (Chicago: University of Chicago Press, 1964)
Mackay, Ruddock F., *Balfour* (Oxford: Oxford University Press, 1985)
Magnus, Sir P., *Kitchener: Portrait of an Imperialist* (London: John Murray, 1958)
Mahan, A.T., *The Story of the War in South Africa 1899–1900* (London: Sampson Low Marston & Co., 1900)
Marais, J. S., *The Fall of Kruger's Republic* (Oxford: Oxford University Press, 1961)
Maurice, Major General Sir F. and Arthur, Sir George, *The Life of Lord Wolseley* (New York: Doubleday Press, 1924)
——, et al, *History of the War in South Africa* (4 vols) (London: Hurst and Blackett, 1906–1910)
McElwee, W.L., *The Art of War: Waterloo to Mons* (London: Weidenfeld and Nicolson 1974)
McFadden, Pam *The Battle of Elandslaagte* (Randburg: Ravan Press, 1999)
——, *The Battle of Talana* (Randburg: Ravan Press, 1999)
Meintjes, Johannes, *Stormberg: A Lost Opportunity* (Cape Town: Nasionale Boekhandel, 1969)
Miller, Stephen, *Lord Methuen and the British Army* (London: Frank Cass, 1999)
Nasson, Bill, *The Boer War* (Stroud: Spellmount, 2011)
O'Brien, Terence H., *Milner* (London: Constable, 1979)
Pakenham, Thomas, *The Boer War* (London: Weidenfeld and Nicolson, 1979)
Pemberton, W. Baring, *Battles of the Boer War* (London: B. T. Batsford Ltd, 1964)
Porter, AN, *The Origins of the South African War* (Manchester: Manchester University Press, 1980)

Powell, Geoffrey, *Buller: A Scapegoat?* (London: Leo Cooper, 1994)
Ransford, Oliver, *Spion Kop* London: John Murray, 1969)
——, *The Battle of Majuba Hill* (London: John Murray, 1967)
Reitz, Deneys, *Commando* (London: Faber and Faber, 1929)
Rethman, Hugh, *The Natal Campaign: A Sacrifice Betrayed* (Stroud: Amberley Publishing, 2017)
Roberts, Andrew, *Salisbury: Victorian Titan* (London: Weidenfeld and Nicholson, 1999)
Robertson, Field Marshal Sir William, *From Private to Field Marshal* (London: Constable, 1921)
Scott, Admiral Sir Percy, *Fifty Years in the Royal Navy* (London: John Murray, 1919)
Smuts, J.C., *Jan Christian Smuts* (London: Castle and Co., 1952)
Steevens, G.W., *From Cape Town to Ladysmith* (Edinburgh: William Blackwood and Sons, 1900)
Surridge, Keith T., *Managing the South African War 1899–1902: Politicians vs Generals* (London: Royal Historical Society, 1998)
Symons, Julian, *Buller's Campaign* (London: The Cresset Press, 1963)
Taylor, Robert, *Lord Salisbury* (London: Allen Lane, 1975)
Trew, Peter, *The Boer War Generals* (Stroud: Sutton Publishing, 1999)
Watt, Steve, *The Battle of Vaal Krantz* (Pinetown: 30° South Publishers, 2014)
Wessels, Andre, ed., *Lord Roberts and the War in South Africa 1899–1902* (Stroud: Army Records Society, 2000)
——, ed., *Lord Kitchener and the War in South Africa 1899–1902* (Stroud: Army Records Society, 2006)

Index

BOOKS IN THIS SERIES:

1. *The Battle of Majuba Hill The Transvaal Campaign 1880–1881* John Laband (ISBN 978-1-911512-38-7)
2. *For Queen and Company Vignettes of the Irish Soldier in the Indian Mutiny* David Truesdale (ISBN 978-1-911512-79-0)
3. *The Furthest Garrison Imperial Regiments in New Zealand 1840–1870* Adam Davis (ISBN 978-1-911628-29-3)
4. *Victory Over Disease Resolving the Medical Crisis in the Crimean War, 1854–1856* Michael Hinton (ISBN 978-1-911628-31-6)
5. *Journey Through the Wilderness Garnet Wolseley's Canadian Red River Expedition of 1870* Paul McNicholls (ISBN 978-1-911628-30-9)
6. *Kitchener The Man Not The Myth* Anne Samson (ISBN 978-1-912866-45-8)
7. *The British and the Sikhs Discovery, Warfare and Friendship c1700–1900* Gurinder Singh Mann (ISBN 978-1-911628-24-8)
8. *Bazaine 1870 Scapegoat for a Nation* Quintin Barry (ISBN 978-1-913336-08-0)
9. *Redcoats in the Classroom The British Army's Schools For Soldiers and Their Children During the 19th Century* Howard R. Clarke (ISBN 978-1-912866-47-2)
10. *The Rescue They Called a Raid The Jameson Raid 1895–96* David Snape (ISBN 978-1-913118-77-8)
11. *Hungary 1848 The Winter Campaign* Christopher Pringle (ISBN 978-1-913118-78-5)
12. *The War of the Two Brothers The Portuguese Civil War 1828-1834* Sérgio Veludo Coelho (ISBN 978-1-914059-26-1)
14. *Forgotten Victorian Generals Studies in the Exercise of Command and Control in the British Army 1837–1901* Christopher Brice (editor) (ISBN 978-1-910777-20-6)
15. *The German War of 1866 The Bohemian and Moravian Campaign* Theodore Fontane (ISBN 978-1-914059-29-2)
16. *Dust of Glory The First Anglo-Afghan War 1839–1842, its Causes and Course* Bill Whitburn (ISBN 978-1-914059-33-9)
17. *Saarbruck to Sedan The Franco-German War 1870–1871 Volume 1* Ralph Weaver (ISBN 978-1-914059-88-9)
18. *The Battle of Lissa 1866 How the Industrial Revolution Changed the Face of Naval Warfare* Quintin Barry (ISBN 978-1-914059-92-6)
19. *The Zulu Kingdom and the Boer Invasion of 1837–1840* John Laband (ISBN 978-1-914059-89-6)
20. *The Fire of Venture Was in His Veins* Major Allan Wilson and the Shangani Patrol 1893 David Snape (ISBN 978-1-914059-90-2)
21. *From the Atacama to the Andes Battles of the War of the Pacific 1879–1883* Alan Curtis (ISBN 978-1-914059-90-2)
22. *The Rise of the Sikh Soldier The Sikh Warrior Through the Ages, c1700–1900* Gurinder Singh Mann (ISBN 978-1-915070-52-4)
23. *Victorian Crusaders British and Irish Volunteers in the Papal Army 1860–70* Nicholas Schofield (ISBN 978-1-915070-53-1)
24. *The Battle for the Swiepwald Austria's Fatal Blunder at Königgrätz, the climactic battle of the Austro-Prussian War, 3 July 1866* Ernst Heidrich (ISBN 978-1-915070-49-4)
25. *British Military Panoramas Battle in The Round, 1800–1914* Ian F.W. Beckett (ISBN 978-1-915113-84-9)
26. *Onwards to Omdurman The Anglo-Egyptian Campaign to Reconquer the Sudan, 1896–1898* Keith Surridge (ISBN 978-1-915070-51-7)
27. *Hungary 1849 The Summer Campaign* Wilhelm Ramming, Christopher Pringle (editor) (ISBN 978-1-915113-80-1)
28. *Line in the Sand French Foreign Legion Forts and Fortifications in Morocco 1900–1926* Richard Jeynes (ISBN 978-1-915113-83-2)
29. *The Republic Fights Back The Franco-German War 1870-1871 Volume 2* Ralph Weaver (ISBN 978-1-915070-50-0)
30. *Controlling the Frontier Southern Africa 1806–1828, The Cape Frontier Wars and The Fetcani Alarm* Hugh Driver (ISBN 978-1-915113-78-8)
31. *The Battle of Magersfontein Victory and defeat on the South African veld, 10–12 December 1899* Garth Benneyworth (ISBN 978-1-915113-79-5)
32. *Too Little Too Late The Campaign in West and South Germany June–July 1866* Michael Embree (ISBN 978-1-804513-77-4)
33. *The Destruction of the Imperial Army* Volume 1: The Opening Engagements of the Franco-German War 1870–71 Grenville Bird (ISBN 978-1-915113-81-8)
34. *Kitchener* The Man Not the Myth Anne Samson (ISBN 978-1-804513-84-2)
35. *From Ironclads to Dreadnoughts* The Development of the German Battleship, 1864–1918 Dirk Nottelmann & David M. Sullivan (ISBN 978-1-804511-84-8)
36. *The Destruction of the Imperial Army* Volume 2: The Battles around Metz Grenville Bird (ISBN 978-1-804511-85-5)
37. *More Work Than Glory* Buffalo Soldiers in the United States Army, 1866–1916 John P Langellier (ISBN 978-1-804513-34-7)
38. *The Spioenkop Campaign* The Battles to Relieve Ladysmith 17–27 January 1900 Robert Davidson (ISBN 978-1-804513-31-6)
39. *The Destruction of the Imperial Army* Volume 3: *The Sedan Campaign 1870* Grenville Bird (ISBN 978-1-804513-32-3)
40. *The Destruction of the Imperial Army* Volume 4: *Sedan, Strasbourg and Metz* 1870 Grenville Bird (ISBN 978-1-804514-59-7)
41. *Memorandum on the Prussian Army in Relation to the Campaign of 1866* Lieutenant Colonel W.E.M Reilly (ISBN 978-1-804516-27-0)
42. *Black Week: The British Army and Defeat in Anglo-Boer War 1899-1900* Quintin Barry (ISBN 978-1-804511-86-2)